Relationship Marketing

Relationship Marketing

Perspectives, Dimensions and Contexts

Tracy Harwood, Tony Garry and Anne Broderick

The McGraw·Hill Companies

London   Boston   Burr Ridge, IL   Dubuque, IA   Madison, WI   New York   San Francisco
St. Louis   Bangkok   Bogotá   Caracas   Kuala Lumpur   Lisbon   Madrid   Mexico City
Milan   Montreal   New Delhi   Santiago   Seoul   Singapore   Sydney   Taipei   Toronto

Relationship Marketing: Perspective, Dimensions and Contexts
Tracy Harwood, Tony Garry and Anne Broderick
ISBN-13 978-0-0 7-7114 22-0
ISBN-10 0-07-7 114 22-1

Mc Graw Hill McGraw-Hill Higher Education

Published by McGraw-Hill Education
Shoppenhangers Road
Maidenhead
Berkshire
SL6 2QL
Telephone: 44 (0) 1628 502 500
Fax: 44 (0) 1628 770 224
Website: *www.mcgraw-hill.co.uk*

British Library Cataloguing in Publication Data
A catalogue record for this book is available from the British Library

Library of Congress Cataloging in Publication Data
The Library of Congress data for this book has been applied for from the Library of Congress

Acquisitions Editor: Melanie Havelock
Associate Development Editor: Jennifer Rotherham
Marketing Manager: Alice Duijser
Senior Production Editor: James Bishop

Cover design by Fielding Design Ltd
Typeset by Fakenham Photosetting Ltd, Fakenham, Norfolk
Printed and bound in Great Britain by Bell and Bain Ltd, Glasgow

ISBN-13 978-0-0 7-7114 22-0
ISBN-10 0-07-7 114 22-1

This book is dedicated to
Sylvia and John
Mel, Jo, Matt and Sam

Brief Contents

Detailed Table of Contents

Preface

There are many perspectives on Relationship Marketing (RM). It has arisen from a number of different academic disciplines, primarily the social sciences, such as economics, psychology and sociology. There is no agreed definition or set of boundaries to RM and authors draw upon a range of diverse perspectives. This book acknowledges this – it presents and discusses a range of theoretical views put forward by academics with a variety of research interests in RM and combines this with practitioner experiences of implementing RM ideas.

Origins

A classical explanation of marketing sees it as the meeting of customer needs through exchange of goods and services for other goods and services or money. More recent elements added to describe a marketing orientation within a firm are: processes of customer satisfaction; strong internal co-ordination of marketing efforts; and the achievement of marketing objectives.

An initial starting point for RM was the notion that marketing exchanges needed to be viewed not just as transactions between buyers and sellers but as a set of activities in which key buyer–seller relationships are constantly developing. RM has been described as a "paradigm shift", with a focus on the way business is transacted (McKenna, 1991).

Other commentators see an overemphasis on RM as a new mode of thinking. It has, for some authors, been heralded as a new dawn and associated with this has been a kind of institutional reification of the view that if you adopt some stronger relationship-management processes, an inevitable improvement in customer retention follows.

Identifying innovative ideas as new paradigms is not surprising – marketing has had a marked tendency to experience successive new paradigms – heralded by writing on services marketing in the work of Shostack (1977) and others in the 1970s; post-modern marketing insights led by Brown (1993) in the 1990s and more recently by the paradigmatic shift being proposed by Vargo and Lusch (2004). Thus, there is often a tendency for new ideas/concepts to represent themselves as original and innovative: the degree to which they are indeed paradigm shifts is the focus of much debate among marketing academics.

Theorists developed a range of conceptual models to represent the nature of RM. RM has evolved from a form of marketing where customers responded directly to marketers (direct marketing) and where, more recently, the formation of long-term relationships with customers is considered to be of greater economic value to organizations. Within RM ideas there is a focus not just on the nature of relationships but on quite detailed models of the dimensions of relationships and the association between relationship development and customer profitability. A common characteristic of much of the recent writing in this area is the focus on the firm's strategic adoption of relationship development activities.

Since the early 1990s there has been consistent criticism of relationship-marketing concepts. Some theorists would argue that RM as an entity does not exist. Indeed, McDonald (2000) goes as far as to state that RM protagonists are nothing more than "happy-clappy, touchy-feely, weepy-creepy, born again zealots without any underlying process" (p. 29).

There is some truth in this view in that some of the potential benefits associated with a greater relationship development focus have been simplistically interpreted. In addition, the transaction vs relationship mode of marketing exchange presented by Christopher *et al.* (1991) has ceased to be viewed as a useful conceptual representation of the orientation by which a firm might adopt a greater relationship focus. Another unfortunate association has been made between relationship development and points-based loyalty programmes. There is an equation of loyalty points accumulation with better relationships with customers. This has been over-extended to an interpretation that sees loyalty programmes as the quintessential RM activity (these issues are further discussed in the Mid-Part Review: Critical Focus on Relationship Marketing).

Enduring Value in RM Theory

Where does this leave RM? Clearly, facile interpretations do no justice to the quite rigorous models that have emerged around the components of RM. The value in RM theory lies in the conceptualization of key elements within a customer–provider relationship upon which a relationship depends. Central themes to emerge include the building of trust and commitment (Morgan and Hunt, 1994), some of the original thinking on the parameters of RM (Christopher *et al.*, 1991; Ballantyne, Nordic School), the customer-orientation and customer-service ethos in the ideas of Grönroos (1990) and Gummesson (1994); the representations of antecedents of customer commitment (Morgan and Hunt, 1994); and the important theoretical contributions on interaction over a significant period of time of the IMP group (Ford, 1990). Other important themes could be cited as outcomes of effective relationships (loyalty development, customer retention). What these themes have in common is the illustration of constructs that are critical to relationship development and to successful relationship maintenance.

Evolution of RM and what to Include

In a similar way, there are varied perspectives on the evolution of RM and disagreement as to the degree of focus that should be given to many relevant theories such as agency theory and even resource-based conceptions of strategic competence. These approaches are accurate in the extent to which relationships are a critical basis for business growth and relationship development skills can be a significant resource for firms across the profit and non-profit spectrum. Nonetheless, they are theoretical strands that have been largely developed for other disciplines (economics, strategic management) and other management applications and may not always be regarded as core ideas to RM models.

The approach in this text has been to identify key perspectives on RM from a range of social science disciplines and to discuss the theoretical frameworks that underpin the perspectives covered. A useful initial summary of perspectives from the 1980s to late 1990s is set out in Table 2.5 at the end of Chapter 2 (pp. 46–47). Cutting across these different perspectives is coverage of significant dimensions within RM (relationship type and duration, trust, commitment), that are fundamental to present-day marketing approaches.

The degree of inclusion of specific approaches to relationship management was also one of choice. The text sought to balance a diversity of perspectives and dimensions within RM with adequate discussion of areas where RM is now evolving due to knowledge-based competition. For consistency the book sought to maintain a link throughout the chapters with the classic frameworks on RM – thus some elements have more curtailed coverage. A case in point is customer relationship marketing (CRM). Other authors have dealt with CRM in great depth and with great application (Gamble, Stone, Woodcock, Foss, 2006). There seems limited value in repeating those explanations in depth. Therefore, in the explanation and discussion of the diverse theoretical strands that underpin RM, this book concentrates less on CRM activities, or on the emergence of e-CRM. The theoretical focus in this book is on two elements:

1 the fundamental elements seen as the enduring value of RM – the structuring of an RM approach and those underpinning elements within a customer–provider relationship upon which a relationship depends (Chapters 1–5)

2 the way in which relationship development approaches are evolving to address knowledge-based competition and emerging social networks (Chapters 6–8)

Potential Readers of this Book

This book is aimed primarily at readers who already have a reasonable level of knowledge of marketing, either university-acquired or experience-based. Potential readers will be keen to understand not just the evolution of RM and the theoretical frameworks, but equally how RM ideas can be applied in manufacturing, services and virtual contexts.

The text is suitable for:

- undergraduates in the later stages of their degree who wish to study RM in depth,

- postgraduate students who wish to pursue a career in business or marketing and have a particular interest in one of the most creative areas of marketing,

- practitioners who want to familiarize themselves with the key elements of RM and see how it relates to different profit and non-profit contexts.

Structure of the Text

This marketing text tries to do three things:

- Trace the evolution of RM concepts and how they have emerged from widely different perspectives

- Differentiate the components or dimensions of RM theory from earlier marketing approaches

- Encourage the reader to examine diverse contexts in which RM activities have been implemented and thus illustrate though a range of cases the versatility of RM

The text structure is uncomplicated. *Perspectives and Dimensions of Relationship Marketing* are investigated in eight chapters in Part 1 (a "perspective" is a term used to describe and analyse different ways of viewing something so that it can be better understood).

Part I sets out to introduce and describe the emergence of RM from its traditional marketing background, touching on economics, consumer and buyer behaviour and marketing strategy streams of literature. It considers key theoretical frameworks that underpin the perspectives covered. Within the first eight chapters, dimensions of RM that are covered in depth include the nature

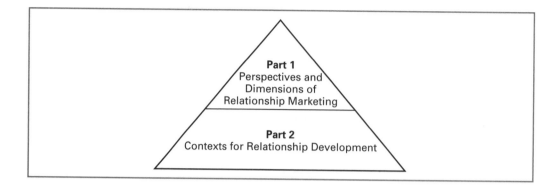

and type of relationships; the links between dyadic and networked relationships; the management of relationships in the supply chain; and specific elements of client–provider relationships in service contexts. Also included within this are social ties and emotional labour; mobilization of information and knowledge management; the role of quality and performance indicators; the nature of virtual communities; their role in relational development; and the roles of various technologies in facilitating relationships.

Part 2 of the book, *Contexts for Relationship Development*, presents case studies of organizations across different marketing contexts. These cases are focused upon an implementation of the key theory and issues discussed throughout the book. They are intended to encourage the reader to develop their own interpretation of how RM concepts may (or may not) be applied in practice.

Key Content of Chapters in Part 1

The initial five chapters of the text offer a coherent review of well-established RM theory, grounded in consumer, industrial or business to business and service contexts. This review does not claim to be comprehensive; rather it focuses on areas of theory where classic themes and much original RM conceptualization emerged. Chapters go into detail on how relationship definitions and relationship development processes incorporated within each perspective have emerged.

As illustrated in Figure 1, this section starts in Chapter 1 – Introduction to Marketing – by reviewing how RM has evolved from our earlier understanding of marketing. This chapter sets the scene for later discussion in Chapter 2 – Defining Relationship Marketing – which describes the classical dimensions and themes that have emerged in our understanding of RM, especially the different approaches and boundaries to organizational and client relationships that exist.

The next two chapters focus on the origins of RM that emerge in strands of theory in industrial and services marketing relationships respectively. Chapter 3 – An Overview of Industrial Marketing and Supply Relationships – examines the foundations and nature of marketing relationships in business-to-business markets, an area where many key practical relationship management tools have been successfully applied.

Tracing the origins of relational marketing approaches, Chapter 4 – Services Marketing and Relational Perspectives – identifies how both implicit an explicit relational focus has evolved since the 1960s in services marketing thinking. It highlights underpinning concepts on service interactions, service quality, and service recovery that are critical dimensions of current approaches to relationship development and customer retention in business-to-consumer con-

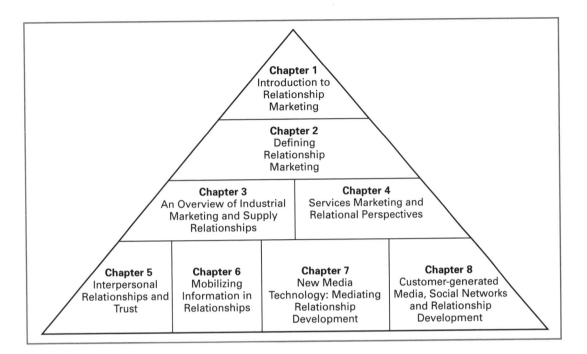

texts (online and offline). As highlighted within chapters 1 to 4, one of the key considerations for RM is the role that employees play in the relationships themselves. Chapter 5 – Interpersonal Relationships and Trust – therefore, begins the discussion by focusing on individual aspects, both soft and hard, that are important to relationships including trust, commitment and the organization, its structure and relationship with employees.

As the reader moves though the text, some later chapters examine RM in the light of knowledge-based competition. Chapter 6 – Mobilizing Information in Relationships – presents a discussion about how knowledge of relationships is managed by individuals, as well as inside and between organizations, which is an increasingly complex and important consideration in light of the drivers for changes in marketing relationships (globalization, outsourcing, etc). Chapter 7 – New Media Technology: Mediating Relationship Development – considers the impact of some emerging technologies as an interface with relationship development.

In contrast with previous texts, the final chapters encourage the reader to consider how relationship development activities become more fluid and more customer-centric in virtual markets. Chapter 7 identifies the way in which intelligent customer interactions and solutions are now necessary to capture the flexibility and mobility of customer relationships in the virtual environment, catering for the emergence of what some theorists describe as "new" consumers. Chapter 8 – Customer-Generated Media, Social Networks and Relationship Development – explores the way online networks act as mediators for conversations between customers and identifies their power to influence organizations through the strength of their relationships and networks. It also highlights the importance of engagement with customer-generated online activities in relationship building and the need for creative relationship strategies that embrace the versatility of digital media.

References

Brodie, R.J., N.E. Coviello, R.W. Brookes and V. Little (1997) "Towards a Paradigm Shift in Marketing? An Examination of Current Marketing Practices", *Journal of Marketing Management*, vol. 13, pp. 386–406.

Brown, S. (1993) "Posmodern Marketing?", *The European Journal of Marketing*, vol. 27, no. 4, pp. 19–34.

Christopher, M., A. Payne and D. Ballantyne (1991) *Relationship Marketing: Bringing Quality, Customer Service and Marketing Together*, Oxford: Butterworth Heinemann, p. 4.

Gamble, P., M. Stone, N. Woodcock and B. Foss (2006) *Up, Close and Personal? Customer Relationship Marketing @ Work*, 3rd edn, London: Kogan Page.

Grönroos, C. (1990) "The Marketing Strategy Continuum: Towards a Marketing Concept for the 1990s", *Management Decision*, vol. 29, no. 1, p. 9.

Gummesson, E. (1994) "Making Relationship Marketing Operational", *International Journal of Service Industry Management*, vol. 5, no. 5, pp. 5–20.

McDonald, M. (2000) "On the Right Track", *Marketing Business*, 28–31 April.

McKenna, R. (1991) "Marketing is everything", *Harvard Business Review*, Jan–Feb, pp. 65–70.

Morgan, R.M. and S.D. Hunt (1994) "The Commitment–Trust Theory of Relationship Marketing", *Journal of Marketing*, vol. 58, July.

Shostack, L. (1997) "Breaking Free from Product Marketing", *Journal of Marketing*.

Vargo S.L. and R.F. Lusch (2004) "Evolving to a New Dominant Logic of Marketing", *Journal of Marketing*, vol. 68, Jan, pp. 1–17.

Cases used in text	
The Traditional Marketing Approach 888's New Tables – Not for Boys Tesco	Chapter 1 Introduction to Relationship Marketing
LEGO Positioning to Die for? IKEA Strategic Business Partnerships (Leicester) NTL and Virgin Media	Chapter 2 Defining Relationship Marketing
Boeings Dreamliner Sony	Chapter 3 An Overview of Industrial Marketing and Supply Relationships
Emirates Airline Eating Out in UK Pubs Aegon Insurance	Chapter 4 Services Marketing and Relational Perspectives
Hotel Employee of Year – Malmaison David Lloyd Leisure Centres TNT Express Worldwide British Airways	Chapter 5 Interpersonal Relationships and Trust
Knowledge Machine at NUCOR Steel The Old Vicarage Hotel, UK Great British Outdoor Market	Chapter 6 Mobilizing Information in Relationships
Hewlett Packard Zoom and Go Silkflowers.com	Chapter 7 New Media Technology: Mediating Relationship Development
Real.com (1) Small World Labs Hewlett Packard Real.com (2) Online Travel Services – Customer Self- customization	Chapter 8 Customer-generated Media, Social Networks and Relationship Development

Guided Tour

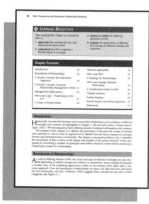

Learning Objectives

Each chapter opens with a set of learning objectives, summarizing what knowledge, skills or understanding readers should acquire from each chapter. A chapter introduction explores these themes further.

Chapter Summary

This briefly reviews and reinforces the main topics you will have covered in each chapter to ensure you have acquired a solid understanding of the key topics. Use it as a quick reference to check you've understood the chapter.

Insight Boxes

Found throughout the chapters these boxes highlight useful points and define key terms to help students pinpoint important aspects of discussion in the text.

Tasks

Tasks can be found throughout the chapters. They are opportunities to test your learning in more depth. They may involve further web research or require you to reflect on ideas in the chapter and come up with your own views and interpretations of RM concepts.

Packed with Examples

The book is packed with practical examples demonstrating the application of concepts, followed by discussion questions to analyze and discuss real issues.

Contexts Section

The cases provided in the Contexts Section are up to date examples, which give students the opportunity to apply what they have learnt to real life examples. Each case is followed by its own set of questions and tasks to reinforce learning.

Figures and Tables

Each chapter provides a number of figures, tables and illustrations to help you visualize RM examples and summarize important concepts.

References and Further Reading

Found at the end of every chapter, these provide students with the resources to research the subject further.

Make the grade!

30% off any Study Skills book!

Our Study Skills books are packed with practical advice and tips that are easy to put into practice and will really improve the way you study. Topics include:

- Techniques to help you pass exams
- Advice to improve your essay writing
- Help in putting together the perfect seminar presentation
- Tips on how to balance studying and your personal life

www.openup.co.uk/studyskills

Visit our website to read helpful hints about essays, exams, dissertations and much more.

Special offer! As a valued customer, buy online and receive 30% off any of our Study Skills books by entering the promo code **getahead**

Acknowledgements

Our thanks go to the following reviewers for their comments at various stages in the text's development:

Mark Godson – Sheffield Hallam University
Simon Chadwick – Birbeck, University of London
Stephen Tagg – University of Strathclyde
Martin Wetzels – Maastricht University
Adam Lindgreen – Eindhoven University of Technology
Jim Hamil: University of Strathclyde
David Abson – Northumbria University
Gaby Odekerken-Schröder – Maastricht University
Per Servais – University of Southern Denmark
Krystal Sirota – Rovaniemi University of Applied Sciences

With thanks to our publishers for their patience and support.

Every effort has been made to to trace and acknowledge ownership of copyright and to clear permission for material reproduced in this book. The publishers will be pleased to make suitable arrangements to clear permission with any copyright holders whom it has not been possible to contact.

About the Authors

Tracy G. Harwood is a Senior Research Fellow within the Institute of Creative Technologies and a national teacher fellow at De Montfort University.

Tony Garry is a Senior Lecturer in Marketing at De Montfort University.

Anne Broderick is a Principal Lecturer in Marketing at De Montfort University.

PART I
Perspectives and Dimensions of Relationship Marketing

CHAPTER 01

Introduction to Relationship Marketing

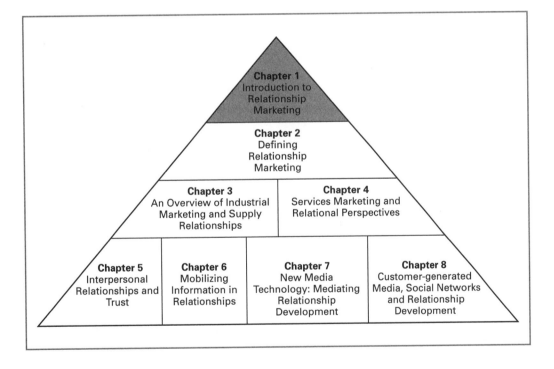

Chapter 1
Introduction to
Relationship
Marketing

Chapter 2
Defining
Relationship
Marketing

Chapter 3
An Overview of Industrial
Marketing and Supply
Relationships

Chapter 4
Services Marketing and
Relational Perspectives

Chapter 5
Interpersonal
Relationships and
Trust

Chapter 6
Mobilizing
Information in
Relationships

Chapter 7
New Media
Technology: Mediating
Relationship
Development

Chapter 8
Customer-generated
Media, Social Networks
and Relationship
Development

❖ **LEARNING OBJECTIVES**

After studying this chapter you should be able to:

1 **define** RM

2 **compare** and **contrast** the traditional marketing mix approach to a relational approach

3 **appreciate** how the concept of RM evolved

4 **understand** the advantages of an RM

Chapter Contents

Introduction

The concept of relationships with customers is nothing new! One only has to read the ancient Middle Eastern proverb "As a merchant, you'd better have a friend in every town" (Grönroos, 1994: 18) to appreciate the importance attached to relationships in a commercial context through history. Indeed, during the Middle Ages there is substantial evidence to suggest that merchants were well aware that some customers were worth "courting" more than others (Buttle, 1996).

INSIGHT: "Service firms have always been relationship orientated. The nature of service business is relationship based" (Grönroos, 1995: 252).

One only has to think of a trip to the hairdresser, dentist or even the traditional corner shops to recognize that sole traders and small businesses have always had an intimate knowledge of customers culminating in outcomes such as product suggestions, credit and social interaction (e.g. Palmer and Bejou, 1994). Close, complex and long-term relationships between buyers and sellers have always been a natural outcome of business interaction.

However, with the advent of mass-produced goods and the concurrent growth and expansion of many business organizations, levels of personal contact have diminished, as the increased usage of call centres highlights. This was particularly the case within consumer markets which increasingly became transaction based. Even within the service sector there was a growing anonymity between buyers and sellers. The customer was turned from a relationship partner into a market share statistic (Grönroos, 1995). With these developments the foundations of the traditional marketing mix or 4Ps (product, price, place and promotion) were laid.

> ᑲ INSIGHT: "Relationship Marketing is an 'old new' idea but with a new focus" (Berry, 1995: 23).

There were some markets, however, where this was never the case. Industrial markets, and some services markets in particular, did not fit the concepts of the marketing mix and these formed the springboard from which many RM theories and concepts were developed.

The purpose of this chapter is to explore the roots and development of RM. It does this by initially carrying out a brief evaluation of the traditional marketing approach based on the four Ps. It then proceeds to explore the development of the RM paradigm before briefly exploring possible future directions within the RM field.

An Overview of the Traditional Marketing Approach

The origins of marketing can be traced back hundreds of years to a time when the functional attributes of a product or service, its market price and its psychological benefits were all used to determine its "just price". An exchange process then took place that usually involved money for goods (Ambler, 2004). However, *the marketing mix* approach (see Figure 1.1), so familiar in introductory marketing texts (such as Jobber, 2004 and Kotler *et al.*, 2003) only came to the fore of marketing in the latter half of the twentieth century.

The foundations of the marketing mix were proposed as a set of variables by McCarthy as early as 1960 and subsequently Borden (1964) termed these variables "the marketing mix". The marketing mix concept was generally accepted for many years as *the* central marketing concept on which many other marketing theories were based and developed. Indeed, its validity was rarely questioned despite having a limited basis in empirical research to back it up (Kent, 1986). This was primarily because a limited number of marketing variables (i.e. the four Ps) appeared to fit the typical characteristics of the contexts facing many marketing managers of that period (see the mini-case on the traditional marketing approach, p. 7). Typically these characteristics

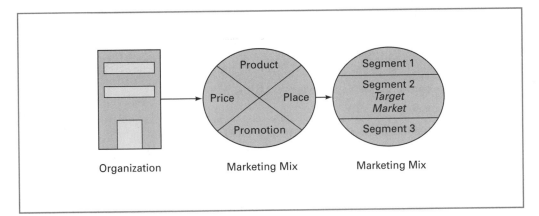

FIGURE 1.1 The Marketing Mix.

MINI-CASE: THE TRADITIONAL MARKETING APPROACH

America was the first country to use sponsor-funded programming as its model for both radio and television. During the 1950s a single company would pay for the production costs of a show. In return the sponsor's products would be pitched to the audience during the course of the programme and often by a celebrity associated with that programme, such as the presenter. Proctor & Gamble and Lever Brothers, the soap manufacturers, invested heavily in game shows and daytime dramas which subsequently became known as "soap operas" or the "soaps" that we know today.

However, the model of one advertiser for each show became so expensive that only the largest companies could afford to promote their products. In the late 1950s NBC's president launched "magazine" sponsorship where several different firms bought time on a single show. In return, the TV network paid for the show.

The format proved successful for many products. The manufacturer of the bottled cleaner Lestoil undertook a $9 million television campaign in the early 1960s and saw sales rise from 150 000 bottles per annum to over 100 million in only three years. To quote Professor John Galbraith at the time, "The industrial system is profoundly dependent upon commercial television and could not exist in its present form without it. Radio and television are the prime instruments for the management of consumer demand."

Thus the traditional marketing mix became the focus of much subsequent theory and development.

Source

N. Johnson (1970) *How to Talk to Your Television Set*, Bantham Books, New York and "TV History: Celebrity Commercials in TV's Golden Age" (accessed at www.teletronic.co.uk/ustvads.htm).

Question

While the traditional marketing mix approach is appropriate in some contexts, it may be found to be problematic in others. How appropriate is it within:

1 A b2b industrial context (e.g. a manufacturer of computer components for IBM)?

2 A b2c company selling children's clothes over the Internet?

revolved around North American consumer markets that formed the basis of many of the studies conducted into marketing during this period. Typically these characteristics included:

- fast-moving consumer packaged goods (FMCGs);
- large mass markets;
- highly competitive distribution systems (e.g. supermarkets); and
- very commercialized media channels (e.g. North American television and radio networks such as ABC, CBC and NBC).

Even today, the 4Ps framework remains popular with practitioners and teachers alike because it is a simple concept, it is easy to understand, it is relatively easy to apply, it is appropriate to many contexts and it is easy to teach (Grönroos, 1994)!

Problems with the Traditional Marketing Approach

However, the traditional marketing mix approach of the 4Ps may be criticized for a number of reasons. These may be summarized as follows:

- The approach assumes that all clusters or segments of customers are similar and may be treated in a standardized way.
- The approach assumes consumers are passive absorbers of marketing information. However, with advances in multimedia technology, there are increasing opportunities for two-way communication and interaction between consumers and marketing organizations using interactive media. Consumers are also increasingly communicating with each other about marketing organizations (e.g. blogs).
- It assumes short-term and often one-off transactions based around the exchange of goods for money. So, the focus of this approach is on a core product or service that is exchanged almost entirely for money with little value added in terms of additional services. However, the notion of a product with features that customers inspect and then buy is too simplistic! In many markets there is a periodic and ongoing demand for products or services giving the opportunities for some sort of ongoing relationship to develop between the provider and the customer (again, think of a trip to the hairdresser, dentist or corner shop!) So, in a relational context, the offering includes both a core product and additional value-adding aspects. This may be something as simple as a social chat about where you are planning to go on holidays, to collecting points on a loyalty card. Thus, in a relational context, the value-adding offering and its management can become extremely complex.

INSIGHT: "The marketing mix suggests that far from being concerned with a customer's interests (i.e. somebody for whom something is done) the views implicit in the four P approach is that the customer is somebody to whom something is done!" (Dixon and Blois, 1983: 4).

INSIGHT: "What counts is the ability of the firm to manage its resources to create a holistic offering over time that evolves into an acceptable perceived customer value" (Grönroos, 1995: 410).

Task 1.1

Imagine you have just received a prescription from your doctor. Regardless of the pharmacy you decide to go to, the medicine prescribed and its price will be identical.

- The prescription may be viewed as a core product or service. What factors influence you as you decide which pharmacy you will take the prescription to in order to collect the medication?
- What opportunities are available to a pharmacy to ensure you use them (think of why people may or may not use Boots)?

- Finally, it over-simplifies the variables required within certain marketing contexts and fails to capture the broader complexity inherent in many markets.

> INSIGHT: "Marketing in practice has been turned to managing this tool box the 'marketing mix' instead of truly exploring the nature of the firm's market relationships and genuinely taking care of the real needs and desires of customers" (Grönroos, 1994: 348).

In summary, the traditional marketing approach does not encapsulate the essence of ongoing or relational exchanges. In an attempt to address these deficiencies, academics have periodically suggested additional elements or variables to the traditional marketing mix in an attempt to reflect the ever-more complex nature of marketing interfaces. Indeed, there have been various attempts to extend the idea of the multiple Ps concepts. Some examples may be seen in Table 1.1.

TABLE 1.1 Examples of Extended Marketing Mixes

The 4Ps	McCarthy (1960)	Product, Price, Promotion, Place
The 5Ps	Judd (1987)	Product, Price, Place, Promotion, People
The 6Ps	Kotler (1986)	Product, Price, Promotion, Place, Political Power, Public opinion formation
The 7Ps	Booms and Bitner (1982)	Product, Price, Promotion, Place, Participants, Physical Evidence and Process
The 15Ps	Baumgartner (1991)	Product/service, Price, Promotion, Place, People, Politics, Public Relations, Probe, Partition, Prioritize, Position, Profit, Plan, Performance, Positive Implementations.

Based on: Gummesson (1994)

Task 1.2

Think about the following products and services:

- An ipod
- A journey by air
- An election campaign

- Choosing between the 5P, 6P and 7P models, choose one model to apply to each product or service. Identify the way in which each element of the model might be relevant to each product or service.

- For each product or service, what elements of the model do you see as critical to whether consumers will feel satisfied with their choice?

However, the consequences of this focus on the marketing mix approach has meant other, possibly less compliant variables (which do not begin with a P!) were neglected. In many cases, these variables were more relevant to particular market contexts. For example, it is now widely accepted within the contexts of business-to-business and inter-organizational marketing that the marketing mix perspective of the 4Ps is too restrictive and fails to capture the broader complexities inherent in these markets. Business markets are often large, complex and populated by many different organizational structures. They are characterized by power-play and negotiation, risk management, specification buying and reciprocal arrangements between buyers and sellers. These aim to achieve cost and performance benefits (Jobber, 2004). It is very difficult to capture this degree of depth and complexity with a four Ps approach. As a result of these criticisms, the context within which the research and practice of marketing occurred has broadened.

The Evolving Focus of Marketing

Christopher *et al.* (1991) highlight how this broadening manifested itself by identifying "the developing central themes of marketing interest" over the last five decades which have culminated in current marketing thinking.

As can be seen from Figure 1.2, in the 1990s academic and practitioner interest in RM took off to the extent that many marketers viewed it as *the* key marketing issue of the decade which was to culminate in a fundamental reshaping of the field. Indeed, a number of authors (e.g. Gummesson, 1987; Moller, 1992; Grönroos, 1994) propose that there was a "paradigm shift" within the field of marketing away from the traditional transaction-based approach towards a more relationship-orientated one. To appreciate the intensity of the terminology used by these authors, it is important to examine its development in more depth.

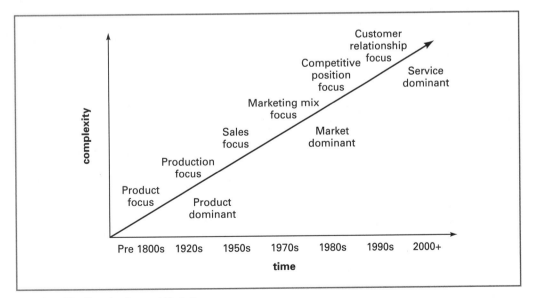

FIGURE 1.2 The Changing Focus of Marketing.
Based on Christopher *et al.* (1991) and Ambler (2004)

> INSIGHT: "A 'paradigm shift' is a term used to describe a major or radical change in the way that something is thought about. In the case of Relationship Marketing, the shift has included new tools for development of theory and research into its application"
> (Backhaus, 1997).

Factors Influencing the Development of RM

The developments that have led to the emergence of RM are complex in nature, largely inter-related and difficult to consider in isolation. However, a number of factors may be identified, namely:

- the maturing of service marketing;
- research within industrial markets;
- a recognition of the benefits of RM for firms;
- a recognition of the benefits of RM for customers;
- advances in information technology.

The maturing of services marketing

The importance of people has been repeatedly emphasized within services marketing literature because the service is performed and the performers are employees (often referred to as "actors"). Indeed, Gummesson (1987) coined the phrase "part time marketers" to stress the critical marketing role performed by front-line employees who interact with customers and their contribution towards delivery and service satisfaction.

Related to this was the emergence of the customer care and quality philosophies of the 1980s. Christopher *et al.* (1991) highlight how there was a shift of focus, particularly within service industries, towards customer care and quality as dimensions that overlap with the marketing philosophy. Interestingly, they attribute part of this shift to the popularity of Peters and Waterman's text *In Search of Excellence* (1982). They further propose that the natural outcome of quality service delivery and customer care is the development of relationships through inter-action between employees and customers. As a result, these entities are inextricably linked (see Figure 1.3).

More recently, the importance of people as a variable has been extended beyond the marketing of services. The debate on the differences between the marketing of goods and services has taken a new turn. Vargo and Lusch (2004) suggest that goods are a part of *service*, rather than *services* being an extension of goods. As Gummesson (1994) states: "customers do not buy goods or services: they buy offerings which render services". This requires effective knowledge management and infor-mation flow between members of the supply chain, from suppliers, through the organization's value-adding components (departments, functions), to the end user. Indeed, the customer is a co-pro-ducer of the service, through their continued involvement in the consumption of the organization's product (Vargo and Lusch, 2004). A fuller discussion of the way that relational elements of marketing are strongly rooted in services marketing literature is undertaken in Chapter 4.

Research within industrial markets

As indicated previously, the failure of the traditional marketing approach to capture the complex-ities and depth of industrial markets led to the growth of research within this field. Research in

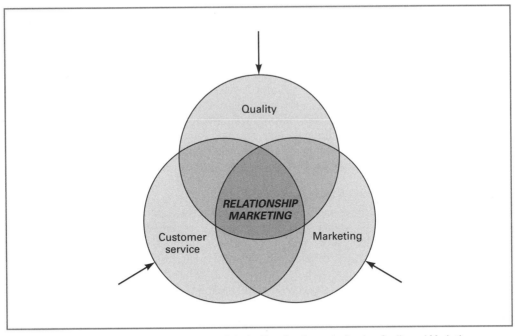

FIGURE 1.3 The Relationship Marketing Orientation: Bringing Together Customer Service, Quality and Marketing Philosophies.
Source: Christopher *et al.* (1991).

this area focused on aspects such as inter-organizational exchange and buyer–seller relationships (e.g. Håkansson, 1982; Ford, 1990), social exchange, channels literature, network relationships (e.g. Johanson and Mattsson, 1988), and strategic-management literature including concepts such as value chains. These are all discussed in more depth in Chapter 3.

A recognition of the benefits of RM for firms

There has been an increasing recognition of the benefits of RM from both the firm's and the customer's perspectives.

From a firm's perspective, increased competition through the globalization of world markets, market fragmentation and the deregulation of many service markets (e.g. banking, law, airlines, etc.) has meant that protection of the customer base has become paramount. As Buttle (1996) stresses, RM is not based on any philanthropic outlook but on two sound economic arguments:

- First, it is more expensive to win a new customer than it is to retain an existing customer.

- Second, the longer the association that exists between company and customer, the more profitable is the relationship for the firm.

More specifically, its advantages to the firm may be summarized as follows:

Increased profitability

It has been widely demonstrated across a variety of industries that profits increase if a firm retains its existing customers rather than attempts to acquire new ones. For example, analysis of more than 100 companies in 24 industries found that firms could improve profits from 25 per cent to 85 per cent by reducing customer defections by 5 per cent. This may be attributable to a number of factors. For example, ongoing relationships may have a direct impact on financial outgoings by helping to reduce transaction costs associated with repeat ordering (Marshall *et al.*, 1979).

However, there is an increased questioning of the validity of such findings. Reinartz and Kumar (2003) highlight the difficulty in defining relationship length as a customer rarely "signs off" (p. 79) when they stop using an organization. A second issue relates to research which demonstrates that both short-term and longer-term customers may be profitable (Reinartz and Kumar, 2000) and that the value of long-term customers varies "substantially with the category" (East *et al.*, 2006: 12). Finally, Dowling and Uncles (1997) and Reinartz and Kumar (2002) argue that long-term customers may not always be cheaper to serve and are just as price sensitive.

Competitive advantage through added value

Some authors suggest RM adds value to a product or service package. This added value is achieved by providing certain "demand peripherals" such as social exchange, customer care, etc. (e.g. Crosby and Stevens, 1987). As a result of this added value, a premium may be charged to the customer. Ballantyne *et al.* (2003) develop this further by suggesting "recent dismay at unethical short-cut approaches to creating shareholder value" (p. 161) has created a climate where interest in the distribution of value among stakeholders is likely to increase the possibility of developing relationships. Value perspectives are suggested which revolve around supplier-managed relationships, mutually interactive processes and values emerging from within networks.

Task 1.3

Work with one other person for this exercise. Imagine you are both working in a hotel for the summer holidays (on the reception desk).

■ Identify a customer group who would use the hotel services regularly. Note what hotel services they might use and where they are likely to spend money when staying at the hotel or using the hotel facilities.

■ Identify a group of customers who might be short-term users and are less likely to be repeat customers. Note what services they may use and what they are likely to spend money on.

■ Discuss with your partner which customer group will be more profitable in a one-year period – a large number of short-term users or small number of regular users?

   Will there be any difference in the level of customer service expected by each group?

   Where could added value be generated for regular users in the hotel services?

Creation of firm advocates

As well as retaining customers, it is proposed by some authors that RM may go beyond creating mere customer loyalty and, as the relationship strengthens, may create "customer advocates" of the company. As Christopher *et al.* (1991) state "The objective of Relationship Marketing is to turn new customers into vocal advocates for the company, thus playing an important role as a referral source" (p. 22). They suggest the existence of a conceptual RM ladder of customer loyalty. Customers are moved up the ladder by enhancing and developing relationships with the customer (see Figure 1.3).

Task 1.4

In the ladder in Figure 1.4, the highest level of loyalty are customer advocates. Looking at the hotel example in Task 1.3, if the hotel had repeat customers and also had advocates, how would you distinguish between the two? In what way would their behaviour differ?

You may wish to read about this further in Christopher *et al.*, 1991.

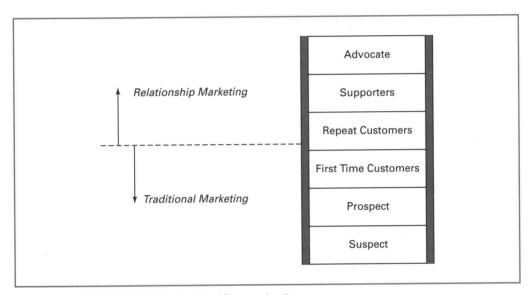

FIGURE 1.4 The Relationship Marketing Ladder of Customer Loyalty.
Based on: Christopher *et al.* (1991).

However, the association between relationship length and recommendation is also questionable as some more recent studies have shown no association between the two (e.g. Verhoef *et al.*, 2002). Indeed, East *et al.* (2005: 11) state that "in a minority of fields, significantly more recommendations will come from recent recruits than from long-tenure customers".

A recognition of the benefits of RM for customers

From a customer's perspective, if a product or service is variable in quality and/or complexity and if the product is of an intangible nature, these combine to create risk and uncertainty.

Risk reduction and reduced uncertainty are posited as potential outcomes that customers find particularly important within the context of some markets (Morgan and Hunt, 1994). Berry (1995) suggests a relationship allows providers to become more knowledgeable about customers' requirements and needs. Thus, having a long-term, ongoing, stable relationship with a provider may reduce uncertainty and risk and hence reduce customer stress as the relationship becomes more predictable. As a result, problems are solved, special needs accommodated and the expectation levels set to the extent that "in some cases, customers may even be aware of competitors who might provide the same or better service but yet they choose to stay in the relationship due to its predictability and comfort" (Bitner, 1995: 249).

Advances in information technology

Berry (1995) summarizes a number of ways that information technology (IT) as a tool may facilitate the effectiveness of a relational perspective:

- Tracking the buying patterns of existing customers
- Customizing services, promotion and pricing to customers' specific requirements
- Co-ordinating or integrating the delivery of multiple services to the same customer
- Providing two-way communication channels (company to customer and customer to company)
- Minimizing the probability of service errors and breakdowns
- Augmenting core service offerings with valued extras
- Personalizing service encounters as appropriate

The extent to which emerging technologies have impacted on relationship development since Berry's (1995) appraisal is discussed in more detail in Chapter 7.

Emerging Themes of RM

As RM evolved, marketers and academics studied and applied it from different geographical, disciplinary and contextual perspectives (see Figure 1.5). Studies were taking place simultaneously within Scandinavia, the USA, the UK and Australia. These studies were drawing on theories from a diverse range of disciplines such as economics, sociology, psychology and more established marketing concepts. At the same time, research was taking place within a variety of contexts such as business-to-business manufacturing, FMCG and services marketing.

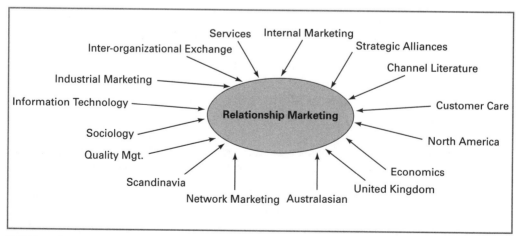

FIGURE 1.5 Perspectives of RM

Within each of these perspectives and contexts, different elements and components of RM were considered to be more relevant than others and so the focus of the research of these had a different emphasis. This resulted in RM evolving into a number of different areas or themes. Various authors have attempted to categorize and classify these using a variety of criteria. Table 1.2 provides an example of these and the classification criteria that have been used.

As can be seen in Table 1.2, Relationship Marketing concepts have been developed from multiple perspectives, but also have emerged across time and have incorporated various sub-areas of focus. RM is really a composite of several different frameworks.

One of the contributors in Table 1.2, Palmer *et al.* (2005), identify relationship marketing "schools of thought". In Table 1.3 below they identify key components by which the "different schools of thought" they propose may be compared and contrasted. Initially, there is an identification of whether the focus is, for example, on the four Ps or relationships: what the basis of exchange is and whether the timescale involved is short term or long term. The number of relationships within markets is explored and this may range from a single relationship between a buyer and a seller to a whole host of suppliers, competitors, customers and stakeholders (this is discussed in more detail in the next chapter). Also considered are the features of the organization in terms of its structure and processes and its culture in terms of the extent and priority attached to internal marketing.

What this table shows is that, when we look at the components of each of the schools of thought, each perspective on RM is complex and implementing parts of a particular framework requires significant strategic thinking on the part of the firm. For all perspectives, resources need to be allocated in areas such as product quality and measurement of relationship success. For some perspectives, (e.g. Nordic school) there is a strategic need to look internally as well as externally. Thus, variation in resource allocation will follow variation in perspective.

TABLE 1.2 Classification of Emerging Relational Themes by Author

Grönroos and Strandvik (1997) based on "broad perspectives"	Brodie *et al.* (1997) classification scheme based on "terminology"	Morgan and Hunt's (1994) classification scheme based on "relational strands"	Palmer, Lindgreen and Vanhamme (2005) "schools of thought"
■ the Nordic School (e.g. Grönroos, 1995); ■ the Network approach within industrial marketing (e.g. Håkansson *et al.*, 1976); ■ the Anglo-Australian approach (e.g. Christopher *et al.*, 1991); and, ■ strategic alliances and partnerships.	■ service contexts (e.g. Berry, 1983; 1995; Grönroos, 1990); ■ inter-organizational exchange (e.g. Håkansson, 1982; Ford, 1990). ■ channels literature; ■ network relationships (e.g. Johanson and Mattsson, 1988); ■ strategic management literature including value chains (e.g. Normann and Ramirez, 1993); ■ information technology related contexts.	■ relational contracting (e.g. Macneil, 1980), ■ relational marketing (e.g. Dwyer *et al.*, 1987); ■ working partnerships (e.g. Anderson and Narus, 1990); ■ symbiotic marketing (e.g. Varadarajan and Rajaratnam, 1986); ■ strategic alliances (e.g. Day, 1990); ■ co-marketing alliances (e.g. Bucklin and Sengupta, 1993); ■ internal marketing (e.g. Berry and Parasuraman, 1991).	■ the Nordic school (e.g. Grönroos, 1995); ■ the IMG Group and IMP (Industrial Marketing and Purchasing) (e.g. Håkansson, 1982; Ford, 1990); ■ the Anglo-Australian school (e.g. Christopher *et al.*, 1991).

TABLE 1.3 Comparison of Main Components of Major Schools of RM versus Transaction Marketing

Key Component	Transaction Marketing	IMP Group	Nordic School	Anglo-Australian Approach
Basis	Exchange and the 4Ps	Relationships between firms	Services	Service /Quality/ Marketing
Time-frame	Short term	Short term and long term	Long term	Long term
Market	Single customer	Multiple Network	30 markets with four categories	Six Markets
Organization	Hierarchical and functional		Functional and cross-functional	Cross-functional process based
Basis of exchange	Price	Product /service, information, financial and social	Less sensitive to price	Perceived value
Product quality dimension	Product/technical/ output quality	Technological	Interaction quality	Function of value and cost ownership
Measurement	Revenue and market share	Customer profitability	Quality, value, customer satisfaction	Customer satisfaction
Customer Information	*Ad hoc*	Varies by relationship stage	Individual	Customer value and retention
Internal Marketing			Substantial strategic importance	Integral to the concept
Service	Augmentation to core product	Close buyer–seller relations	Integral to product	Basis for differentiation

Sources: Aijo (1996); Christopher (1996); Christopher *et al.* (1991); Ford (1994); Grönroos (1994); Kotler (1992); Palmer *et al.* (2005); Ravald and Grönroos, (1996); Turnbull *et al.* (1996)

Task 1.5

Collect together some adverts from various published sources such as lifestyle magazines, trade journals and newspapers.

- With reference to Table 1.3, what approach to RM do you think the company strategy is focusing on?

- What would you say the adverts are attempting to achieve in terms of customer response?

- In what areas should the company allocate resources to implement a good RM approach?

However, it should be remembered that not all customers want or require relationships with their suppliers (Jackson, 1985a; Blois, 1996) and it may not always be possible or desirable to develop relationships within certain markets (Palmer and Bejou, 1994). Examples of this may include:

- price-sensitive products where items are purchased purely on the basis of price;
- commodities that are homogeneous; and
- where there are purely transaction-based demand patterns.

Task 1.6

Think of a recent example of where you have been interested in just purchasing a product or service and not forming "a relationship" with the supplier.

- What was the background surrounding the purchase?
- What are the features of the market?
- What are the bases of competitive advantage for organizations within the market?

From looking at the growth and development of RM, it becomes apparent that many differing strands of relational marketing have developed in differing contexts and with differing areas of precise focus. One can conclude that organizations have relationships with different individuals and groups of individuals within many different organizations and within different contexts requiring different strategies and tactics. Have a look at the mini-case on 888 for an illustration of this (see p. 18).

Definitions of RM

As a result of its varied roots, there are at least 26 definitions of RM (Ballantyne *et al.*, 2003). Some of the definitional perspectives are shown in Table 1.4.

TABLE 1.4 Examples of Definitional Perspectives for RM

Perspective	Definition
Berry (1983) from a services perspective	"Relationship Marketing is attracting, maintaining and multi-service organizations enhancing customer relationships" (p. 25)
Jackson (1985a) from an industrial marketing perspective	"Marketing concentrated towards strong, lasting relationships with individual accounts" (p. 120)
Berry and Parasuramen (1991) from a services perspective	"Attracting, developing and retaining customer relationships" (p. 133)
Grönroos (1995) from a network perspective	"To identify and establish, maintain and enhance relationships with customers and other stakeholders, at a profit so that the objectives of the partners interest are met; and this is achieved by a mutual exchange and fulfillment of promises"

MINI-CASE: 888'S NEW TABLES – NOT FOR BOYS

The 2005 Gambling Act acted as a catalyst for huge market growth within the gambling industry after many years of regulatory restrictions. The Act allowed for an increase in the supply of new casinos, a relaxation of advertising restrictions and the opening up of new channels including the Internet. However, the push for this expansion is perceived by many as coming from the government and the gambling industry and not the market itself.

The public appear deeply divided over government plans to allow deregulation of the gambling industry. Many are behind senior Church of England and Roman Catholic figures who, together with the heads of the Methodist Church, the Church of Scotland and The Salvation Army, are vociferous in their raising of concerns related to the social consequences of gambling. However, a YouGov poll highlighted some of the anomalies the public have. Many people are worried about the potential problems gambling may create but, at the same time, this is balanced with the right to choose what they do in their own leisure time.

With market research suggesting the most likely targets for the new Las Vegas style casinos to open across the country are ABC1 males in the 18–24 age group who have visited casinos abroad, the growth in popularity of online gambling has largely been sidelined. Online virtual casinos are likely to attract other potential customers such as females who may be daunted by the prospect of visiting "bricks and mortar" casinos. Principal among the providers of such services is 888.com.

888 Holdings plc is licensed and regulated by the Government of Gibraltar where its main headquarters is located. It is one of the world's most popular online gaming companies offering products such as blackjack, roulette and video poker. Preferring not to outsource, 888 develops and runs its own software, marketing, payment processing, risk management and member relationship management. Although losing 55 per cent of its revenues when the United States outlawed online gambling in October 2006, 888's profits rose by 34 per cent to $90.5m despite the loss of 26 million of its registered customers

While the company attempted to reduce costs by slashing 210 jobs (equating to 23 per cent of the workforce) and cutting its marketing costs by 16 per cent to $84.3 million, it stepped up research and development spending by 71 per cent to $19.4 million. The latest product offerings include multi-hand poker and backgammon. Gigi Levy, the chief executive, highlighted how 888 was continually exploring new ways to attract new customers and retain existing ones. This includes a women-only poker table. The new table is set to feature pink baize, players can enjoy disco balls and there is a virtual bar where players can enjoy cocktails.

Sources

"New help 888 top $90m", A. Osborne, *Daily Telegraph*, 1 May 2007.

"Britain deeply divided over casinos", G. Jones, and H. McCormack, *Daily Telegraph*, 2 May 2007.

www.888holdingsplc.com

www.totalgambler.com/tips/bettingnews

Question

Which loyalty schemes that you are familiar with do you think are appropriate within this context?

When examining definitions of RM, nearly all involve common underpinning themes such as attracting, maintaining and enhancing mutually beneficial relationships which are characterized by interactions. Very often these individual relationships are viewed within a much wider network of relationships.

Chapter Summary

From studying the literature, there are clearly some areas of commonality across the themes that have emerged (e.g. a services context, network and industrial marketing, etc.) Principal among these is the desire to develop stable, long-term relationships with all stakeholders so as to acquire competitive advantage (Egan, 2003). It has been argued that strategic marketing, which emphasizes profitability and market share, overshadows the customer and that the four Ps are product and production focused with limited application to emerging services. Traditional marketing theory emphasizes the transactional nature of exchanges, but marketing exchange is more meaningful at an organizational level when multiple exchanges are viewed over time. This identifies the importance of the development of the client relationship. Perspectives on RM are complex, and several schools of thought have emerged. These apply RM ideas that require different resource allocations.

However, it is the diversity of these themes and their appropriateness and applicability to differing contexts that is problematic. Unsurprisingly, given such a plethora of differing terms, perspectives and strands, there has historically been much discussion not only as to what RM constitutes but who and what should be involved in the relational context and within which boundaries.

Chapter 2 explores in more depth the concepts central to Relationship Marketing, and discusses the appropriateness and applicability of some key dimensions. Chapters 3 and 4 review different marketing contexts in which Relationship Marketing has emerged and where relationship approaches play a key role: on the one hand, industrial marketing and supply relationships and, on the other consumer service contexts.

Review Questions

1 Think of an FMCG market and a services market. Is RM of more relevance to one market than the other? What are the key areas of commonality and differences from a firm and customer perspective?

2 Is RM relevant to a publicly funded hospital? If so, how?

3 In what circumstances might a transactional approach to marketing strategy be appropriate?

Further Reading

Egan, J. (2003) "Back to the Future: Divergence in Relationship Marketing Research", *Marketing Theory*, vol. 3, no.1, pp. 145–157.

Palmer, R., A. Lindgreen, and J. Vanhamme (2005) "Relationship Marketing: Schools of Thought and Future Research Directions", *Marketing Intelligence and Planning*, vol. 23, no. 3, pp. 313–330.

Vargo, S.L. and R.F. Lusch (2004) "Evolving to a New Dominant Logic of Marketing", *Journal of Marketing*, vol. 68, Jan, pp. 1–17.

END OF CHAPTER CASE AND KEY QUESTIONS

Tesco

Tesco plc is a UK-based global supermarket chain with annual revenues in excess of £30 billion. By October 2006 Tesco was posting half-year profits of £1.15bn. With an established presence in the huge brick-and-mortar infrastructure, Tesco is also the world's most successful and profitable online grocer.

Tesco.com is by far the most popular online grocery site in the UK, capturing 66 per cent of all online grocery orders, with 750 000 regular customers placing an average of 30 000 orders per day. Total sales online everyday have risen to approximately £2.5 million.

Tesco attribute part of their success to a focus on the customer experience: "Customers value the time savings of not having to drive to a store, manually pick the groceries, queue up to pay, drive home and unload the car. Customers do, however, usually enjoy the opportunity to touch and feel the fresh produce and to make 'impulse buys' " says Patricia Seybold, a journalist for the *Financial Daily*.

Tesco has managed to streamline the customer's shopping experience while ensuring customers get the quality and the prices they want. At the same time they have seamlessly integrated customers' in-store and online shopping experiences.

Many online grocery services assume that it is more cost-effective to handle inventory and fulfilment operations from a distribution warehouse. But Gary Sargeant of Tesco realized that customers would prefer to purchase online from the store in which they would normally shop in person. That way, customers would receive the same price for each item online as the price in the store nearest their home.

Customers were also familiar with the selection of products available in their local stores. By linking the online shopping application directly to each store's inventory systems, it was unlikely that customers would order a product that was not available, saving considerable time and effort for both customers and for Tesco. Finally, the servers in each store could save a history of each customer's favourite products to ensure that these were always in stock. Tesco keeps track of what each family has bought, both in the store and online.

This "shop online from my store" scenario permits regional pricing variations to be maintained, boosting overall profits (in the supermarket business, certain neighbourhoods support higher prices than others). At the same time, customers' online prices remain competitive with the prices charged by local stores.

The Tesco Direct team takes the customer experience very seriously. They monitor on-time deliveries, accuracy of orders and customer satisfaction. They also simulate customers' online shopping experiences to monitor the state of the end-to-end customer experience proactively.

Tesco's online shopping site also does a good job of cross-selling and up-selling. When you check off an item (such as bread), other related items (such as marmalade or butter) pop up on the screen.

Every purchase the household makes – online and offline – is captured. That information is used to improve the shopper's convenience and their experience with Tesco.

Tesco will also launch a 184-page catalogue to promote non-food goods. It will be handed out in 15 stores where customers will be able to order goods for delivery to their home or to be picked up from the store later. Tony Shiret, an analyst at Credit Suisse, described Tesco's venture into the kind of multi-channel sales pioneered by Argos, the catalogue store, as "a toe in the water". He said: "This looks like a limited trial, but I would be fairly surprised if they didn't extend it.

Sources

"Tesco bags two-thirds of on-line grocery market", Tash Schfrin, *Computer Weekly*, 4 October, 2006.

"Tesco hungry for non-food on-line sales", Sarah Butler, *The Times*, 31 August 2006.

"Shopping on-line with Tesco", Patricia Seybold, *Financial Daily from the HINDU Group*, 7 March 2002.

Questions

1 What type of relationship do Tesco and its customers have?

2 Who are the winners and who are the losers or is this the "win-win" situation for all stakeholders that RM theorists often mention?

References

Aijo, H.E. (1996) "The theoretical and philosophical underpinnings of Relationship Marketing", *European Journal of Marketing,* vol. 30, no.2, pp. 8–18.

Ambler, T. (2004) "A long perspective of marketing", *European Business Forum,* accessed at http://www.ebfonline.com/main_feat/in_depth.asp?id=548, 15 December 2005.

Anderson, J.C. and J.A. Narus (1990) "A Model of Distributor Firm and Manufacture Firm Working Partnerships", *Journal of Marketing,* vol. 54, no. 1, pp. 42–58.

Ballantyne, D., M. Christopher, and A. Payne (2003) "Relationship Marketing: Looking Back, Looking Forward", *Marketing Theory,* vol. 3, no. 1, pp. 159–166.

Baumgartner, J. (1991) "Nonmarketing Professional Need More than 4Ps", *Marketing News,* 22 July, p. 28.

Berry, L.L. (1983) "Relationship Marketing", in *Emerging Perspectives on Services Marketing,* L.L. Berry, G.L. Shostack and G.D. Upah, Chicago, IL, American Marketing Association, pp. 25–28.

Berry, L.L. (1995) "Relationship Marketing of Services – Growing Interest, Emerging Perspectives", *Journal of the Academy of Marketing Science,* vol. 23, no. 4, pp. 236–245.

Berry, L.L. and A. Parasuraman (1991) *Marketing Services,* New York: The Free Press.

Bitner, M.J. (1995) "Building Service Relationships: It's All About Promises", *Journal of the Academy of Marketing Science,* vol. 23, no. 4, pp. 246–251.

Blois, K.J. (1996) "Relationship Marketing in Organisational Markets: When is it Appropriate?", *Journal of Marketing Management,* vol. 12, pp. 161–173.

Booms, B.H. and M.I. Bitner (1982) "Marketing Strategies and Organisation Structures for Service Firms", in J. Donnelly and W. George (eds) *Marketing of Services,* Chicago, IL: American Marketing Association.

Borden, N.H. (1964) "The Concept of the Marketing Mix", *Journal of Advertising Research,* June, vol. 4, pp. 2–7.

Brodie, R.J., N.E. Coviello, R.W. Brookes and V. Little (1997) "Towards a Paradigm Shift in Marketing?, An Examination of Current Marketing Practices", *Journal of Marketing Management,* vol. 13, pp. 386–406.

Bucklin, L.P. and S. Sengupta (1993) "Organizing Successful Co-marketing Alliances", *Journal of Marketing,* vol. 57, no. 2, pp. 32–46.

Buttle, F. (1996) "Relationship Marketing", in F. Buttle (ed.) *Relationship Marketing: Theory and Practice,* London: Paul Chapman Publishing.

Christopher, M. (1996) "From brand values to customer values", *Journal of Marketing Practice: Applied Marketing Science,* vol. 2, no. 1, pp. 55–65.

Christopher, M., A. Payne and D. Ballantyne (1991) *Relationship Marketing: Bringing Quality, Customer Service and Marketing Together,* Oxford, UK: Butterworth Heinemann, p. 4.

Crosby, L.A. and N. Stevens (1987) "Effects of Relationship Marketing on Relationship Satisfaction, Retention and Prices in the Life Insurance Industry", *Journal of Marketing Research,* vol. 24, November, pp. 404–411.

Day, G.S. (1990) *Market Driven Strategy,* New York: The Free Press, in R.M. Morgan and S.D. Hunt (1994) "The Commitment–Trust Theory of Relationship Marketing", *Journal of Marketing,* vol. 58, July, pp. 20–38.

Dixon, D. and K. Blois (1983) "Some Limitations of the 4P's as a paradigm for marketing", Marketing Education Group Annual Conference, Cranfield Institute of Technology, UK, July.

Dowling, G. and M. Uncles (1997) "Do Customer Loyalty Programs Really Work?", *Sloan Management Review,* vol. 38, Summer, pp. 71–82.

Dwyer, F., P. Schurr and S. Oh (1987) "Developing Buyer–Seller Relationships", *Journal of Marketing,* vol. 51, no. 2 (April), pp. 11–27.

East, R., P. Gendall, K. Hammond and W. Lomax (2005) "Consumer Loyalty: Singular, Additive ot Interactive?", *Australian Marketing Journal,* vol. 13, no. 2, pp. 10–26.

Egan, J. (2003) "Back to the Future: Divergence in Relationship Marketing Research", *Marketing Theory,* vol. 3, no. 1, pp. 145–157.

Ford, D. (1990) *Understanding Business Marketing – Interaction, Relationships and Networks,* London: Academic Press.

Ford, D. (1994) *Understanding Business Marketing – Interaction, Relationships and Networks,* 2nd edn, London: The Dryden Press.

Grönroos, C. (1990) "The Marketing Strategy Continuum: Towards a Marketing Concept for the 1990s", *Management Decision,* vol. 29, no. 1, p. 9.

Grönroos, C. (1994) "Quo Vadis, Marketing? Towards a Relationship Marketing Paradigm", *Journal of Marketing Management,* vol. 10, pp. 347–360.

Grönroos, C. (1995) "The Rebirth of Modern Marketing: Six Propositions About Relationship Marketing", Swedish School of Economics and Business Administration, *Working Paper,* 307, Helsinki.

Grönroos, C. and T. Strandvik (1997) "Editorial", *Journal of Marketing Research,* vol. 13, p. 341.

Gummesson, E. (1987) "The New Marketing – Developing Long Term, Interactive Relationships", *Long Range Planning,* vol. 20, no. 4, pp. 10–20.

Gummesson, E. (1994) "Making Relationship Marketing Operational", *International Journal of Science Management,* vol. 5, no. 55, pp. 5–20.

Håkansson, H. (ed.) (1982) *International Marketing and Purchasing of Industrial Goods: An Interaction Approach,* Chichester: Wiley.

Håkansson, H., J. Johanson and B. Wootz (1976) "Influence Tactics in Buyer–Seller Processes", *Industrial Marketing Management,* vol. 5, pp. 319–332, in D. Ford (ed.) (1990) *Understanding Business Markets: Interaction, Relationships and Networks,* London: Academic Press.

Jackson, B.B. (1985) "Build Customer Relationships That Last", *Harvard Business Review,* vol. 63, November/December, pp. 120–128.

Jobber, D. (2004) *Principles and Practice of Marketing,* 4th edn, London: McGraw-Hill.

Johanson, J. and L.G. Mattsson (1988) "Internationalisation in Industrial Systems: A Network Approach", in V. Hood (ed.) *Strategies in Global Competition,* New York: Helm.

Judd, V. (1987) "Differentiate with the 5th P:People", *Industrial Marketing Management,* November.

Kent, R.A. (1986) "Faith in Four P's: An Alternative", *Journal Of Marketing Management,* no. 2, pp. 145–154.

Kotler, P. (1986) "Megamarketing", *Harvard Business Review,* March–April, pp. 117–24.

Kotler, P. (1992) "Marketing's New Paradigm: What's Really Happening Out There", *Planning Review,* vol. 20, no. 5, pp. 50–52.

Kotler, P., G. Armstrong, J. Saunders and V. Wong (2003) *Principles of Marketing,* London: *Financial Times,* Prentice Hall.

MacNeil, I.R., (1980) *The New Social Contract: An Inquiry into Modern Contractual Obligations,* New Haven, CT: Yale University Press.

McCarthy, E.J. (1960) *Basic Marketing: A Managerial Approach,* Homewood, IL: Irwin.

Marshall, RA., A. Palmer and S.N. Weisbart (1979) "The Nature and Significance of Agent–Policyholder Relationships", *CLU Journal,* no. 33, January, pp. 44–53.

Moller, K. (1992) "Research Traditions in Marketing: Theoretical Notes", in H.C. Blomqvist, C. Grönroos and L.J. Lindqvist (eds) *Economics and Marketing: Essays in Honour of Gosta Mickwitz,* Helsingfor, Finland.

Morgan, R.M. and S.D. Hunt (1994) "The Commitment-trust Theory of Relationship Marketing", *Journal of Marketing,* vol. 58, July, pp. 20–38.

Normann, R. and R. Ramirez (1993) "From Value Chain to Value Constellation: Designing Interactive Strategy", *Harvard Business Review,* July–August, pp. 65–77.

Palmer, A. and D. Bejou (1994) "Buyer–Seller Relationships: A Conceptual Model and Empirical Investigation", *Journal of Marketing Management,* vol. 10, pp. 495–512.

Palmer, R., A. Lindgreen and J. Vanhamme (2005) "Relationship Marketing: Schools of Thought and Future Research Directions", *Marketing Intelligence and Planning,* vol. 23, no. 3, pp. 313–330.

Peters, J. and R. Waterman (1982) *In Search of Excellence: Lessons from America's Best Run Companies,* New York: Harper and Row.

Ravald, A. and C. Grönroos (1996) "The Value Concept and Relationship Marketing", *European Journal of Marketing,* vol. 30, no. 2, pp. 19–30.

Reinartz, W. and V. Kumar (2000) "On the Profitability of Long-life Customers in a Noncontractual Setting: An Empirical Investigation and Implications for Marketing", *Journal of Marketing,* vol. 64 (October), pp. 17–35.

Reinartz, W. and V. Kumar (2002) "The Mismanagement of Customer Loyalty", *Harvard Business Review,* July, pp. 86–94.

Reinartz, W. and V. Kumar (2003) "The Impact of Customer Relationship Characteristics on Profitable Lifetime Duration", *Journal of Marketing,* vol. 67, no. 1, pp. 77–99.

Turnbull, P., M. Cunningham and D. Ford (1996) "Interaction, Relationships and Networks in Business Markets: An Evolving Perspective", *Journal of Business and Industrial Marketing,* vol. 131, no. 3, pp. 44–62.

Varadarajan, P. and D. Rajaratnam (1986) "Symbiotic Marketing Revisited", *Journal of Marketing,* vol. 50 (January), pp. 7–17, pp. 20–38.

Vargo, S.L. and R.F. Lusch (2004) "Evolving to a New Dominant Logic of Marketing", *Journal of Marketing,* vol. 68, January, pp. 1–17.

Verhoef, P., P. Frances and J. Hoekstra (2002) "The Effect of Relational Constructs on Consumer Referrals and Number of Services Purchased from a Multi-service Provider: Does Age of Relationship Matter?", *Journal of the Academy of Marketing Science,* vol. 30, no. 3, pp. 202–216.

CHAPTER 02

Defining Relationship Marketing

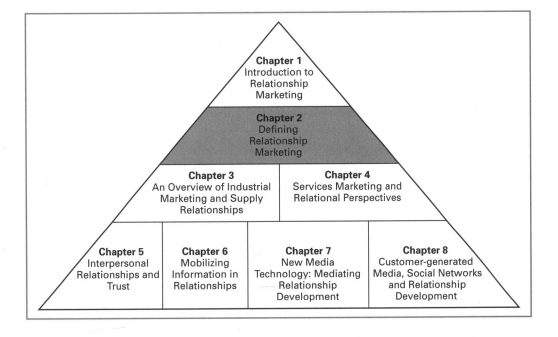

Chapter 1
Introduction to Relationship Marketing

Chapter 2
Defining Relationship Marketing

Chapter 3
An Overview of Industrial Marketing and Supply Relationships

Chapter 4
Services Marketing and Relational Perspectives

Chapter 5
Interpersonal Relationships and Trust

Chapter 6
Mobilizing Information in Relationships

Chapter 7
New Media Technology: Mediating Relationship Development

Chapter 8
Customer-generated Media, Social Networks and Relationship Development

❖ LEARNING OBJECTIVES

After studying this chapter you should be able to:

1 **appreciate** the multidisciplinary and multicultural roots of RM

2 **understand** that RM comprises a flexible series of concepts

3 **analyse** and **define** the differing parameters of RM

4 **evaluate** the applicability of differing RM concepts to different markets and customers

Chapter Contents

Introduction

Historically, the term RM has been much used within marketing to cover a plethora of different concepts and contexts. As highlighted in Chapter 1, the term still covers a "broad church" (Egan, 2003: 149) encompassing many differing strands of relational philosophies and contexts.

The purpose of this chapter is to identify the parameters of RM given the variety of markets and customers in which it may be applied and to identify how the various features of concepts, themes and dimensions have commonality. The chapter is structured as follows: first, it identifies the boundaries of RM in terms of the nature and number of the parties involved. It then progresses by examining a number of typologies used within relational contexts before proposing a classification system for relationships.

Boundaries of Relationships

As well as differing themes of RM, the scope and type of relational exchanges are also flexible depending on which concept and context it is viewed from. Some concepts incorporate a broader view of the marketing organization within its environment while others take a narrower approach. How the boundaries of relationships are drawn will affect the form and extent that the relationship will take. Hollensen (2003) suggests these concepts fall into one of three categories (see Figure 2.1).

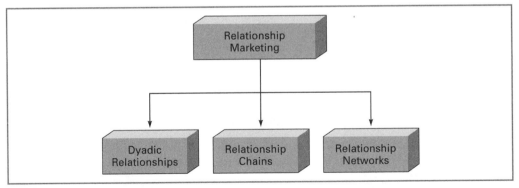

FIGURE 2.1 Categories of Relationships

Each of these concepts is now explored in more detail.

Dyadic relationships

The relationship is primarily between two parties who are usually the seller and the buyer (see Figure 2.2).

FIGURE 2.2 A Relational Dyad

This is the building block on which customer or inter-firm relationships are developed and may be at a number of levels. For example, at one level it will be a service provider and a customer (think of a trip to the dentist) or a sales representative and a purchasing officer. At another level it may involve strategic alliances between the senior managers of two large organizations.

> 𝒢𝒪 INSIGHT: A Dyad is "two units treated as one, a group of two", New English Dictionary

A chain of relationships

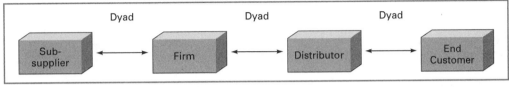

FIGURE 2.3 A Chain of Relationships

With chains of relationships, the simple dyadic model is extended to include parties other than purely the buyer and seller. For example, it may contain a number of dyadic relationships between the members of a vertical supply chain each attempting to create value enhancing relationships (see Figure 2.3). This type of model is typically found, for example, in a manufacturing context where there may be the manufacturer of a finished product who is supplied by a manufacturer of components, who is in turn, supplied by a manufacturer of sub-components or raw materials.

Networks of relationships

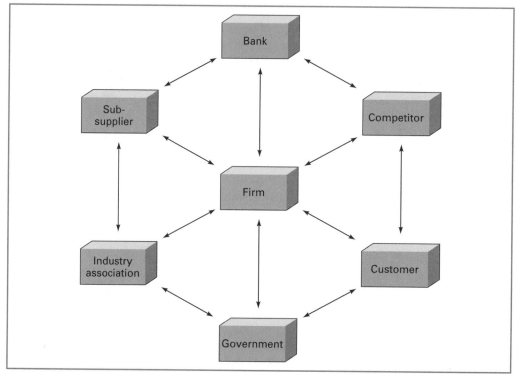

FIGURE 2.4 A Network of Relationships

A more complex structure is one of networks of relationships where dyads of relationships interact with three or more other parties (see Figure 2.4). So, for example, a builder may have a network of relationships incorporating customers, suppliers often in the form of builders merchants, the bank, other builders with whom there may be a competitive or co-operative relationship, other tradespeople in the form of plumbers, electricians and so on.

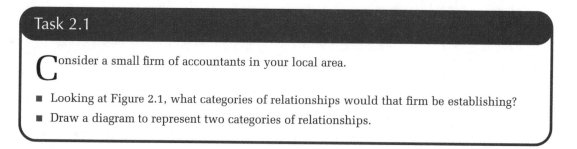

Task 2.1

Consider a small firm of accountants in your local area.

- Looking at Figure 2.1, what categories of relationships would that firm be establishing?
- Draw a diagram to represent two categories of relationships.

Each of these general relationship concepts is now explained in more depth.

A Dyadic Concept: The Interaction Approach

The interaction approach has its roots in industrial and services marketing and views marketing as an interactive process in a social context. So, if we take the examples given in the first chapter, sole traders and small businesses (e.g. hairdressers, shopkeepers, etc.) acquire intimate knowledge about their customers. With this they are in a position to make product suggestions, as well as making credit judgements, and to interact socially with customers (small talk, for example). As a result close, complex, long-term relationships between buyer and seller have often developed. The same is true at a different level where, for example, large manufacturers of industrial products acquire knowledge about their organizational customers and the key individuals involved in purchasing decisions within them.

Research in Scandinavia by the Industrial Marketing and Purchasing (IMP) Group (1990) suggested that the traditional concept of the 4Ps model of marketing was not appropriate for this type of context. They suggested a number of alternative variables which describe and influence the interaction between the buyer and seller within such contexts (see Figure 2.5):

- The interaction and exchange process
- The parties involved in terms of the buying and selling firm and the individuals within them
- The environment within which the interaction takes place
- The atmosphere within which the interaction takes place

Each of these is now explored in more detail.

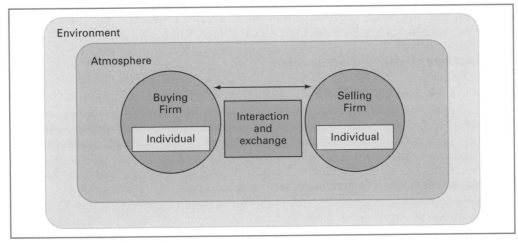

FIGURE 2.5 The Interaction Approach
Based on: IMP Group (1990)

The foundations of relationships are the individual or "discrete transactions" or "episodes" on which they are based. In its purest form, the discrete transaction may be money on one side and an easily recognized commodity on the other. More commonly, these episodes consist of a core product and information, financial and social exchange. Each individual episode can affect the likelihood of a relationship developing and its nature. So, for example, if a customer receives poor service during an interaction with the selling organization when they have only just started to use them, they may have second thoughts about whether they wish to use that firm again.

There are a number of other factors that will influence the likelihood of a relationship developing:

- The product service or offering
- The frequency of demand
- The nature of the interaction

The product offering has a major influence on the likely development of relationships. It may not be always possible or desirable to develop relationships within certain markets (e.g. price sensitive commodities). However, where there is a complex product and there are difficulties in interpreting the exact nature of the need (for example, professional services such as lawyers and dentists), a relationship is more likely to develop.

Demand patterns will also impact on the likelihood of relationships developing. For a relationship to develop, the customer must have an ongoing, periodic desire for the service. This is what differentiates it from a purely transaction-based demand pattern. So, at one level this may be for a dentist and at another it may be for component parts or commercial legal advice.

Where there is interaction of a personal nature, the likely development of relationships is increased because there is an opportunity to add value to the product offering by providing certain demands peripherals e.g. social exchange (having a chat!), customer care, etc.

The participants in the process

This not only refers to the characteristics of the individuals involved in the relationship – such as their motivation, experience, preferred interaction style and risk aversion – but also to the features of the participating organizations such as culture, size, structures and strategies.

The atmosphere in which interaction occurs

The atmosphere evolves as the relationship develops and is unique to the relationship insofar as it is a hybrid culture which reflects the personalities of the individuals and cultures of the organizations involved. It encompasses factors such as relative power dependence and the "asymmetry" of the participating organizations, the closeness and mutual expectations of those involved in the relationship and the state of any conflicts or co-operation both between the individuals and their organizations.

The environment in which interaction occurs

A number of external factors will affect the likely development of a relationship.

Market structure refers to the number of suppliers and the differences between them. Relationships are more likely to develop in a concentrated market structure where there are a few key providers. Where there are more alternative suppliers with attractive offerings, there will be a decrease in the motivation to bond within a particular relationship as there may be the temptation to defect to cheaper or better value suppliers.

In a stable market environment a close relationship increases the ability of one organization to forecast the likely behaviour of another. However, where there is a high degree of market "dynamism", the opportunity cost of reliance on a single or small number of relationships may be increased.

Other environmental factors which affect the likelihood of relationship development include market globalization and internationalization, channel positioning and social functions.

A Dyadic Concept: Customer Relationship Management (CRM)

Although, historically, many have viewed this type of RM as tactical (e.g. the use of loyalty schemes as a sales promotion tactic), CRM is increasingly being recognized as a strategic approach to developing market relationships with individual customers. Critically, it requires some form of response from the potential customer so that the firm is enabled to take action. Have a look at the mini-case on Lego which illustrates this (see pp. 33–4).

> INSIGHT: "CRM is an enterprise-wide commitment to identify your named individual customers and create a relationship between your company and these customers so long as this relationship is mutually beneficial" (Gamble, Stone and Woodcock, 1999).

According to Tapp (2005), a firm that has adopted a philosophical approach to CRM will demonstrate the following characteristics:

- Employees who consider customer service as their main priority
- Processes that cut across functional departmental boundaries to serve the customer better
- Customers identified by their value to the company and prioritized accordingly
- A centralized database that has an integral part to play in terms of processing "live" inbound and outbound customer contact often across multiple channels

It is not within the scope of this text to discuss dimensions of CRM in depth. However, below is an illustration of some of the key factors surrounding its implementation.

Technological developments

The increased accessibility of computer technology coupled with increasingly sophisticated software allows for the capture of data (through for example, texting or emailing entries to competitions, loyalty cards, etc.), its storage and its retrieval for marketing purposes (such as personalized letters, phone scripts and the offer of customized products or service packages to carefully defined target segments).

Market and media fragmentation

Increasingly fragmented markets coupled with the growth of specialized media such as interactive cable and satellite TV channels (e.g. music, sport, fashion and travel), Internet websites, radio stations, etc. means that more targeted offerings may be promoted through more targeted channels. This gives an opportunity for low-cost micromarketing to select segments in a defined geographic area.

Increasingly sophisticated analytical techniques

By using psychographical and geo-demographical techniques, and cross-referencing these with, for example, product usage and media usage, complex profiles of potential customers may be identified and targeted with customized offerings. Key enablers for this are increasingly sophisticated software packages. At present we see this use of sophisticated geo-demographic profiling in well-targeted daytime regional, television TV adverts on networks such as Midlands Asian TV (MATV), which is a very successful regional television network in the central UK. In future, authors (Jiang, 2000) predict that firms can engage in similar one-to-one marketing through Internet channels.

A key component of successful CRM hinges on the effectiveness of the marketing database. Database marketing allows direct contact with the customer through various media channels such as:

- direct mail,
- websites,
- telemarketing, and
- direct response advertising (e.g. Interactive TV).

INSIGHT: "Database Marketing is an interactive approach to marketing that uses individually addressable marketing media and channels" (Stone *et al.*, 1995).

Typical information held on such marketing databases includes profitability measures of customers, product usage information, promotional information, transactional information and psychographic and geo-demographic profiles of existing and prospective customers. Databases may be used for a number of marketing techniques including:

- the targeting of likely respondents;
- increasing loyalty through the use of loyalty cards;
- developing interest through the provision of information. This might include company newsletters, customised offers, etc.

Hansotia (2002) suggests CRM works best in sectors where,

- there are frequent customer interactions;
- a high level of expertise may be needed to guide purchase decisions;
- multiple products and services are purchased by the customer.

Management Implications

From these two dyadic concepts we can see that the strategic development of dyadic relationships with customers relies on diverse firm competences. In the environment of long-term business-to-business relationships, the atmosphere of reassurance, comfort and the recognition of the perceived expertise of either party is sometimes informally transmitted as well as formally evident. Thus, for a positive interactive atmosphere, strong people skills allied to proactive internal service culture will be needed. These are not short-term investments – it takes time to guide staff to recognize and reciprocate cultural cues. For the effective encouragement of positive dyadic relationships, CRM requires strong internal systems and good technology integration as a starting point. It is clear that the underlying CRM approach cannot graft well on to the theoretical concepts of the interaction model. This highlights perhaps that the different philosophies behind relationship development activities can diverge significantly.

Having examined dyadic relationships, the next section explores chains of relationships.

Task 2.1

High street banks are typical examples of where CRM has been implemented. For a high street bank of your choice, comment on the following:

- What does their range of products and services typically include?

- What are its distribution and communication channels with customers?

- How does it promote its products and services?

- Using an example, explain what type of relationship banks are trying to engender with their customers.

MINI-CASE: LEGO – POSITIONING TO DIE FOR?

Lego is one of the world's largest toy manufacturers. It is estimated that more than 400 million children and adults play with Lego each year. However, despite being voted the nation's favourite toy for a number of successive years and a YouGov poll into the top ten favourite toys of the past century showing Lego as the clear winner (ahead of computer games, teddy bears, Meccano and train sets !) Lego is in serious financial difficulty!

With an annual revenue of over £1billion and employing around 8000 people in North and South America, Asia and Europe, the company has posted a loss for a number of consecutive years. After attempting unsuccessfully to redress its losses with new products such as computer games, the company is attempting to restructure so as to focus on its core values. As Frank Martin, of Hornby toys states, "Children are still interested in playing. Blaming the TV or computer games is a poor excuse for poor performance."

Lego's chief executive, 35-year-old Jorgen Vig Knustorp summarizes the strategy: "The new ownership structure enables the Lego group to increase its focus on its core business. We have to return to the core of our brand and to deliver what consumers are expecting us to deliver."

A key enabler of this strategy is "professional customer interaction". "Lego has to focus on combining old know-how with new sales channels", says Jens Loff of PLS Ramboil Management, a Danish consulting firm.

Customers will help create value by participating in product development and forming virtual communities. A key tool for achieving this will be the Lego website and the Legoclub. Legoclub is a fan club established by Lego. Profit maximization is not its prime purpose as membership is free. Once members have provided details and signed up, they have access to various Lego offers on its products, a range of information on Lego and interactive games. Competitions have first prizes that invite the winners to Legoland to help design the next generation of Lego products (a focus group!). It also includes facilities that enable users to design and order their own Lego products which are subsequently custom-made at the Lego factory, boxed in Lego boxing and shipped to the designer's home address.

Lego's value exchange site (Szmigin, Canning and Reppel, 2005) is highly customized but allows for extensive customer interaction and dialogue not just with the organization but with other enthusiasts. This is backed up with hard copies of the Lego magazine sent to members' addresses, discounts to Legoland and customized offers on its products and clothes.

As one competitor commented, "Lego has a position to die for. Children think they are having fun, parents think it's educational and now they are adding value to the core product during the whole process."

Questions

1 **How has technology enabled Lego to adopt an interactive approach?**
2 **Why do you think Lego still uses a hard copy of its magazine?**

A Chain of Relationships

Much of the focus on chains of relationships revolves around the concept of vertical channels and their associated relationships, culminating in the "Lean Enterprise" (Womack and Jones, 1996). This is a collaboration of organizations within the supply chain.

The philosophy behind the lean enterprise is that organizations within the supply chain organize themselves around value-adding activities, thus eliminating waste and providing the end customer with a stronger value proposition (see Figure 2.6). In this way, the supply chain becomes the competitive advantage rather than the competing individual organizations. This is achieved through collaboration and co-operation between the channel members rather than the more traditional inter-firm competition approach. Consequently, good relationships between the member organizations are essential.

Examples of good practice often cited in this context include Toyota and Pratt and Whitney. Another example is IKEA (see the mini-case study on IKEA below) which uses 2300 suppliers in 67 countries to supply over 10 000 products to its stores at up 30 per cent cheaper than its competitors (*The Economist*, 2004).

Network Approaches

Network theory builds on and develops the interaction approach further. Instead of concentrating on one buyer–seller (dyadic) relationship, there is a recognition that organizations operate in a complex, dynamic commercial environment and that decisions are made within the context of a complex web of interrelationships. One early perspective on the scope of relationships in which organizations may be involved was provided by Christopher *et al.* (1994) in their "Six Markets" model (see Figure 2.7). Here it is suggested that the firm has a number of markets at whom it needs to direct marketing activities and with whom it needs to formulate positive relationships. These are now explored in more detail.

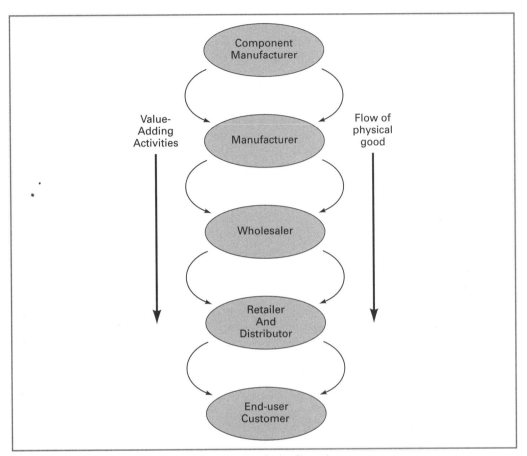

FIGURE 2.6 The Relationship Chain Applied to a Vertical Distribution Channel

MINI-CASE: IKEA

The IKEA group of companies has over 220 stores in over 33 countries of which 24 are stores owned and run by franchisees. Nearly 400 million people visited these stores in 2006. The group turnover for the fiscal year 2005 was EUR 14.8 billion. The organization employs over 90 000 people in 44 countries. In 2006 over 160 million copies of the IKEA catalogue were printed in 52 editions and 25 languages.

The company has over 2000 manufacturing suppliers in 53 countries globally contributing to its product range of 9500 lines. With such a vast network of suppliers, IKEA ensures that it is able to communicate and collaborate with all its suppliers in the supply chain. Primarily revolving around the concept of supply-chain management, IKEA is able to organize and manage its diverse communities of suppliers. Its supply systems allow it to improve sourcing, control its order management and react to changing customer demands. Using a secure, real-time Internet-based platform, it is able to share information between multiple tiers of trading partners to support its cost reduction and service-enhancement objectives.

However, there is more to IKEA's relationships with its suppliers than the control of physical product movements or the flow of order-related information. IKEA believes that good working conditions and the protection of the outside environment are prerequisites for doing good business and their slogan "low price but not at any price" epitomizes what they are attempting to achieve.

When starting up new relationships, IKEA gives preference to suppliers who fulfil certain requirements surrounding corporate citizenship such as respecting human rights, treating their workforce fairly and minimizing environmental impact. IKEA has produced a 50-page report listing its requirements. The report is extremely user friendly.

The company believes in investing in long-term relationships with suppliers who are committed to their practices and together they develop an action plan to achieve them. Part of the relationship revolves around knowledge transfer whereby IKEA will provide expertise to help suppliers. It will give a period of up to 24 months to suppliers to comply with its requirements and IKEA representatives will visit a supply company 1–2 times a month to ensure the relationship is working smoothly and expectations on both sides of the relationship are being met.

Sources

IKEA press release: IKEA – their co-workers and customers join hands to benefit Hurricane Katrina victims (www.ikea-group.ikea.com/press)

IKEA press release: IKEA sales and stores on the rise (www.ikea-group.ikea.com/press)

Question

How might power imbalances such as the one highlighted in the above case adversely affect such relations between organizations and their suppliers?

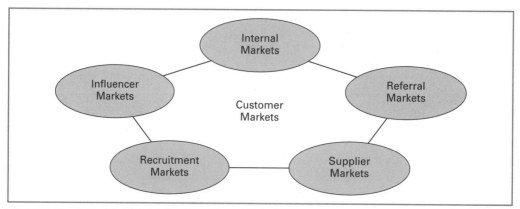

FIGURE 2.7 The Six Markets Model: A Broadened View of Marketing

With customer markets there is a focus on the existing, direct customers of the firm and not just potential ones. Internal markets refer to individuals and departments within the organization that may either be classified as an internal customer or be viewed as an integral part of meeting the external customer's needs and wants (customer or market orientation).

Suppliers of services and products to the firm are increasingly being viewed as collaborators in the value chain rather than adversaries from whom the best price can be extracted (similar to the concept of relationship chains). Referral markets are referral and advocate sources and include existing customers, intermediaries and other third parties that could recommend the organization to potential customers. So, for example, in the course of a house purchase, an estate agent may recommend a solicitor to do the conveyancing, a surveyor to do a survey and even a financial advisor to give mortgage advice.

> INSIGHT: "The best form of marketing is to get the customers to do the marketing for you", (Christopher *et al.*, 1994).

Increasingly, many firms are finding it difficult to attract employees with the right 'attitude' and skills and are therefore developing relationships with potential employees within such markets (e.g. work placement schemes, sponsorship of prizes at universities, etc.). Influencer markets include financial and regulatory organizations and the government. An example is organizations involved in key capital or infrastructure projects. These may include communication systems, transport infrastructure, defence and energy-related projects. This will be a key market for many organizations in the run-up to the London Olympics.

Another early perspective on the scope of relationships in which organizations may be involved was suggested by Morgan and Hunt (1994). They classify various types of relational exchanges into four broad categories. Within this framework, these may be decomposed into ten other sub-partnership categories (see Figure 2.8, p. 40).

Task 2.2

Try applying Morgan and Hunt's model to a practical context you are familiar with or the university in which you are studying.

- Start off with the four broad categories and then the ten other sub-partnership categories.
- Are there any other relationships that the models so far examined do not cover?

A number of authors have devised similar concepts. Gummesson (1999) for example, extends the number of relationships further and identifies 30 separate relationships categorized by the level at which they occur (see Table 2.1, pp. 38–39).

Clearly, where to draw the line in terms of the parameters and relationships that should be included when examining an organization and its relationships becomes critical. This is open to debate among academics and practitioners alike.

TABLE 2.1 Gummesson's Thirty Rs

Classical marketing relationships

R1 The classic dyad – the relationship between the supplier and the customer
This is the parent relationship of marketing, the ultimate exchange of value, which constitutes the basis of business.

R2 The classic triad – the drama of the customer–supplier–competitor triangle
Competition is a central ingredient of the market economy. In competition there are relationships between three parties: between the customer and the current supplier, between the customer and the supplier's competitors, and between competitors.

R3 The classic network – distribution channels
The traditional physical distribution and the modern channel management including goods, services, people and information, consists of a network of relationships.

Special market relationships

R4 Relationships via full-time marketers (FTMs) and part-time marketers (PTMs)
Those who work in marketing and sales departments – the FTMs – are professional relationship makers. All others, who perform other main functions but yet influence customer relationships directly or indirectly, are PTMs. There are also contributing FTMs and PTMs outside the organization.

R5 The service encounter – interaction between the customer and the service provider
Production and delivery of the service involves the customer in an interaction relationship with the service provider, often referred to as the 'moment of truth'.

R6 The many-headed customer and many-headed supplier
Marketing to other organizations – industrial marketing or business marketing – often means contacts between many individuals from the supplier's and the customer's organizations.

R7 The relationship to the customer's customer
A condition for success is often the understanding of the customer's customer, and what supplies can do to help their customers become successful.

R8 The close versus the distant relationship
In mass marketing, closeness to the customer is lost and the relationship becomes distant, based merely on surveys, statistics and written reports.

R9 The relationship to the dissatisfied customer
The dissatisfied customer perceives a special type of relationship, more intense than the normal situation, and often badly managed by the provider, The way of handling a complaint – the recovery – can determine the quality of future relationships.

R10 The monopoly relationship: the customer or supplier as prisoners
When competition is inhibited, the customer may be at the mercy of the supplier – or the other way round. One of them becomes prisoner.

R11 The customer as 'member'
In order to cerate a long-term sustaining relationship, it becomes increasingly common to enlist customers as members of various loyalty programmes.

R12 The electronic relationship
Information technology – telecom, computers, TV – is an element of all types of marketing today and it forms new types of relationships.

R13 Parasocial relationships – relationships to symbols and objects
Relationships do not only exist concerning people and physical phenomena, but also to mental images and symbols such as brand names and corporate identities.

R14 The non-commercial relationship
This is a relationship between the public sector and citizens/customers, but it also includes voluntary organizations and other activities outside the profit-based and monetarized economy, such as those performed in families.

R15 The green relationship
Environmental and health issues have slowly but gradually increased in importance and are creating a new type of customer relationship through legislation, the voice of opinion-leading consumerism

changing the behaviour of consumers and an extension of the customer–supplier relationship to encompass a recycling process.

R16   The law-based relationship
A relationship to a customer is sometimes founded primarily on legal contracts and the threat of litigation.

R17   The criminal network
Organized crime is built on tight and often impermeable networks guided by an illegal business mission. They exist around the world and are apparently growing but are not observed in marketing theory. These networks can disturb the functioning of a whole market or industry.

Mega relationships

R18   Personal and social networks
Personal and social networks often determine business networks. In some cultures even, business is solely conducted between friends and friends of friends.

R19   Mega Marketing – the real 'customer' is not always found in the marketplace
In certain instances, relationships must be sought with governments, legislators, influential individuals and others, in order to make marketing feasible on an operational level.

R20   Alliance changes the market mechanism
Alliance means closer relationships and collaboration is necessary to make the market economy work.

R21   The knowledge relationship
Knowledge can be the most strategic and critical resource and "knowledge acquisition" is often the rational for alliances.

R22   Mega alliances change the basic condition for marketing
The European Union (EU) and the North American Free Trade Agreement (NAFTA) are examples of alliances above the single company and industry. They exist on government and supranational levels.

R23   The mass media relationship
The mass media can be damaging or supportive to marketing and they are particularly influential in forming public opinion. The relationship to media is crucial for the way media will handle an issue.

Nano relationships

R24   Marketing mechanisms are brought inside the company
By introducing profit centres in an organization, a market inside the company is created and internal as well as external relationships of a new kind emerge.

R25   Internal customer relationship
The dependency between the different tiers and departments in a company is seen as a process consisting of relationships between internal customers and internal suppliers.

R26   Quality providing a relationship between operations management and marketing
The modern quality concept has built a bridge between design, manufacturing and other technology-based activities and marketing. It considers the company 's internal relationships as well as its relationships to the customers.

R27   Internal marketing: relationships with the "employee market"
Internal marketing can be seen as part of RM as it gives indirect and necessary support to the relationships with external customers.

R28   The two-dimensional matrix relationship
Organizational matrices are frequent in large corporations, and above all they are found in the relationships between product management and sales.

R29   The relationship to external providers of marketing services
External providers reinforce the marketing function by supplying a series of services, such as those offered by advertising agencies and market research institutes, but also in the area of sales promotion and distribution.

R30   The owner and financier relationship
Owners and other financiers partly determine the conditions under which a marketing function can operate. The relationship to them influences the marketing strategy.

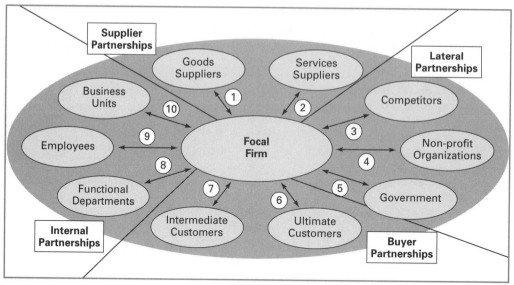

FIGURE 2.8 Morgan and Hunt's Relational Model

Task 2.3

Take one of the above models of network relationships – either:

- Christopher *et al.* – 6 markets Model
- Morgan and Hunt – Relational Model
- Gummesson – 30R Model

Read further about it. Now, look carefully at the model and

- apply the categories in the model to a city hospital near you;
- outline activities that the hospital management could undertake to strengthen their network credibility and influence.

  What, in your opinion would be more difficult to implement in the model?

When examining networks of relationships, the relationships within them will exhibit different characteristics and features. For this reason, some researchers in this field have attempted to create typologies to enable their classification.

A Typology for Relationships

There is no broadly acceptable typology of relational networks. However, a number of perspectives are examined here to indicate the variety of approaches suggested by researchers.

One perspective is offered by Cravens and Piercy (1994). They suggest there are four types of networks. The type of network relationship (ranging from highly collaborative to a one-off, transaction-based relationship) and the volatility of the environment (the dynamism or rate of change within the market environment) will determine under which of the types a relationship should be classified (see Figure 2.9).

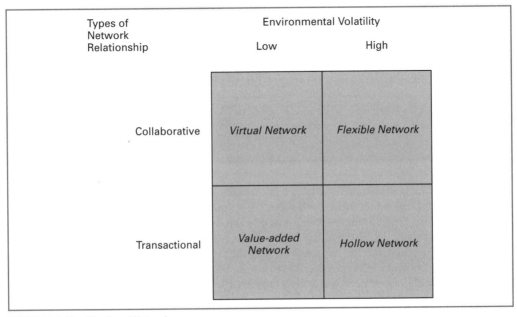

FIGURE 2.9 A Classification of Networks
Based on Cravens and Piercy (1994).

Hollow networks exist where the market environment is volatile, the core organization is often a specialist one and will therefore use other organizations to aid in performing a transaction. Temporary relationships are formed as and when they are needed (e.g. temporary contract work to build a capital project). Flexible networks are where the core organization establishes longer-term relationships with other adaptable and dynamic organizations so that the network as a whole is capable of thriving in the volatile environment. Value-added networks are where the organizations in the network have core attributes which compliment each other and therefore optimize the creation of customer value. So, for example, the core organization may be focused on product design but will use a range of suppliers and distributors to bring the product to market on a transactional basis. The members of a virtual network attempt to create competitive advantage through closer collaboration and the creation of joint systems. This has also been referred to as the "virtual" organization. Such companies share services, knowledge, information, skills, etc. in order to meet customer needs. Table 2.2 provides some examples of these types of networks.

Donaldson and O'Toole (2002) offer another perspective classifying relationships by their strength. Strength in this context refers to social and economic investment behaviours. These are summarized in Figure 2.10.

TABLE 2.2 Types of networks

Type of network	Example or sector in which found
Hollow	Event management such as concerts and exhibitions
Value-added	Off-line music distribution where record labels have traditionally recorded and marketed musicians and suppliers and retailers have distributed the music
Flexible	Increasingly, online distribution music distribution optimizes flexible networks where musicians record and distribute online, often using a variety of organizations such as PR companies for promotion and others for merchandizing
Virtual	The development and use of common reservation systems by global airlines. This is a well established example of a system that is largely invisible to customers but is a key element of how the service is implemented.

A hierarchical relationship may be said to exist when one party dominates the relationship and there is less trust between the buyer and seller. The opportunistic relationship is typically transactional in nature. This culminates in one-off exchanges characterized by low social and economic investments. In contrast, the bilateral relationship is one where both parties invest similarly in the relationship. The recurrent relationship is a situation where there are potentially limited benefits beyond the exchange. Therefore, any repeat business is likely to occur where there is a high social investment and a high degree of social interaction.

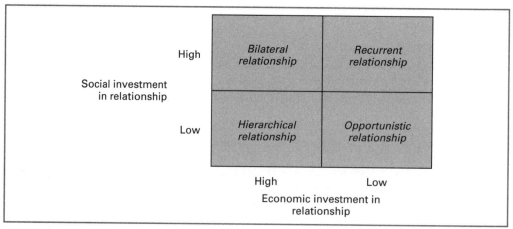

FIGURE 2.10 Relationship classification
Based on Donaldson and O'Toole (2002).

Task 2.4

In relation to Donaldson and O'Toole's typology, what would you consider to be the key characteristics of social and economic investment and how would you measure them? How would you apply them to the following situations?

- A dentist and their client
- A motorist filling up at petrol station on a motorway, autoroute or similar
- A supermarket and its vegetable suppliers (farmers)
- A firm of lawyers and a firm of accountants
- A politician and a voter

MINI-CASE: STRATEGIC BUSINESS PARTNERSHIPS

Located in Leicester, the Strategic Business Partnership is a multidisciplined consultancy, providing business and management expertise in key areas to small and medium-sized enterprises. The firm's work encompasses a range of industries, including manufacturing, retailing, service based and professional services. All of the principal partners are "hands-on" business managers, with appropriate general business experience and qualifications. Additionally, each partner is an acknowledged specialist in a key business area. By utilizing a range of recognized business performance tools, the partners' approach is to introduce and embed appropriate management techniques across the whole client business.

Within such professional service and knowledge-transfer markets, personal contacts and word-of-mouth recommendation are crucial. The partners of the Strategic Business Partnership are well aware of this and have a well established network of relationships on both a formal and informal basis.

As well as their potential customer and supplier markets, the partners are continually developing their referral markets and influencer markets. The partners are members of a number of professional bodies including the Institute of Personnel Managers (IPM) and the Chartered Managers Institute (CMI). This provides the opportunity to network with other members at a local level. With some of these professional bodies such as the CIM (Chartered Institute of Marketing), the partners are active committee and board members at both a local and regional level, again providing the opportunity to network. They also maintain links with the local Chamber of Commerce and Leicester Business Forum.

They are also involved in informal networking and profile raising, including doing unpaid, *pro bono* work (for local charities) and attending mutual support forums such as INTEGRA. They ensure their continuing professional development by teaching on part-time, post-graduate, post-experience courses (such as MBA and CIM programmes) at a range of local universities. Again, another opportunity to network!

Question

Using Cravens and Piercy's Classification of Networks (see Figure 2.9), how would you classify the various networks of relationships that Strategic Business Partnerships has?

The above section on typologies demonstrates the variety of criteria that may be used to classify different types of relationships within different contexts. Relational typologies may also have two key uses for practitioners:

- First, through applying typologies at whatever level, practitioners will recognize that they may have different types of relationships with different types of stakeholders within different types of networks.

- Second, this may help identify the characteristics and features of these relationships and where firms should be investing their resources (both economic and social) so as to optimize such relationships.

A Classification System for RM

Having identified and discussed a variety of themes and typologies that underpin individual relationships, there is perhaps one major criticism of RM from a practitioner's (and student's) standpoint. While it is important to recognize and understand the differences in RM concepts

TABLE 2.3 The Dimensions of the Marketing Exchange

Dimension	Explanation
1. Focus	What is being exchanged? ■ Product (a tin of coke) ■ Service (a meal in a restaurant) ■ Information or advice (legal advice)
2. Parties involved	Who takes part? ■ One buyer and one seller (customer and shopkeeper) ■ Lots of buyers and lots of sellers
3. Communication patterns	How do the parties communicate? ■ Does one party do most of the communicating (a soft drinks manufacturer)? ■ Do they interact with each other (call centres)?
4. Type of contact	What type of contact is there between the parties? ■ Impersonal (TV advertising) ■ Is it customized or personalized (direct marketing)? ■ Is it face to face and interpersonal (a trip to the hairdresser)?
5. Duration	Is the exchange ■ A one-off purchase (a bottle of water at an airport departure lounge while going on holiday)? ■ Ongoing and periodic (a course of dental treatment)?
6. Formality	Is the arrangement formal or informal? ■ Is it purely a business arrangement? ■ Do the parties ever meet at a social level (corporate sporting events)?
7. Balance of power	Does one of the parties dominate the relationship? ■ Buyer dominated (supermarkets) ■ Seller dominated (utilities such as water, gas, etc.)

and contexts, a key difficulty is being able to identify and clarify which aspects of RM may be appropriate to a particular context and how those aspects may be applied to this context.

In an attempt to provide help with this, a number of RM classification systems have been developed. By way of illustration, the next section will focus on one of these proposed by Brodie *et al.* (1997).

Given the diversity of definitions, terms, contexts and perspectives already covered in this text, it is not surprising that there is ambiguity as to

- what RM is;
- who is involved in a relationship;
- when a relationship exists;
- what kind of relationship it is.

A framework to aid clarification of these questions was initially suggested by Brodie *et al.* (1996) and subsequently augmented by Coviello *et al.* (2001) to include an e-marketing approach. Using content analysis of how previous researchers had defined and used various terms associated with marketing, Brodie *et al.* (1997) identified a number of themes and dimensions. Seven of these dimensions are relevant to the nature of the exchange (see Table 2.3).

Table 2.3 highlights the interactive nature RM theory. This is particularly the case when it is compared and contrasted with more traditional approaches to marketing, perhaps encompassed

TABLE 2.4 Management and Process Dimensions

Dimension	Meaning
1. Managerial intent	What is the strategic goal? ■ To maximize short-term profit? ■ To attract new customers? ■ To retain existing customers? ■ To achieve mutual goals with customers?
2. Decision focus	Where is the decision focus? ■ On a product or brand? ■ On customers in a market? ■ On individual relationships? ■ On a firm? ■ On firms in a network of connected relationships?
3. Managerial investment	Where does the organization focus its investments? ■ In internal marketing assets or capabilities? ■ In developing committed relationships with individuals? ■ In developing a position relative to other firms?
4. Managerial level	Are marketing decision made and implemented by ■ Functional marketers? ■ Specialist marketers? ■ Managers from across functions? ■ A general manager?
5. Time frame	Is the planning horizon ■ Short term? ■ Long term?

TABLE 2.5 A Classification of Marketing Perspectives

	Transactional Perspective	Relational Perspective			
	Type: Transaction marketing	Type: Database marketing	Type: Interaction marketing	Type: Network marketing	Type: e-Marketing (Coviello *et al.*, 2001)
Focus	Economic transaction	Information and economic transaction	Interactive relationships between buyer and seller	Connected relationships between firms	Information generating dialogue between a seller and many identified buyers
Parties involved	A firm and buyers in the general market	A firm and buyers in a specific market	Individual sellers and buyers (a dyad)	Firms "with" firms (involving individuals)	Firm "with" individuals
Communication patterns	Firm "to" market	Firm "to" individual	Individuals "with" individuals (across organizations)	Firms "with" firms (involving individuals)	Firm using technology to communicate "with" and "among" many individuals (who may form groups)
Type of contact	Arms-length, impersonal	Personalized (yet distant)	Face-to-face, interpersonal (close, based on commitment, trust and co-operation)	Impersonal-interpersonal (ranging from distant to close)	Interactive via technology
Duration	Discrete (yet perhaps over time)	Discrete and over time	Continuous (ongoing and mutually adaptive, may be short or long term)	Continuous (stable, yet dynamic, may be short or long term)	Continuous (but interactivity occurs in real time)
Formality	Formal	Formal (yet personalized via technology)	Formal and informal (i.e. at both a business and a social level)	Formal and informal (i.e. at both a business and a social level)	Formal (yet customized and/or personalized via interactive technology)
Balance of power	Active seller, passive buyers	Active seller, less passive buyers	Sellers and buyers mutually active and adaptive (interdependent and reciprocal)	All firms active and adaptive	

	Customer attraction (to satisfy the customer at a profit)	Customer retention (to satisfy the customer, increase profit and attain other objectives such as increased loyalty, decreased customer risk, etc.)	Interaction (to establish, develop and facilitate a co-operative relationship for mutual benefit)	Co-ordination (interaction between sellers, buyers and other parties across multiple firms for mutual benefit, resource exchange, market access, etc.)	Creation of IT enabled dialogue
Managerial intent	Customer attraction (to satisfy the customer at a profit)	Customer retention (to satisfy the customer, increase profit and attain other objectives such as increased loyalty, decreased customer risk, etc.)	Interaction (to establish, develop and facilitate a co-operative relationship for mutual benefit)	Co-ordination (interaction between sellers, buyers and other parties across multiple firms for mutual benefit, resource exchange, market access, etc.)	Creation of IT enabled dialogue
Decision focus	Product or brand	Product/brand and customers (in a targeted market)	Relationships between individuals	Connected relationships between firms (in a network)	Managing IT-enabled relationships between the firm and many individuals
Managerial investment	Internal marketing assets (focusing on product/service price, distribution, promotion capabilities)	Internal marketing assets (emphasizing communication, information and technology capabilities)	External market assets (focusing on establishing and developing a relationship with another individual)	External market assets (focusing on developing the firm's position in a network of firms)	Internal operational assets (IT, website, logistics) Functional systems integration
Managerial level	Functional marketers (e.g. Sales Manager, Product Development Manager)	Specialist marketers (e.g. Customer Service Manager, Loyalty Manager)	Managers from across functions and levels in the firm	General manager	Marketing specialists (with) technology specialists Senior Managers
Time frame	Short term	Longer term	Short or long term	Short or long term	Short or long term

Based on Brodie *et al.* (1997) and Coviello *et al.* (2001).

by variations of the marketing mix. These dimensions at an operational level are further augmented by potential relational management activities and processes at a strategic and organizational level (see Table 2.4).

Through these relational and management dimensions, four general marketing perspectives may be identified:

- Transaction Marketing
- Database Marketing
- Interactive Marketing
- Network Marketing

Subsequently , Coviello *et al.* (2001) add a fifth marketing perspective:

- E-marketing

These, together with the key characteristics of each dimension related to the exchange, managerial and process dimensions from the above tables may be seen in Table 2.5.

When thinking about relational perspectives, we can compare and contrast organizations such as a utility company, a firm of business consultants, a leisure centre and a supermarket. The type of marketing perspective that is pertinent to an organization has huge ramifications for that organization. Clearly, there are strategic implications in terms of appropriate strategic planning and the cultural orientation that the organization should adopt. Senior management leadership will determine support levels and organizational buy-in for the implementation of such orientations. HRM strategies in terms of the recruitment, training, retention and, critically, rewarding of employees should reflect the marketing perspective adopted by the organization. Very often there is a need for appropriate "hard and soft" systems' infrastructures to support these. In short, the implementation of an appropriate relational strategy requires both a huge financial investment and a huge strategic commitment on the part of of the organization, often requiring a cultural change.

While some researchers view this classification system as overly simple and dated, its strengths lie in the fact that the 12 dimensions identified may provide a useful way, particularly for practitioners, of understanding and distinguishing between the way marketing is currently being practised by an organization and the implications of adopting an appropriate relational orientation. It is also still widely cited in many more current academic articles.

Chapter Summary

This chapter has explored the parameters of RM in terms of scope and the type of relational exchanges. It has highlighted how these parameters may be flexible depending on which concept and context it is viewed from and that some concepts incorporate a broader view of the marketing organization within its relational environment than others. Initially it was suggested that there are three broad categories of relational exchanges: dyadic relationships, relationship chains and relationships networks. Within each of these broad categories, more detailed relational concepts were explored such as CRM, Interactive Marketing, Value Chains and types of networks. The chapter finished with a Relational Classification Framework to help understand and distinguish between different types of networks.

Review Questions

1 Within a market of your choice, using a diagram draw and explain the networks of interactions that take place. How might a firm add value to each of these relationships?

2 Using your diagram, explain how the concept of the value chain may be of relevance when examining these relationships.

3 Give examples of how a competitor's marketing activities may affect an organization's relationships with its customers.

Further Reading

Ballantyne, D., M. Christopher and A. Payne (2003) "Relationship Marketing: Looking Back, Looking Forward", *Marketing Theory*, vol. 3, no. 1, pp. 159–166.

Beverland, M. and A. Lindgreen (2004) "Relationship Use and Market Dynamism: A Model of Relationship Evolution", *Journal of Marketing Management*, vol. 20, pp. 825–858.

Brodie, R.J., N.E. Coviello, R.W. Brookes and V. Little (1997) "Towards a Paradigm Shift in Marketing? An Examination of Current Marketing Practices", *Journal of Marketing Management*, vol. 13, pp. 386–406.

Ford, D. (1990) "Introduction: IMP and the Interaction Approach", in D. Ford (ed.) *Understanding Business Markets: Interaction, Relationships and Networks*, London: Academic Press.

END OF CHAPTER CASE AND KEY QUESTIONS

Can Virgin Media turn around NTL's customer care record?

With more than 3 million cable subscribers, Virgin Media, formally known as NTL, is the UK's number one cable operator, providing television, telephone, data, and Internet services provision (ISP) to residential and corporate customers. However, as NTL, the company was being continually rated number one for poor customer service.

In 2004, NTL had a quarterly churn rate of around 12–14 per cent ("NTL cheers lower losses", *Netimperative*, 2004). The main reasons cited for switching by customers were the speed/bandwidth of the connection and the price. The third motivator invariably seems to be service availability and quality ("The costs and benefits of customer self-service", Claus Skaaning (CEO, Dezide Aps, Denmark), *The Wise Marketer*, November 2005). For NTL, these typically revolved around:

■ incorrect billing

■ incorrect product packages

■ engineers failing to keep appointments

■ technical queries.

> INSIGHT: Churn rate refers to the percentage of existing customers leaving the company.

When customers attempted to phone the company's helpline, they could be faced with waiting times of 20–30 minutes before getting through to a customer service representative.

The company became infamous for its level of customer care. Its reputation for customer service reached new depths when a story was reported in the press about a disgruntled consumer, who having contacted the company to complain, was put on hold for an hour. It was reported that they stumbled across the facility to change NTL's recorded message while pressing the "star" key to access a number of options. Other callers to the centre were greeted with a message full of four-letter expletives which concluded with "We are not going to handle any of your complaints, leave us alone and **** off and get a life" (*The Times*, 9 June 2005). Earlier in the month, NTL had come second from bottom in a report on complaint handling compiled by the Institute of Customer Service.

In October 2001 one disgruntled NTL customer was so incensed with the level of service he received from the cable firm that he penned the now notorious cat-litter letter of complaint. In the letter the customer complained about an "inadequacy of service which had not previously been considered possible, as well as ignorance and stupidity of monolithic proportions". The three-page letter was fowarded to the company along with the content's of the man's cat-litter tray "as an expression of my utter and complete contempt for both you, and your pointless company". The letter went on to win several awards.

However, since ISP offerings are becoming increasingly similar, it seems likely that poor customer service will become an increasingly important churn factor. With NTL estimating Average Revenue per User (ARPU) at around £40 per month in 2004 (NTL Annual Report, 2004), its annual churn rate was estimated to equate to around £201 million in lost revenue per year.

This has had a huge impact on the company's profitability and its ability to grow. Estimates suggest that a very small increase in customer retention (5 per cent) may mean a 25–55 per cent increase in profitability. If customer satisfaction and retention can be improved by making minor investments, this can have a major impact on profitability. By improving the quality of its customer service, NTL has managed to reduce the customer churn from 14.4 to 13.2 per cent.

Sources

Caller swears revenge on helpline, Joanna Bale, *The Times*, 9 June 2005.

NTL customers outspoken over outrage, Will Sturgeon, *Software Silicon*, 16 June 2003.

Questions

1 How would you classify the type of relationship between Virgin Media and its customers and what are its features?
2 Critically evaluate the systems and structures Virgin Media have in place for managing customer accounts.
3 Suggest ways in which you think Virgin Media could improve their CRM strategy at a strategic and at a tactical level.

References

Brodie, R.J., N.E. Coviello, R.W. Brookes and V. Little (1997) "Towards a Paradigm Shift in Marketing? An Examination of Current Marketing Practices", *Journal of Marketing Management,* vol. 13, pp. 386–406.

Christopher, M., A. Payne and D. Ballantyne (1994) *Relationship Marketing: Bringing Quality, Customer Service and Marketing Together,* Oxford, UK: Butterworth Heinemann.

Coviello, N., R. Milley and B. Marcolin (2001) "Understanding IT enabled Interactivity in Contemporary Marketing", *Journal of Interactive Marketing,* vol. 15, no.4, Autumn.

Cravens, D.W. and N.F. Piercy (1994) "Relationship Marketing and Collaborative Networks in Service Organizations", *International Journal of Service Industry Management,* vol. 5 , no. 5, pp. 39–53.

Donaldson, B. and T. O'Toole (2002) *Strategic Market Relationships: From Strategy to Implementation,* New York: John Wiley & Sons.

Egan, J. (2003) *Relationship Marketing: Exploring Relational Strategies in Marketing,* Harlow: Financial Times, Prentice Hall.

Ford, D. (1990) "Introduction: IMP and the Interaction Approach", in D. Ford (ed.) *Understanding Business Markets: Interaction, Relationships and Networks,* London: Academic Press.

Gamble, P., M. Stone and N. Woodcock (1999) *Up Close and Personal: Customer Relationship Marketing @ Work,* London: Kogan Page.

Grönroos, C. (1995) "The Rebirth of Modern Marketing: Six Propositions About Relationship Marketing", Swedish School of Economics and Business Administration, *Working Paper,* 307, Helsinki.

Gummesson, E. (1999), *Total Relationship Marketing: Rethinking Marketing Management from 4Ps to 30Rs,* Oxford: Butterworth Heinemann.

Hansotia, B. (2002) "Gearing up for CRM: Antecedents to Successful Implementation", *Journal of Database Marketing,* vol. 10, no. 2, pp. 121.

Hollensen, S. (2003) *Marketing Management: A Relationship Approach,* Edinburgh: Financial Times and Prentice Hall.

IMP Group (1990) "An Interaction Approach" in D. Ford (ed.) *Understanding Business Markets: Interaction, Relationships and Networks,* London: Academic Press.

Jiang, P. (2000) "Segment-based Mass Customisation: An Exploration of a New Conceptual Marketing Framework", *Internet Research: Electronic Networking Applications and Policy,* vol. 10, no. 3, pp. 215–26.

Morgan, R.M. and S.D. Hunt (1994) "The Commitment-Trust Theory of Relationship Marketing", *Journal of Marketing,* vol. 58, July, pp. 20–38.

Stone, M., D. Davies and A. Bond (1995) *Direct Hit: Direct Marketing with a Winning Edge,* London: Pitman.

Szmigin, I., L. Canning and A. Reppel (2005) "Online Community: Enhancing the Relationship Marketing Concept Through Customer Bonding", *International Journal of Service Industry Management,* vol. 16, no. 2, pp. 480–496.

Tapp, A. (2005) *Principles of Direct and Database Marketing,* Edinburgh: FT Prentice Hall.

Womack, J.P. and D. T. Jones (1996) "Beyond Toyota: How to Root out Waste and Pursue Perfection," *Harvard Business Review,* Sept–Oct, pp. 140–58.

CHAPTER 03

An Overview of Industrial Marketing and Supply Relationships

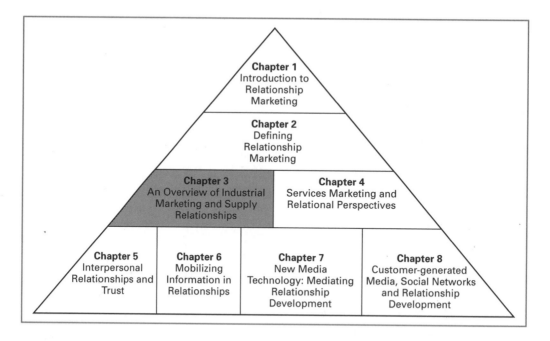

	Chapter 1	
	Introduction to Relationship Marketing	

	Chapter 2	
	Defining Relationship Marketing	

Chapter 3	Chapter 4
An Overview of Industrial Marketing and Supply Relationships	Services Marketing and Relational Perspectives

Chapter 5	Chapter 6	Chapter 7	Chapter 8
Interpersonal Relationships and Trust	Mobilizing Information in Relationships	New Media Technology: Mediating Relationship Development	Customer-generated Media, Social Networks and Relationship Development

❖ LEARNING OBJECTIVES

After studying this chapter you should be able to:

1 **define** industrial marketing and **discuss** the drivers for change in industrial marketing and supply relationships

2 **compare** different models of industrial buyer behaviour

3 **understand** how to manage different types of industrial marketing relationship

4 **assess** how supply relationships are evolving

5 **consider** the value-added through relationships between buyers and suppliers

Chapter Contents

Introduction

Industrial marketing is about marketing transactions between organizations, as identified by Gummesson in the previous chapter, where customers are not necessarily the end users of products and services – that is, marketing is "business-to-business", or b2b. Examples of this may be the supplier of component parts to a car manufacturer or a contract cleaning service to an office. This type of transaction differs from consumer marketing in very specific ways, including the make-up and size of customers, and the complexity and nature of purchasing processes.

> INSIGHT: b2b marketing is business-to-business marketing, where marketing transactions take place between organizations.

Ensuring stable relationships between suppliers and their customers is important to both parties. Consider, for example, the importance, and indeed, critical nature of the supplier of completed airplane wings to an aircraft manufacturer. Clearly, without wings, the airplane cannot fly; moreover, it would not be easy for an airplane manufacturer to find a new supplier of wings, which are complex structures, if their relationship with the supplier breaks down irretrievably. Thus, consequences of relationship continuity relate to long-term financial stability for both the supplier and the customer.

This chapter is, therefore, an important contribution to our understanding of RM from the perspective of industrial suppliers and their customers. The chapter first sets out to describe the nature of industrial markets, then the changes that have influenced their development. Thereafter, models of buyer behaviour and industrial relationship management are presented and discussed. Finally, two specific forms of industrial relationship are examined: outsourced and co-destiny relationships.

An Overview of Industrial Marketing

Industrial marketing is about transactions between suppliers and customers, (as referred to in Chapter 2), who collaborate within a supply chain. Transactions typically comprise goods and services which are used by buyers in their production of some product for another customer or end user. The goods and services fall into a number of discrete product classes (based on Jobber, 2004):

- Materials used in the manufacture of products, such as steel used in the manufacture of cars, or clay used in the manufacture of bricks

- Components, such as semi-conductors (microchips) used in the manufacture of robotics, computers and other electronic goods

- Plant and equipment used in the operation of manufacturing plants, for example, conveyor belts, production lines and forklift trucks

- Products and services used in the repair and operation of production equipment, for example, lubricants used to oil the production line or catering services used to feed the factory workers. These are commonly referred to as maintenance, repair and operation items (MROs).

Although each product class may be important to the buyer, it is evident that some products may be more critical than others. This may depend upon the reliability needed from the product being supplied, the value of the purchase and the availability of alternative sources of supply. Arguably, these may be effectively managed by contracts with penalty clauses, which do not necessarily involve close relationships between suppliers and customers. Williamson (1985), based on the work of Coase (1937), describes an economic theory of an organization. He identified the need for transaction-cost economies as being a key reason why organizations may seek relationships with others. Transaction costs are those that arise from the search for information, the negotiation and decision-making around contracts and the enforcement and policing of contracts. The value of having the contract revolves around the frequency of the transactions between the buyer and the supplier, and the nature and criticality of the supplies to the buyer. Such considerations are the basis of the make-versus-buy decision made by organizations – where a product or service is important, it is probably better to produce it "in-house", rather than "outsource" it from a supplier. This is discussed later in this chapter. Suffice to say that, where a contracted supply is important to the buyer, it may be beneficial to work closely with the supplier in order to minimize the risks of being exploited.

Another perspective on the buyer (or customer) considers them as "production units" (Gadde and Hakansson, 2001), where emphasis is placed on "inputs" (raw materials, components and other constituents to the production process). However, an alternative view is that the customer is a "capital-earning unit", which places much greater emphasis on different types of inputs, such as knowledge and financial efficiency, and where relationships are close because of the need to exchange information and work together to achieve financial goals. Relationships are, therefore, key to the modus operandi.

Where the production perspective is emphasized, the product classes present specific problems, or risks, for customers: some require considerable technical competence, some high administration, while others may be time sensitive in supply and production. These may be categorized according to their impact on profitability, as illustrated in Figure 3.1 below.

Others have categorized risk in different ways, such as by the level and type of organizational member involvement in the integration of the supply into the customer's production processes (Drummond and Ensor, 2003):

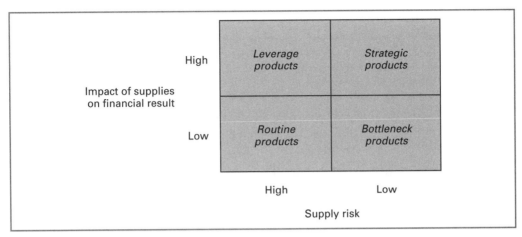

FIGURE 3.1 Categorization of Supply Risks
Source: adapted from Kraljic (1982).

- Routine order products, where there is low risk and few problems in use or performance
- Procedural problem products, where some training is required in use and risk is associated with successful adoption by users
- Performance problem products, which considers the ability of the product to meet the user's needs, including its compatibility with existing equipment
- Political problem products, which arise when there is an impact on another area of the business, and politicking may result from competition within the organization to "own" the product

At this juncture, it is worth noting that individuals and organizations tend to be risk averse because of the potential impact on the bottom line.

There are other characteristics of industrial, compared to consumer markets.

Nature of customers

Organizations tend to have fewer industrial customers and these can often be categorized according to their importance to the supplier. For example, the commonly used Pareto rule suggests that 80 per cent of business is typically transacted with 20 per cent of customers ("80/20 rule"). An understanding of which customers are included in the 20 per cent is useful because it enables organizations to manage these "key customers" effectively.

Complexity of buying

Customers often look for complex solutions to complex problems and, in the process of defining their ideal solution, build quite detailed specifications of products and services. Purchases tend to be high priced and involve many members of organizations.

Derived demand

This is about the influence of the end-user on the supply chain members – industrial customers will require only sufficient products and services from suppliers that enable them to meet their demand.

Professionalism

Given the nature of industrial markets, suppliers and customers usually take a professional approach to selling and purchasing, requiring high-level interpersonal skills, such as effective negotiation. These are supported by formalized structures within businesses, such as centralized purchasing departments and order-tracking systems, so that selling and buying processes meet standards of accepted legal and ethical business practice.

The next section discusses how developments in purchasing and supply have influenced industrial markets in recent times.

Developments in Industrial Markets

As stated in Chapter 2, marketing relationships between suppliers and customers have evolved from purely transaction-based marketing because of a need to achieve value in the supply chain which enhances profitability for channel members (Grönroos, 1997; 2001), largely through operational efficiencies (the concept of the "lean enterprise" was presented, Womack and Jones, 1996). Such an approach emphasizes the importance of close and strong relationships between the supply-chain members. The underlying premise for collaboration is that both parties commit to adapting their behaviour to ensure relationship longevity. Consider, for example, the ultimate impact of the exertion of power in the relationship between supermarket chains and the farmers who supply them at lower and lower margins.

Within this context there are some specific factors which enable organizations to work together more effectively. Gadde and Hakansson (2001) highlight some major changes in the industrial purchasing context. Matthyssens and Van den Bulte (1994) highlight key market changes: the move from short-term contracts to long-term close relationships; "multiple-sourcing" to single sourcing; threat of buying the suppliers to outsourcing and co-makership agreements; tactical purchasing to strategic supply management; and price being central to the quality and competence of the supplier. For example, most organizations are increasingly reliant on outsourcing which enables them to focus on core business activities, with less strategically important aspects of business operations being provided by third parties. Many organizations are also more focused on co-operating with suppliers to ensure supply and in developing efficient working relationships, have reduced the number of suppliers they use in order to focus effort. Donaldson (1996) highlights in addition the issues of total quality management (TQM) and innovations in supply-chain management (just-in-time delivery: JIT), computer-aided design (CAD) and information technology (IT).

Zineldin (2000) draws the Relationship Marketing literature together with TQM, suggesting further enhancements to the approach (referred to as Total Relationship Marketing) using specific processes and tools primarily developed in the automotive industry (e.g. Toyota) such as "Kaizen" (change for better), "Hoshin Kanri" (quality policy deployment) and "Flowcharts" (or blueprinting) to improve the flow of goods and services through the production process and between the supplier and customer. In a consumer context, Payne and Frow (1997) discuss this in terms of customer retention and the resultant potential for increased profitability (Reichheld and Sasser, 1990).

Other trends have evolved from the supplier's approach to selling to customers. Rich (2000) states relationship "selling" has moved from personal selling for short-term goals to a "life-long process" in order to reap bigger rewards at a later date. Selling behaviour has moved from "hard selling", incorporating objection handling and closing behaviours (Strong, 1925), to more "consultative" selling models of investigating customer needs, e.g. the "SPIN-strategy" (Rackham, 1987) and the Counsellor Selling model (DeCormier and Jobber, 1998).

More recently, ethical issues around corporate social responsibility (CSR) in their activities is having a great impact on purchasing and supply behaviour. The Chartered Institute of Purchasing and Supply identify CSR as comprising ten component parts: environmental responsibility, human rights, equal opportunities, diversity and supplier diversity, corporate governance, sustainability, social impact, ethical trading, biodiversity and community involvement. Clearly these components have a far-reaching impact on relationships. Attempt Task 3.1 to consider these further.

Task 3.1

Imagine you are a buyer for a supermarket looking to secure supply of English grown strawberries. In your role, you visit the farm to inspect the growing, picking and shipping operations to ensure CSR policies are met. Discuss the aspects of CSR you would investigate.

It is evident from this that the ability of the organization to communicate and exchange information strategically is fundamental to good relationships. Gadde and Hakansson (1993) differentiate types of information important to supply as being technical – say, about the particular specification of a product; commercial, which might include market information; and administrative, which may be about the support mechanisms for a product. Key roles this information performs are in co-ordinating effort between functions within the organization; influencing internal stakeholders so that they may accept changes; and learning, which is about the transfer of knowledge between the supplier and customer.

Sheth (1973) also highlights four main factors that influence the decision-making process within the organization:

- Expectations of the decision-making unit – especially those individuals within the organization, such as Finance and Production
- Factors influencing the buying process – perceptions of risk, type of purchase being made, time pressures, also size of organization and degree of centralization in the purchasing department
- The decision-making process and how conflicts are resolved, including problem-solving, persuasive abilities, bargaining skills and exertion of power
- Situational factors – to do with a supplier and their context, for example, their cash flow, industrial relations, etc.

INSIGHT: Monczka and Morgan (2000) have identified a number of challenges for suppliers and customers in industrial markets, including:

- Increasing efficiency requirements, that is, adding value to the bottom line
- Making use of information technology
- Integrating and consolidating supplies, most especially in light of a global purchasing context
- Insourcing and outsourcing, and the nature of relationships with suppliers
- Strategic cost management
- "Network" management – the strategic role of the interrelationships among suppliers, the customers (and their customers)

Thus, significant trends in industrial marketing may be summarized as:

- the recognition that not all customers are the same, i.e. some are high-value and others are unprofitable;
- the move towards retention of customers, rather than acquisition of new;
- the just-in-time concept necessitating greater openness between buyers and sellers in order to achieve efficiencies in the supply chain;
- the trends in outsourcing, necessitating "co-makership" agreements that require involved negotiation and conflict resolution processes and, ultimately, lead towards mutually beneficial outcomes;
- the evolution of technologies and interconnectivity between these which facilitate exchanges, e.g. databases, content management systems, the Internet-based and now mobile communications technologies;
- corporate social responsibility and its impact upon relationship development and management.

The nature of these influences enables us to focus on different types of relationships, which will be discussed later in this chapter. The next section discusses a key trend that has only been touched upon in this section so far: the role of industrial buyer behaviour, from which much of our understanding of marketing relationships from this perspective has emanated.

Industrial Buyer Behaviour

Early research into marketing took the perspective of either one or other side of the buyer–seller classic marketing relationship. Indeed, research focused on "passive" buying and "active" selling roles (Ford, 1980), a classic example of which is seen in the sale of double-glazed windows! From the marketer's perspective, research into organizational buyer behaviour (OBB) was predicated upon the idea that a greater understanding of decision-making (influences, processes and behaviours), would result in greater profit from more effective marketing effort. Although much has been done to understand b2b buyer decision-making, and behaviour in particular, more recently it has been decided that there remains limited up-to-date research into this area (Baker, 2005). It is important to understand buyers in order to enhance organizational benefits, including increasing sales and profitability. Such an understanding enables complex buying situations to be managed by focusing on the development of appropriate marketing strategies.

An influential factor in the early research into OBB was the increased emphasis on organizational decisions about making or buying products and services on a straight or modified rebuy basis (Robinson, Faris and Wind, 1967). Research identified the "buying centre", the nature of decision-making and conflict resolution (Sheth, 1996). The buying centre is recognized as having a number of phases. Broadly, these include: problem recognition, search for solution process and choice process (Webster, 1965). One of the most widely recognized models is that of Robinson, Faris and Wind (1967). These authors identified an eight-stage model, which has been used as a benchmark for various subsequent models (Johnston and Lewin, 1996). A comparison of some of these so-called "buy-phase" models is shown in Table 3.1.

Within these phases, three buying situations ("buyclasses") – new task, modified rebuy and straight rebuy – give context to the decision-making process. Robinson *et al.*, proposed analysing this along three dimensions:

TABLE 3.1 Comparison of Buy-phase Models

Robinson *et al.* 1967	Webster and Wind (1972)	Wind (1978)	Moller (1981)
1. Problem (need) recognition	1. Identity needs	1. Identification of needs	1. Purchase initiation
2. Determine characteristics	2. Establish specification	2. Establish specification	2. Formation of evaluative criteria
3. Describe characteristics			
4. Search for source	3. Identify alternatives	3. Search for alternatives	3. Information search
5. Acquire proposals		4. Establish contact	4. Acquire proposals
		5. Set purchase and usage criteria	
6. Evaluate proposals	4. Evaluate alternatives	6. Evaluate alternatives	
		7. Budget availability	
		8. Evaluate specific alternatives	5. Evaluation of quotation
		9. Negotiate	6. Negotiation of terms
7. Select order routine	5. Select supplier	10. Buy	7. Supplier choice
			8. Allocation of contract
		11. Use	
8. Performance feedback		12. Post-purchase evaluation	

Adapted from Parkinson *et al.* (1986).

- The information requirements of the purchasers in order that they make appropriate decisions
- The consideration of possible alternatives
- The extent of the buying organization's familiarity with the purchasing situation

Nonetheless, as a marketing model, this is now somewhat outdated and has been variously criticized because of its over-simplicity in describing modern business relationships. Consider, using the example in Task 3.2, the use of loyalty schemes by a supplier and the impact this then has on purchasing behaviour. The framework is typically associated with a transactional approach and, as such, is useful in describing the nature of information-exchange processes with this approach. Now, ongoing relationships are emphasized, influenced by the market-development factors outlined above, rather than the one-off transactions implied by the models shown in Table 3.1. Other criticisms of the RFW framework are levied for its:

- lack of consideration of personal or organizational characteristics;
- failure to recognize the complexity of the buyer–seller relationship;
- inability to recognize the strategic importance of the purchase.

This is because the buying situation is not so much a "purchase" or even "repeat purchase" (where the buyer goes through the decision process in isolation from the seller), but is more of a joint exploration of solutions available to the customer and supplier dyad (Iacobucci, 1996). This is brought about, for example, by changes in the market environment.

Task 3.2

Using fast food as an example, identify and describe each of the following classes of product development:

- Straight rebuy
- Modified rebuy
- New task purchase

Attempts have been made to update the model. One such is Wilson (1996), who proposed a process which links the sales cycle with the buying cycle in a systems approach. The model highlights the need for greater efficiency in order to remain competitive; a long-term view of activities; and increased "open" communication in order to improve the speed and flexibility of solution delivery. Such an approach also emphasizes the respective parties' dependence on shared vision and goal compatibility. Factors influencing buying behaviour have been found to include individual resources such as expertise (or expert power); buying centre characteristics such as size; situational characteristics such as propensity for risk-taking and pressures of time; and individual behaviour (Kohli, 1989). This author found that the ability of individuals to influence buying behaviour varies with buying centre and situational factors. This suggests the importance of the relational context in which buying decisions are made – for example, the buying power and resource control of the supermarket buying strawberries, which are a highly perishable soft fruit, from the farmer who acts independently from a co-operative (refer to Task 3.2).

In turn, more complex models encompass the interrelationships between economic, social and emotional factors. Authors emphasize that the driver for collaboration is the increased complexity of the transactions that form the basis of the relationship. The process of relational development necessarily revolves around trust and co-operation. This is an aspect that is inherently complex to implement but advantages of genuine partnership are noted to be:

- avoidance of adversarial relationships;
- elimination of conflict;
- agreement on problem resolution, cost and time savings.

Subsequent developments, therefore, consider organizational buying as being somehow intertwined with the selling cycle, and especially influenced by the economic environment. The idea is illustrated in Figure 3.2.

Sheth's (1973) model of integrative buying behaviour encompasses interrelationships between economic, social and emotional factors. Webster and Wind's (1972) model also incorporates environmental factors as well as individual social and organizational elements. Others

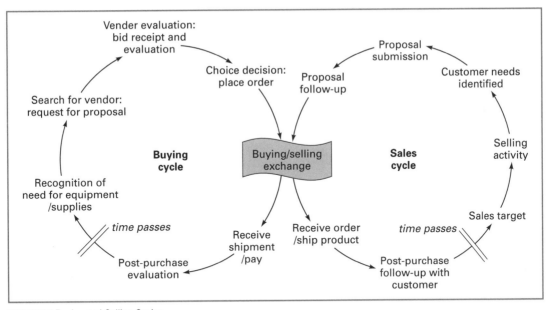

FIGURE 3.2 Buying and Selling Cycles
Source: adapted from Wilson (1996).

Task 3.3

Consider Figure 3.2 and comment on what might happen if a customer's and supplier's cycles got out of synchrony with each other.

recognize the importance of the buyer–seller interaction process (e.g. Hakansson, 1982). Figure 3.3 (p. 62) highlights the complex early research picture that emerged into the study of organizational buying.

Suffice to say, buyer behaviour models identify just one exchange. While this is useful to understand in order to develop a marketing strategy around the decision-making process of the parties, they are inadequate in describing ongoing relationships with many transactions, because of the increased complexity arising from the multiple layers of exchanges which, in turn, impact on relational development and outcomes.

> INSIGHT: A decision-making unit is a term used to describe a group of individuals within an organization who make decisions about what to buy.

In considering this complexity, for example, a commonly used concept is that of the decision-making unit (DMU). There are typically a number of different individuals involved in industrial purchasing decisions, primarily from within the buying organization, although influencers will include those in the wider environment especially where the organization is operating as part of a network. What makes this more complex, however, it that the composition of the DMU may change over time, thereby influencing the nature of interpersonal relationships built between the supplier and the customer. Figure 3.4 illustrates the typical roles within a DMU for a product.

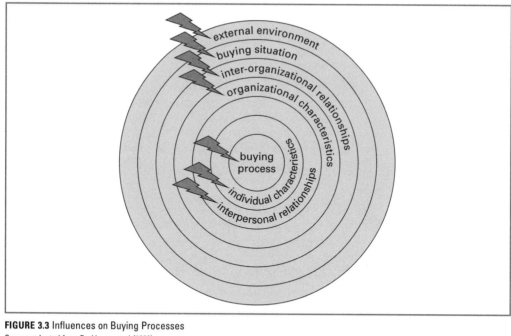

FIGURE 3.3 Influences on Buying Processes
Source: adapted from Parkinson *et al.* (1986).

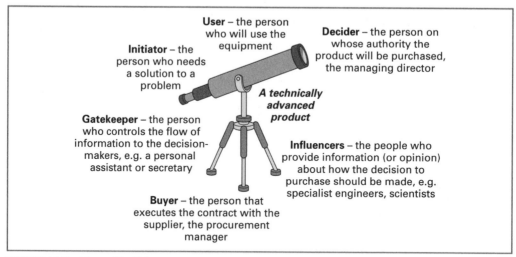

FIGURE 3.4 A Decision-making Unit

Significantly, ongoing relationships have been identified (Sheth, 1996) as being one of a series of major research streams into organizational buying to emerge. Supplier–customer relationships are seen as strategically important to an organization. Nonetheless, a customer organization may have greater flexibility to "shop around" for better prices and different technologies if it avoids engaging in relationships with suppliers.

There are, therefore, a number of considerations to be made when entering into relationships (Gadde and Hakansson, 2001). These are:

- The ongoing economic consequences of relationships, the costs of which may be difficult to measure. It is, therefore, important continually to evaluate the benefits as well as the costs to ensure the relationship remains viable. Direct costs may be seen in pricing and other "hard" terms related to management of the relationship; benefits relate more to savings, such as contribution towards efficiency and impact on revenue generated.

- The variety of relationships between the customer and its suppliers – no two relationships can be managed in the same way! Benefits are likely to arise from the different relational approaches which will need to be managed appropriately.

- Over or under-involvement in a relationship can result in costly inefficiencies which must be corrected. This also necessitates that both parties consider the nature of interactions (or interface) between the two organizations in order to allocate appropriate resources for effective and efficient relationship management.

- The need for mutuality, that is, both parties contributing to the relationship for longevity and benefits.

Task 3.4

Consider the brief descriptions of b2b scenarios below. Would you recommend a more tactical relationship or a strategic relationship approach? Explain your answers.

- A land development company wants to save money on their existing fleet of company cars over the next two years.

- A manufacturer wants to develop a comprehensive nationwide service centre to support their after-sales service.

- A small high-tech diagnostics equipment manufacturer wants to develop an advertising promotional campaign for a new product launch.

More recently, the Chartered Institute of Purchasing and Supply has identified a "spectrum" of relationships which are appropriate in different supply contexts (CIPS, 2006). These vary from purely adversarial and transactional, appropriate where the customer and supplier perceive little benefit from entering into a long-term arrangement, to single-sourced, outsourcing, strategic alliance, partnerships and co-destiny arrangements (see Table 3.2, p. 64).

Donaldson and O'Toole (2000) have classified relationships by their strength in terms of social, such as trust, and economic, that is investment, behaviours. These are summarized in Chapter 2. A classification system discussed by Donaldson and O'Toole (2002) shows that, where one party dominates the relationship, there is likely to be less trust between the customer and supplier. Similarly, an opportunistic relationship is typically transactional in nature, whereas a bilateral relationship is one where both parties invest to an equal degree in the relationship. The recurrent relationship is a typical situation where there are potentially limited benefits beyond the exchange and, therefore, this represents the repeat business likely to occur where there is a high social investment.

Such a classification reveals that not all relationships are based on equal terms between the customer and supplier, either because of market forces, differences in corporate governance or benefits to the parties. For example, suppliers may be powerful when there are few other sources of supply for the organization, or the business is not seen as being important to the supplier;

TABLE 3.2 Some Relationship Definitions

Relationship	Definition	Appropriate Context
Single-sourced	One supplier meets the needs of a customer on a range of products and services for a contract period on an exclusive basis	Where the arrangement results in economies of scale that may result from the relationship benefiting both parties
Outsourcing	Where a supplier retains overall responsibility of a particular aspect of its business but the performance of it is carried out by a supplier	Used where the expertise of the supplier can benefit the customer, usually where the aspect outsourced is peripherally important to the customer, rather than strategically so
Strategic alliance	Where two organizations or more work together for mutual gain	Where the parties wish to protect a market position
Partnership	Commitment by both parties to engage in a long-term relationship by sharing risk and rewards	In practice, this is difficult because as the partnership matures, so the goals change, making objectives for relationship continuation difficult to define
Co-destiny	Where there is genuine alignment between the parties	An association between suppliers, where agreement is reached on, for example, industry standards

Adapted from Chartered Institute of Purchasing and Supply (2006).

buyers may be powerful when there are few main customers in the marketplace. Differences in governance exist between public- and private-sector organizations. While many private-sector organizations are relatively free to form relationships with suppliers and customers, subject to adherence to legal structures, many public-sector organizations have additional layers of accountability that often preclude exclusive relationships with the private sector, lest these are seen to be anti-competitive and open to abuse.

A review of relationship-development theory identifies that the relationships evolve along a typical pathway and yet, as suggested by Table 3.2 and the discussion above, there may be many approaches to industrial relationships. The next section introduces the commonly understood relationship-development cycle and the subsequent section expands the discussion on two similar and yet quite contrasting types of industrial relationship: outsourcing and co-destiny.

Relational Development Cycles

The body of literature on relational development highlights the cyclic evolution of relationships from early stages of encounter, or "courtship", to partnership or "marriage" and, ultimately, dissolution or "divorce" (e.g. Ford, 1980; Dwyer *et al.*, 1987). The marriage metaphor has received some criticism because different perspectives on its relative importance within society ultimately change its meaning when used to describe industrial relationships (see Egan, 2004 for a review of this discussion). A number of models have been developed which identify the key stages of relationship development (Table 3.3).

TABLE 3.3 Relationship Development Models

Ford (1980)	Dwyer *et al.* (1987)	Borys and Jemison (1989)	Wilson (1995)	Evans *et al.* (2004)
Pre-relationship stage	Awareness		Search and selection	Attraction
Early stage	Exploration	Defining purpose	Defining purpose	Interaction
Development stage	Expansion	Setting boundaries	Setting boundaries	Progression
Long-term stage	Commitment	Value creation	Value creation	Deterioration
Final stage	Dissolution	Hybrid stability	Hybrid stability	Cessation reclamation

Source: Based on Evans *et al.* (2004).

While early stages of relationship development primarily comprise acquisition strategies (Evans *et al.*, 2004), it is the later stages of retaining the business that dominate the discussion on industrial relationships. What these simple models hide is that, as relational development becomes increasingly collaborative between customer and supplier, so the complexity of the transactions increases, and the benefits for the parties become more obscure. An example of this is illustrated in Table 3.4, which identifies the objectives and relational tone, based on work undertaken from, primarily, the seller's perspective of relationship development.

> INSIGHT: A Key Account Manager (KA Manager) is a person who manages the relationship with a customer for a supplier organization. The customer is typically understood to be strategically important to the supplier, often accounting for a considerable amount of business, although they may be strategic for other reasons, such as their ability to give access to new markets.

The models of relationships referred to above are important in understanding how relationships between suppliers and customers may evolve over time. Key account management (KAM), for example, is now well recognized as an area of Relationship Marketing with increasing significance (Gummesson, 2002). When successfully implemented, it enhances the opportunity to achieve longer-term competitive advantage through rationalization of resources (McDonald, Millman and Rogers, 1996; Schultz and Evans, 2002). Long known to be practised in industry, KAM (or national account management, NAM, as it is widely known in the USA), highlights useful working practices or deficient areas within organizations and provides benchmarking guidelines for future development of customers into key accounts.

The emphasis in KAM research is increasingly on the competences and skills required to successfully implement and manage successful relationships which net economic value. This includes account selection and planning, processes for effective development, global management, reward, recruitment and selection mechanisms. Nonetheless, it is important to recognize that every relationship is contextually different – it may be characterized by different actors with different priorities, preferences and styles of interaction. Relationships develop in a dynamic environment and the relational task may be approached in different ways to achieve a desired outcome, which itself may vary according to the needs of the interacting organizations. Time, its availability and balance between task and relational issues, is also highly variable. This has been emphasized in the work of Homburg *et al.* (2002). These authors identified different levels within supplier–customer relation-

TABLE 3.7 Relational Development Model

Stage	Objectives	Relational Tone
Pre-relationship stage	■ Identify key accounts ■ Establish account potential ■ Secure initial order	■ Friendly – due to informal social contact ■ Spartan – confidential information exchange and limited trust
Early relationship stage	■ Penetrate account ■ Increase volume of business ■ Become preferred supplier	■ Liking between key individuals develops (main contacts) ■ Trust is still an issue
Mid-relationship stage	■ Build towards partnership ■ Become single source supplier ■ Establish key account status	■ Social interaction becomes the emphasis – trust builds rapidly ■ Key information is shared, possibly through dedicated (Electronic Data Interchange) links
Partnership stage	■ Develop spirit of partnership ■ Lock in customer by providing external resource base	■ Profit is a focus for both parties ■ "Spirit of partnership" and co-operation exists ■ Effort on managing shared information
A further, "synergistic" stage	■ Effect continuous improvement ■ Achieve shared rewards (potential for quasi-integration)	■ Systems become transparent – openness and honesty presides ■ Borders between the customer and supplier become "blurred" – focus of interaction is on the "end customer"

Based on MacDonald, Millman and Rogers (1996); Donaldson (1996); Wilson (1999).

ships which exist at, for example, top-, middle- and operating-levels within organizations. Perhaps unsurprisingly, they found the higher the level within the organization at which relationships are recognized, the more likely a relational approach is to be successful (because middle and junior managers tend to adopt the approaches preferred by senior management).

Similar to customer development, and at the other end of the supply chain, supplier development is now also a strategically important aspect of business operations and management. Compton and Jessop (2001) suggest that supplier relationship development is about providing assistance to suppliers in order to facilitate their supply to the organization of products and services it needs. This may take the form of providing personnel for support or training, providing capital investment, equipment or expertise (Monckza et al., 1998). Factors that make supplier development important are (Fogg, 2006):

- the growth of outsourcing, meaning that the cost of goods and services are a high proportion of business costs;
- the need to manage delivery of products and services to ensure business continuity;
- the role of technologies in enabling buyers and suppliers to become specialists in their core activities.

The process of relational development necessarily revolves around trust and co-operation (Lamming, 1993). This is an aspect of relationship development that is inherently complex to implement because, as summarized by Langfield-Smith and Greenwood (1998), Western business environments have traditionally not included life-long employment, face-to-face negotiation, co-ownership between buyers and sellers and sharing of career paths. This is, of course, an allusion to the Japanese principles on which the theories of fostering industrial relationships have evolved. Nonetheless, advantages of relationships necessitate its consideration as the premise for longevity which supports the move from a transactional model to a co-operative framework.

The next section reviews different forms of supply relationships that are now common in industrial contexts.

Supply Relationships

Following on from earlier discussion in this chapter, this section expands on two significant forms of supply relationship that are now common in industry, plus one further form that is yet evolving in the wake of technological enhancements. These reflect the typologies identified in Chapter 2 of dyadic, channel and network relationships.

Outsourcing relationships

Outsourcing is a channel relationship which is, essentially, dyadic in nature. Outsourcing enables a company to specialize but also obliges it to identify its critical resources that are to be kept in-house – and this is likely to change over time as the organization develops. IBM has identified a number of characteristics that it uses to help managers determine an outsourcing decision, and where, overall, an activity is considered to be strategic rather than peripheral to its business, the decision is, generally, to remain in-house. Such activities include:

- those that provide management and strategic direction;
- those that help the organization to differentiate itself in the marketplace;
- those that help to maintain core competencies and control.

Outsourcing a business process or activity enables an organization's management to concentrate its resources (such as people, time, facilities) and effort on core business. It does this by enabling the customer to use the specific expertise of the outsourcing provider – this may help to achieve cost reductions in the supply chain that make the product or service more cost effective to the customer. The process of outsourcing enables the customer to evaluate the market, say, by tendering for a supply solution which thereby generates views on possible alternatives. Outsourcing also facilitates changes in working practices and/or people involved in the processes that are affected.

Factors influencing the adoption of outsourcing as a solution include (Jenster *et al.*, 2005; McIvor, 2005):

- *Globalization* – trade agreements between geographic regions of the world, coupled with deregulation and an imperative for free trade, have encouraged organizations to take advantage of global markets. This is not without problems, such as language, culture, legal requirements and currency movements, which all present challenges for trading partners. First manufacturers, and latterly service providers, have been keen to maximize benefits from sourcing supplies from less developed areas of the world in an attempt to achieve greater competitive advantage through cost cutting.

■ *Technological developments* – information and communications technologies have had a significant impact on business operations and they are increasingly blurring the boundaries of traditional organizations (for example, virtual organizations and e-commerce are now common terms). The Internet provides access to information about a broader spectrum of supply solutions than ever before. The challenges remain how to best exploit the opportunities provided by the rapidly evolving commercial technologies.

■ *Public sector reforms* – introduction of competitive market structures have fundamentally changed the way public-sector organizations function in Europe. The aim is to improve performance and achieve "best value" in service provision for the general public.

■ *Changes in customer demand and levels of sophistication* – because of increased access to a wider range of information, customers have become more discerning about prices, quality and availability. In turn, this has influenced expectations for interaction with organizations and, increasingly, public-sector services.

Downsides to this are highlighted in the mini-case study about Boeing and its use of outsourced providers in the development of its new Dreamliner aircraft.

MINI-CASE: BOEING'S DREAMLINER

Boeing is using outsourced products and services for at least 80 per cent of one of its newest aircraft from a range of different suppliers around the globe (Holmes, 2006). Providers are supplying key complex systems for use in a new aircraft's, Dreamliner, aerostructure and sub-system. The Dreamliner is a relatively small, lightweight and agile commercial aircraft. It is scheduled to take its first commercial flight in 2008, with its launch customer, All Nippon Airways. The first airplane began production in 2005. Suppliers and their products include:

■ Rolls Royce's new Trent 1000 engine

■ Safran's Messier-Dowty and Messier-Bugatti landing gear, wheel and brakes units

■ Smiths Aerospace's Common Core System (the technological "backbone" of the aircraft)

■ Dassault Systemes' product lifecycle management software.

Recently, Boeing has developed a new supplier management arrangement, responsible for supplier sourcing and partnering. The aim is to facilitate risk-sharing among supplying partners, with the overall focus being to encourage greater supplier involvement in product development initiatives. Ultimately, such a focus is likely to reap future rewards in terms of cost savings, alignment in the supply chain and enhanced return on investments made by the stakeholders.

The managing director of the partnering organization identifies a number of characteristics as being important for its outsourced providers:

■ work-flow that embraces lean manufacturing techniques;

■ happy employees across the full range of roles – individuals who enjoy their jobs and are committed to doing it well;

■ the opportunity to share in the organization's future vision and the commitment to helping the organization to achieve it – it's about "sharing the 'why' of things".

Boeing's increased focus on partnering and relationships (from their contract basis), necessitates the organization's staff have more technical knowledge about the airplane and its production processes. A key role of outsourcing providers is, therefore, to share knowledge with the organization's staff. According to the managing director, "different cultures or archetypes bring different strengths to the team … we have found the more diversity of background and thought you have, the better the solutions you get" (Bernstein, 2006). The partnering organization's managers participate in a rotational programme, where staff become managers in the supplying organizations for a period of time before returning to their own company.

Business Week (Holmes, 2006) reported that the organization's engineers have uncovered a number of significant problems that could impact on the organization's ability to meet their 2008 delivery date. Problems identified include:

- a mid-section of the aircraft has failed its testing, impacting on quality and safety;

- test versions of other sections of the aircraft have not been accepted by the organization;

- software systems provided by different providers are not seamlessly integrated, necessitating additional work;

- the airplane's weight is considered to be too high, especially its carbon-fibre wing section.

These problems are all having a "domino effect" on the supply chain – one problem is impacting on the ability of suppliers to meet their respective deadlines which, ultimately, will impact on the organization's bottom line. Furthermore, it is reported that tensions are high among staff and arguments have ensued, although this is not necessarily uncommon for such major projects as the new aircraft. Matters appear to be compounded, however, by the unique outsourcing provision, which is higher than the organization have used on their other aircraft. Now serious questions are being asked about the appropriateness of its supply solution.

Questions

1 **What risks are identified in the Boeing mini-case? How are they likely to impact on Boeing and its suppliers?**

2 **What influence do the following four factors appear to have had on Boeing's decision to outsource:**

   - **Globalization?**

   - **Technology development?**

   - **Public-sector reform?**

   - **Changes in customer sophistication?**

Co-destiny relationships

These relationships are somewhat looser than partnerships and, essentially, premised on the network approach discussed in this and the previous chapter. As intimated, co-destiny relationships are about the connection between the business models used by the organizations, where the adoption of a particular practice by one organization has implications for others in the network. A classic example of this is currently unfolding in the construction sector in the UK, where the approach to business by the key competitors has traditionally been quite adversarial. More recently, the use of partnerships and relationship-management approaches has had a significant impact on the way competitors work together as consortia (Lysons and Farrington, 2006) to influence the whole market, enhance buying power and respond to an international market.

A particular type of co-destiny relationship is a Supplier Association (SA). SAs are mechanisms used to enhance network benefits between and among customers and suppliers. The purpose of these associations is to disseminate best practice in order to promote development, usually in an industry sector (such as car manufacturing, where it was originally introduced back in the 1950s). Hines (1994) has identified a number of objectives of the approach:

- To improve and enhance supplier skills and competences
- To develop synergy between suppliers, so promoting standards within industry sectors
- To facilitate information flow
- To build trust between suppliers and purchasers
- To develop purchaser reputations among suppliers and potential suppliers
- To promote knowledge flow about market developments
- To support smaller suppliers or niche players
- To provide examples of good practice to promote learning across the sector

These networks are especially good at enabling the parties to respond to uncertainty, given that all parties may participate to a preferred level, depending on their particular resources. A number of characteristics are, however, common to all networks in customer–supplier relationships (Grabher, 1993):

- Loose coupling, where levels of autonomy retained by the partners enable partners to benefit at a broader level
- Reciprocity, where patterns of behaviour reward reactions from others
- Power, which enables exploitation of the relationship and may be used to contain the network and facilitates trust building and management
- Interdependence, where stable, long-term interactions are mutually beneficial to the partners

Other forms of networked relationships are evolving as a result of the influence of Internet-based technologies. An example of this is "business-webs" ("b-webs"). These extend the supplier association idea and incorporate producers, service providers, suppliers, other stakeholders and customers by using the Internet to communicate (Tapscott *et al.*, 2000). The use of technology to form relational communities will be discussed further in Chapter 7.

Adding Value Through Relationships

Throughout this chapter there has been an underlying assumption that relationships between buyers and suppliers in an industrial marketing context are "a good thing". Factors cited include the following:

- Cost reduction due to focusing on fewer suppliers
- Reduction of uncertainty in a market where products and services are of critical importance to business continuity
- Management of risk in an individual contractual relationship

- Assurance that quality is maintained
- Development of specialism and expertise, say, as a result of being able to outsource and collaborate with suppliers, which may in turn enhance profitability by improving efficiencies
- Innovation and reduced time to market for new products and services arising from closer collaborations
- Reputation building, potentially enabling wider reach in a market

Nonetheless, while the literature highlights these obvious benefits, relationships remain a notoriously complex area of business to identify, establish and build in practice. Not only is it difficult to identify which of the many suppliers of an organization may prove to be the best business partners, but it is then difficult to determine an appropriate pathway to establishing the basis of a strong working relationship. Indeed, most relationships start out being transactional in nature and it is only when the supplier has proved itself to be trustworthy and reliable that a relationship may begin to develop. Furthermore, once established, there are a great many challenges to overcome in ensuring the relationship remains a valuable asset to the organizations. Such challenges include the following (Harwood and Garry, 2005):

- Increased pressure to compromise or make accommodations within the organization because the emphasis on co-operation with an external party may result in lower returns
- Avoidance of confrontation because it can create barriers to exchanges which may be taken as failure, when conflict can result in truly creative solutions to problems
- Misleading behaviour by one party may undermine the competitive position of the other
- Reliance on value-laden outcomes means it can be difficult to quantify the benefits
- The requirement of great skill and competence to manage, especially in interpreting the other party's position, interests and needs

Task 3.5

Examine each of the following "supply" relationships and determine whether there is greater benefit to you from approaching the relationship transactionally or relationally:

- Your bank
- Your landlord
- Your favourite clothing store

In assessing the value added through relationships it is pertinent to remember the end user or customer! In the industrial context, as stated at the outset in this chapter, buyer and supplier relationships take place within a supply chain designed to meet the needs of the end user. As highlighted by the likes of Drummond and Ensor (2003), each component of the supply chain should add some value and, therefore, if the benefits do not enhance that value then, ultimately, there is little point in engaging in the relationship.

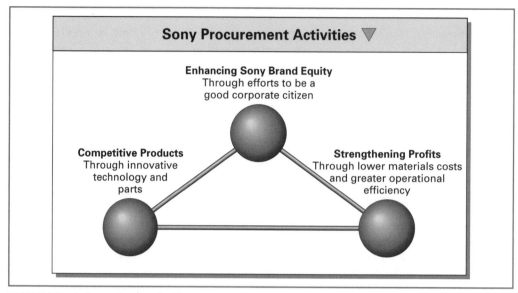

FIGURE 3.5 Sony's Approach to Supplier Management
Source: www.sony.jp

Chapter Summary

This chapter has presented a review of the industrial and supply chain perspective of RM. Discussion of industrial marketing has highlighted some of the important drivers for change. The review emphasized the importance of information to the search process of buyers, and models of organizational buyer behaviour were presented and discussed. Subsequently, the evolution of relationships was discussed in terms of the economic consequences, the types of relationships, the involvement of the parties in the relationship-management process and the need for mutuality in achieving benefits. The relational development cycle was reviewed, wherein the complexity of relationships were reflected upon. Finally, two specific forms of industrial and supply relationship were discussed: outsourcing and co-destiny relationships.

Review Questions

1 What are the drivers for change in industrial markets?
2 Comment on how supply relationships are evolving.
3 Identify and describe two different types of industrial marketing relationship.

Further Reading

Donaldson, B. and T. O'Toole (2000) "Classifying Relationship Structures: Relationship Strength in Industrial Markets", *The Journal of Business and Industrial Marketing,* vol. 15, no. 7, pp. 491–506.

Dwyer, F.R., P.H. Schurr and S. Oh (1987) "Developing Buyer–Seller Relationships", *Journal of Marketing,* vol. 51, April, pp. 11–27.

Kraljic, P. (1982) "Purchasing Must Become Supply Management", *Harvard Business Review*, Sept–Oct, pp. 109–117.

END OF CHAPTER CASE AND KEY QUESTIONS

Sony: a networked approach to supply chain management

Sony is a high-tech computer components manufacturer; it is a global organization headquartered in Japan, known for its audio-visual, information and communications products, electronic components and semi-conductors. Sony's aims, through its dealings with suppliers, are to:

- meet the needs of its customers worldwide by offering a high level of value and good corporate citizenship through its operations;
- build relationships based on mutual trust and co-operation with suppliers for parts and materials for its products using numerous suppliers worldwide.

Sony stresses that suppliers should be "good partners" by providing quality products that satisfy customers through ethical standards of trading. Their procurement philosophy emphasizes the importance of innovation in the supply chain in order to build competitive advantage and profitability. Figure 3.5 illustrates its approach.

Partnership is Sony's fundamental approach to ensuring it achieves its procurement principles, recognizing that without partners it will be difficult to adapt to a dynamic business environment. The organization identifies that the following practices will enhance its ability to meet customer needs:

- Sharing of business practices, processes and policies, including strategies and technological solutions
- Collaboration to generate high value, that is, higher than they would be able to do if they were more competitive in their approach to working with suppliers
- Working towards combining technological skills in order to enhance, build and sustain supply chains, while focusing on the quality of component parts and compliance within regulatory frameworks

An example of Sony's partnering strategy is its relationship with Idemitsu, a supplier, formalized in November 2005. The supplier is collaborating to develop and promote a new type of Organic Light-Emitting Diode (OLED). The Diode has a thin self-luminous display which gives high-quality colour reproduction and rapid response to moving imagery. The technology can be used in flat panel display products and is presently competing for market space against the commonly used LCD (liquid crystal display) technology. Idemitsu is renowned for having developed the world's brightest blue-light organic luminous material back in 1997, based on its "molecular engineering and organic synthesis technologies". Since then, it has been working on new technologies including the Diode. In the meantime, Sony has been working on various similar technologies, based on "low temperature polysilicon Thin Film Transistor technologies". These have been used in its Personal Digital Assistant (PDA) products since September 2004.

By sharing their complementary diode-related technologies, the two organizations aim to develop new superior luminous materials which they plan will use less power, have higher brightness and colour reproduction for the high definition (HD) era, give high response time for moving images and be capable of long life.

In turn, Idemitsu reached agreement in March 2006 with a chemicals manufacturer, Mitsui, to begin supplying samples of world-class, high-performance red light-emitting materials. It identifies the product as a tangible result of ongoing collaboration in the development of OLEDs, based on an R&D partnership, including manufacturing the technology. Idemitsu did not previously have the capability to make red light-emitting materials, but in combination with other colours, including the blue-light emitting diode, it anticipates benefits in terms of synergizing production of the colours using new fluorescent-type materials.

The agreement reached with Mitsui gives the Idemitsu the right to market the product and, subsequently, it has purchased the patent of the technology. Mitsui promotes an active network of research within and between universities around the world through its exchange programmes and by hosting international symposia. It actively pursues joint research projects in order to create business opportunities. Its research findings are presented at conferences worldwide and published in journals related to catalysis science and advanced materials. Through its various collaborations with industry and academe, it provides an exchange of knowledge and expertise in chemical technology research.

The agreement between the Sony and the Idemitsu specifies that both will be able to benefit from the technology-related patents and, in addition, both have agreed to exchange the rights to use each other's component-related patents. The result of the collaboration is expected to be rapid joint development of new products.

In a press release the President of Idemitsu highlighted the importance of the partnership to new product developments, while Sony's President and Electronics CEO said: "We are very pleased to work on this joint development with this supplier, which has leading edge technology in many areas ... Our organization is positioning OLED as the most important technology for the next generation flat display. Thanks to the development of new superior luminous materials through the joint efforts of the two companies, we will be able to accelerate the OLED development and will advance the materialization of our OLED applied products."

Sources

www.sony.jp; www.mitsui.jp; www.idemitsu.jp

Questions

1 Examine the relationship between Sony and Idemitsu and comment on the likely value-adding benefits to each.

2 Assuming that Idemitsu is partnering with Mitsui to enhance its collaborative capacity with Sony, evaluate the factors that are likely to have influenced Sony's decision to reach agreement with Idemitsu.

3 Discuss the steps that Sony could take to ensure that Mitsui will not exploit its relationship with Idemitsu.

Follow-up task

■ Review Sony's website (www.sony.jp) and briefly describe who may comprise its decision-making unit.

■ Examine how each of these stakeholders may influence its relationship with suppliers.

References

Baker, M.J. (2005) comment.

Bernstein, A. (2006) New global job shift, *Business Week* [online], US, available http://www.businessweek.com/magazine/content/03_05/b3818001.htm, accessed 17 August.

Borys, B. and D.B. Jemison (1989) "Hybrid Arrangements as Strategic Alliances: Theoretical Issues in Organizational Combinations", *Academy of Management Review*, vol. 14, pp. 234–249.

CIPS (Chartered Institute of Purchasing and Supply) (2006), www.cips.org.

Coase, R.H. (1937) "The Nature of the Firm", *Economica*, vol. 4, pp. 386–405.

Compton, H.K. and D.A. Jessop (2001) *The Official Dictionary of Purchasing and Supply Terminology for Buyers and Suppliers*, Cambridge: Liverpool Business Publishing.

DeCormier, R. and D. Jobber (1998) "The Counsellor Selling Model: Components and Theory", *The Journal of Selling and Major Account Management*, vol. 1, no. 2, pp. 22–40.

Donaldson, B. (1996) "Industrial Marketing Relationships and Open-to-Tender Contracts: Co-operation or Competition", *Journal of Marketing Practice: Applied Marketing Science*, vol. 2, no. 2, pp. 23–34.

Donaldson, B. and T. O'Toole (2000) "Classifying Relationship Structures: Relationship Strength in Industrial Markets", The Journal of Business and Industrial Marketing, vol. 15, no. 7, pp. 491–506.

Donaldson, B. and T. O'Toole (2002) *Strategic Market Relationships: From Strategy to Implementation*, New York: John Wiley & Sons.

Drummond, G. and J. Ensor (2003) *Strategic Marketing Planning and Control*, 2nd edn, Oxford: Butterworth Heinemann.

Dwyer, F.R., P.H. Schurr and S. Oh (1987) "Developing Buyer–Seller Relationships", *Journal of Marketing*, vol. 51, April, pp. 11–27.

Egan, J. (2004) *Relationship Marketing: Exploring Relational Strategies in Marketing*, Harlow: Financial Times, Prentice Hall.

Evans, M., L. O'Malley and M. Patterson (2004) *Exploring Direct and Customer Relationship Marketing*, 2nd edn, London: Thomson.

Fogg, M. (2006) *Managing Purchasing and Supply Relationship*, Stamford: The Chartered Institute of Purchasing and Supply.

Ford, D. (1980) "The Development of Buyer–Seller Relationships in Industrial Markets", *European Journal of Marketing*, vol. 14, no. 5/6, pp. 339–354.

Gadde, L. and H. Hakansson (1993) *Professional Purchasing*, London: Routledge.

Gadde, L.-E. and H. Hakansson (2001) *Supply Network Strategies*, Chichester: John Wiley and Sons.

Grabher, G. (1993) "Rediscovering the Social in the Economics of Interfirm Relations", in Grabher (ed.), *The Embedded Firm: On the Socioeconomics of Industrial Networks*, London: Routledge.

Grönroos, C. (1997) "Value-driven Relational Marketing: From Products to Resources and Competencies", *Journal of Marketing Management*, vol. 13, pp. 407–419.

Gummesson, E. (2002) *Total Relationship Management*, London: Butterworth-Heinemann.

Hakansson, H. (ed.) (1982) *International Marketing and Purchasing of Goods: An Interaction Approach*, Chichester: John Wiley and Sons.

Harwood, T. and T. Garry (2005) "Relationship Marketing: Why Bother?", *Handbook of Business Strategy*, Bradford: Emerald.

Hines, P. (1994) *Creating World Class Suppliers*, London: Pitman.

Holmes (2006) Comment [online] US, available www.boeing.com/news/releases, accessed 18 August.

Homburg, C., J.P. Workman Jnr and O. Jenson (2002) "A Configurerational Perspective on Key Account Management", *Journal of Marketing*, vol. 66, no. 2, pp. 38–60.

Iacobucci, D. (ed.) (1996) *Networks in Marketing*, London: Sage Publications.

Jenster, P.V., H.S. Pedersen, P. Plackett and D. Hussey (2005) *Outsourcing Insourcing*, Chichester: John Wiley & Sons.

Jobber, D. (2004) *Principles and Practice of Marketing*, London: McGraw-Hill.

Johnston, W.J. and J.E. Lewin (1996) "Organizational Buying Behavior: Toward an Integrative Framework", *Journal of Business Research*, vol. 35, pp. 1–16.

Kohli, A. (1989) "Determinants of Influence in Organizational Buying: A Contingency Approach", *Journal of Marketing*, vol. 53, July, pp. 50–65.

Kraljic, P. (1982) "Purchasing Must Become Supply Management", *Harvard Business Review*, Sept–Oct, pp. 109–117.

Lamming, R. (1993) *Beyond Partnership – Strategies for Innovation and Lean Supply*, London: Prentice Hall.

Langfield-Smith, K. and M.R. Greenwood (1998) "Developing Co-operative Buyer–Supplier Relationships: A Case Study of Toyota", *Journal of Management Studies*, vol. 35, no. 3 (May), pp. 331–353.

Lysons, K. and Farrington (2006) *Purchasing and Supply Chain Management*, 7th edn, Harlow: Financial Times Prentice Hall.

Matthyssens, P. and C. Van den Bulte (1994) "Getting Closer and Nicer: Partnerships in the Supply Chain", *Long Range Planning*, vol. 27, no. 1, pp. 72–83.

McDonald, M., T. Millman and B. Rogers (1996) *Key Account Management: Learning from Supplier and Customer Perspectives*, Cranfield: The Centre for Advanced Research in Marketing at the Cranfield School of Management.

McIvor, R. (2005) *The Outsourcing Process*, Cambridge: Cambridge University Press.

Moller, K. (1981) *Industrial Buying Behaviour of Production Materials. A Conceptual Model and Analysis*, The Helsinki School of Economics Publication Series.

Monczka, R.M. and J.P. Morgan (2000) "Competitive Strategies for the 21st Century", *Purchasing*, pp. 48–59.

Monckza R.M., R. Trent and R. Handfield (1998) *Purchasing and Supply Chain Management*, Cincinnatti: International Thompson Publishing.

Parkinson, S.T. and M.J. Baker with K. Moller (1986) *Organizational Buying Behavior*, London: MacMillan Press.

Payne, A. and P. Frow (1997) "Relationship Marketing: Key Issues for the Utilities Sector", *Journal of Marketing Management*, vol. 13, pp. 463–477.

Rackham, N. (1987) *Making Major Sales*, Aldershot: Gower Publishing.

Reichheld, F.F. and W.E. Sasser Jnr (1990) "Zero Defections: Quality Comes to Services", *Harvard Business Review*, Sept–Oct, pp. 105–111.

Rich, M.K. (2000) "The Direction of Marketing Relationships", *Journal of Business and Industrial Marketing*, vol. 15, nos 2/3, pp. 170–179.

Robinson, P.J., C.W. Faris and Y. Wind (1967) *Industrial Buying and Creative Marketing*, Boston, MA: Allyn and Bacon.

Schultz, R.J. and K.R. Evans (2002) "Strategic Collaborative Communication by Key Account Representatives", *The Journal of Personal Selling and Sales Management*, vol. 22, no. 1, pp. 23–31.

Sheth, J.N. (1973) "A Model of Industrial Buyer Behaviour", *Journal of Marketing*, vol. 37, October, pp. 50–56.

Sheth, J.N. (1996) "Organizational Buying Behaviour Past Performance and Future Expectations", *Journal of Business and Industrial Marketing*, vol. 11, no. 3/4, pp. 7–24.

Strong, E.K. (1925) *The Psychology of Selling*, New York: McGraw-Hill.

Tapscott, D., D. Ticoll and A. Lowy (2000) *Digital Capital*, CA: HBS Press.

Webster, F.E. and Y. Wind (1972) "A General Model for Understanding Organizational Buying Behavior", *Journal of Marketing*, vol. 36, April, pp. 12–19.

Webster, F. (1965) "Modeling the Industrial Buying Process", *Journal of Marketing Research*, vol. 2, pp. 370–376.

Williamson, O.E. (1985) *The Economic Institutions of Capitalism*, New York: Free Press.

Wilson, D.T. (1995) "An Integrated Model of Buyer–Seller Relationships", *Journal of the Academy of Marketing Science*, vol. 23, no. 4, pp. 335–345.

Wilson, E.J. (1996) "Theory Transitions in Organizational Buying Behavior Research", *Journal of Business and Industrial Marketing*, vol. 11, no. 6, pp. 7–19.

Wilson, K. (1999) "Developing Key Account Relationships: The Integration of the Millman-Wilson Relational Development Model with the Problem Centred (PPF) Model of Buyer–Seller Interaction in Business-to-Business Markets", *The Journal of Selling and Major Account Management*, vol. 1, no. 3, pp. 11–32.

Wind, Y. (1978) "Issues and Advances in Segmentation Research", *Journal of Marketing Research*, vol. XV, pp. 317–337.

Womack, J.P. and D.T. Jones (1996) *Lean Thinking: Banish Waste and Create Wealth in your Corporation*, New York: Simon and Schuster.

Zineldin, M.Z. (2000) "Total Relationship Management (TRM) and Total Quality Management (TQM)", *Managerial Auditing Journal*, vol. 15, nos 1–2, pp. 20–28.

04

Services Marketing and Relational Perspectives

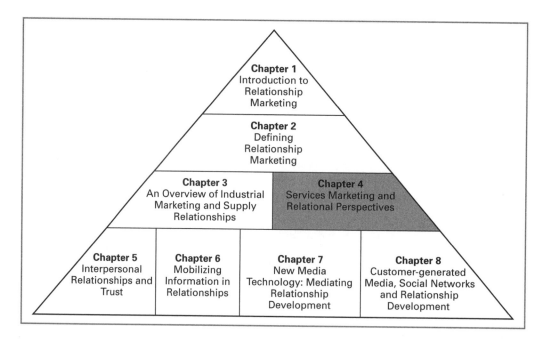

Chapter 1
Introduction to Relationship Marketing

Chapter 2
Defining Relationship Marketing

Chapter 3
An Overview of Industrial Marketing and Supply Relationships

Chapter 4
Services Marketing and Relational Perspectives

Chapter 5
Interpersonal Relationships and Trust

Chapter 6
Mobilizing Information in Relationships

Chapter 7
New Media Technology: Mediating Relationship Development

Chapter 8
Customer-generated Media, Social Networks and Relationship Development

❖ LEARNING OBJECTIVES

After studying this chapter, you should be able to:

1 **understand** the relational focus in early service marketing ideas

2 **consider** differences in customer interfaces in services and the way relationship building varies according to these different kinds of services

3 **identify** how relationship development links to service quality ideas

4 **be aware** of the role of service employees in ongoing relationship building

5 **appreciate** the changes in trust-building in service relationships

Chapter Contents

Introduction

Grönroos (1988) views services as processes, arguing that services are activities rather than things. According to Gummesson (1993) customers do not buy goods or services but rather they buy an offering and the value may consist of many components.

> INSIGHT: Service = "any activity or benefit that one party can offer to another that is essentially intangible and does not result in the ownership of anything. Its production may or may not be tied to a physical product" Kotler *et al.* (2005)

Service relationship concepts have always existed; the particular focus has varied. In some periods, relationship aspects were more explicit; in others, the interactive domain was highlighted; and in yet others, the behavioural elements came to the fore in academic research.

This chapter draws out these varied relational perspectives in services. It initially identifies some variation in the nature of services, outlining the development of interrelationships and the management of parallel internal–external processes. It then traces early relational perspectives on services and how such perspectives have evolved. A key section then identifies the qualities of services, how this thinking is now being adapted in virtual environments and how customers are now using different cues to assess value and are relying on different sources for trust.

Service marketing ideas which focus on the interactive domain are then explored, with particular examination of the interactive elements within the service encounter, notably through the service blueprint. In the third part of the chapter, more explicit relationship dimensions in the form of behavioural elements of services are noted and this covers relationship elements in service quality in the 1980s. An important final element is the behaviour of service personnel as the key to good relationship development.

Looking Across the Services Spectrum

In considering how services marketing has contributed to some of our current Relationship Marketing ideas, it is first useful to identify the nature of services and how they vary in terms of users, organization goals and the range of marketing activities engaged in. Table 4.1 indicates some common service organizations that would engage in different forms of service marketing. Three different kinds of services are profiled – a bank, a grocery retailer and a school (fee-paying). We can see that the non-profit-making service – the school – has different goals, a wide variety of benefits are demanded and it would be unlikely to engage with the full range of marketing activities.

Task 4.1

Complete the remaining columns in Table 4.1 and identify for yourself how the other organizations vary in the scope of marketing activities, the nature of their organizational goals, the diversity of their customer and stakeholder groups and the benefits which they seek to generate for their customers in their service process and delivery.

■ In your opinion, what would you regard as any *common* customer-focused activities that all of the above service organizations would need to undertake?

One of the key differences that can be seen is within the key interrelationships that each service organization builds and maintains.

Service manager role – internal and external interface

The service manager's role is very broad and if we highlight a few key responsibilities (see Insight box below), we can see that they are simultaneously working at an internal as well as external level of relationship management. On a day-to-day basis, while they focus primarily on service communication, service process, delivery, customer perception, and engagement and satisfaction with the service encounter, their work may also integrate with elements of human resource management in an organization.

TABLE 4.1 The Services Spectrum

Service	Main organizational goal(s)	Principal benefit	Principal user customer or stakeholder	Scope of marketing activities
Bank	To gain profit To increase business and retain customers	Protect financial assets Offer competent financial service	Individual and business customers who pay	Full range
Grocery Retailer	To gain profit To increase business and retain customers	Enable stimulating and effective shopping experiences	Individual households who pay local communities	Full range
School (where fees are paid by parents)	To meet parent, child educational needs To sustain performance To remain competitive with the offering in other schools To generate enough revenue to prosper	Effective educational service Opportunity to develop in a secure environment Opportunity to progress in life	Meets both parent and child needs and fulfils society's requirement for adequate education of youth	Less than full range – will use service planning and positioning but not on same scale as bank. May use many elements of the 7 Ps, but unlikely to use national advertising, or have great flexibility in pricing
University Library				
Online Dating Agency				
Amazon.com				

INSIGHT: A service marketing manager's role is multidimensional, involving some of the following activities:

- Managing interfaces with employees and with customers both online and offline
- Commissioning or undertaking market research both online and offline with customers regarding service development
- Initiating improvements to service processes
- Initiating modifications to service delivery
- Pushing for improvement in customer service, feedback and service recovery systems
- Benchmarking the organization's service processes against the best in the marketplace

These simultaneous roles also require different levels of relationship management.

Source: Broderick, author.

Managing a service is inevitably a balancing of different internal and external stakeholders. Because services are delivered as they are created (as in organizing a concert), the relationship management of upstream and downstream elements occurs very close together and can be simultaneous. These parallel activities are shown in Figure 4.1 (p. 82).

Services Marketing Theory and Relationship Focus

We have seen in the previous section that, as the nature of services varies, the nature of relationships to be developed also varies – thus, relationship development is inherent to services. For this reason, much of the earlier academic thinking about relationships in services marketing theory (1960s–1980s) is implicit and tends to focus on the interface and process elements in relationships, such as service behaviours of employees and interactive delivery

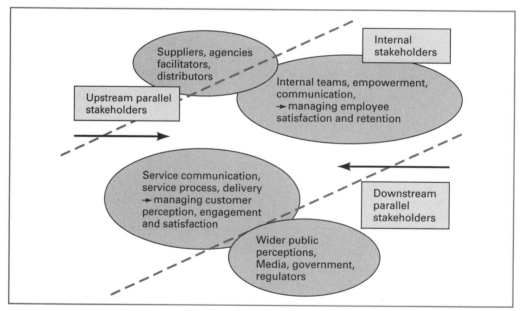

FIGURE 4.1 Internal–external Relationship Management in Services
Source: Broderick, author.

processes. This is evident in early work of Lovelock, Shostack in the 1970s and also in the service quality focus in the 1980s of Parasuraman, Berry and Zeithaml. In services marketing theory, particular focus on relationship development and relationship models only emerged in the 1990s, some of the best-known being the work of Grönroos and Gummesson. Numerous authors in all other areas of marketing have focused on relationship development both before this (e.g. IMP group interaction model in Chapter 2), and dedicated RM authors emerged as key theorists after this in the 1990s (e.g. see Six Markets model of Christopher et al., 1991 in Chapter 2).

Services marketing has never been one set of key ideas, but draws upon several perspectives. Within these perspectives there has always been a strong focus on relationship dimensions that relate to the management of a service organization. When we consider Relationship Marketing ideas that arise from services thinking, therefore, we need to trace some of the implicit elements of earlier theorists as well as the more explicit later models. Some relationship elements that we can note include:

- Early relationship dimensions within service categorization in the 1960s and 1970s
- The interactive domain in service frameworks such as service blueprint in the 1970s
- Focus on service behaviours in service quality and critical incident analysis of customer interface in the 1980s
- Relationship development role of service personnel in the 1990s

Relational Dimensions in Service Formats

Key elements

Early scholars in services marketing (Lovelock, Shostack 1970s, 1980s). defined services marketing as different from product marketing. Shostack's (1977) seminal article entitled "Breaking free from product marketing" characterized services as having distinct properties such as intangibility and inseparability, which required a different approach to marketing from that adopted in product markets. A tangibility continuum was proposed by Shostack (1977), anchored at one end by highly intangible 'pure' service products and at the other by products with strong tangible elements. In Figure 4.2 below, two examples of services are noted – a service that is associated with quite tangible physical elements, a car repair service and a more intangible service – a personal counselling service.

Is this valid for relationship development? Yes, because as we look at the right-hand side of the continuum, where tangibility is lower, services are often tailored towards specific groups, and the expertise of the service provider is more critical. The level of confidence in the service comes from the service provider interactions, the suggested benefits and their behaviour. Many implicit cues are relational.

Alternatively, in early studies, there was a strong emphasis on relational dimensions. Chase (1978) defined services in terms of the degree of contact with the client that was involved. Lovelock (1983) undertook a seminal study in 1983, in which he reviewed the classification approaches from the 1960s to 1983. He grouped these studies under five key categories: the nature of the service act; the type of relationship the organization has with its customers; the degree of customization and judgement on part of the service provider; the nature of demand and supply for the service and how the service is delivered. More recently, Perez-Rivera (1994) offered a more up-to-date review of service classifications. She identified six broad categories under which classification schemes are detailed: the nature of the organization; the nature of the service; the customer relationship; the nature of demand; the service package; and the delivery method. A table showing the combined classification approaches, as noted by both Lovelock (1983) and Perez-Rivera (1994) is shown in Table 4.2.

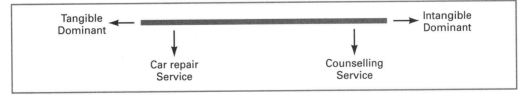

FIGURE 4.2 Tangibility Spectrum
Source: adapted from Shostack (1977).

TABLE 4.2 Service Format Elements in Previous Studies

Service Format	Author	Year
Tangibility	Shostack	1977
Degree of customization and standardization	Lovelock	1983
Performed on equipment/people	Thomas	1978
Degree of contact, whether high or low	Chase	1978
Type of relationship envisaged	Lovelock	1983
Degree of production/consumption flexibility	Zeithaml, Bitner	1996
Nature of benefit	Hill	1977
Degree of customer involvement	Palmer	1994

We can consider, on the one hand, a visit to the Post Office to post an important package by registered post; and, on the other, a visit to a hair salon. We can define each according to the Elements in Table 4.2. This immediately suggests that in terms of level of contact, relationship envisaged, degree of customization, and degree of customer involvement; the visit to the hair salon indicates a stronger relationship focus (Table 4.3).

TABLE 4.3 Applying Service Format Elements to Common Services

Basis	Post Office	Hair Salon
Tangibility	Medium — premises, weigh machine, receipt but cannot see result	High — can see results immediately
Degree of customization and standardization	Low	High
Performed on equipment/people	Registering letter – on equipment/people	On people
Degree of contact, whether high or low	Low, few words	High, plenty of conversation in hair salons.
Type of relationship envisaged	None – basic transaction	If a regular customer, long
Degree of production/consumption flexibility	Limited – need to go and have parcel weighed	Limited – need to go to premises
Nature of benefit	Official process and guarantee of secure delivery	Experience personal care Gain personal confidence
Degree of customer involvement	Low to medium – an objective outcome of safe delivery	Relatively high – you want to look and feel good about yourself

Is this relevant today? Many of the above elements are. It is useful to assess the level of contact, the degree of customization and the nature of benefit for any service. Classifying service patterns and formats is regarded as valuable to marketers. Palmer (2004) argues that they can enable a firm to gain strategic insights and this has also been acknowledged more recently by Lovelock, Vandermerwe and Lewis (2004). Nonetheless, the way service patterns and formats are examined has evolved, as categories first developed in the 1970s become less relevant.

> INSIGHT: "We need to classify services into marketing-relevant groups, looking for points of similarity between different industries. We can use the insights from these classifications to help us focus on marketing strategies that are relevant to specific service situations" (Lovelock, Vandermerwe and Lewis, 2004: 30).

Services operate in multidimensional mode

If we look at Lovelock's (1983) ideas on customization and standardization, this becomes clear. The level of customization in service relationships is now more complicated than can be represented in a simple matrix where the level of customization varies with discrete or continuous delivery elements (see Figure 4.3). Service organizations have been challenged by diversifying market demands to include multiple dimensions such as high contact, high customization for some customer groups, and processes that deal with low customer involvement elements. Many service organizations can operate simultaneously in either a customized or standardized mode. For instance, bankers working on a merger may require high, customized contact with both client organizations in terms of the complex financial planning involved; but in relation to lodging the legal paperwork, it may be dealt with remotely by telephone or third-party courier.

Recent literature in Relationship Marketing shows that relationship duration and development is complex and varied. Some of the varied components on relationship development are shown in Chapter 1, Table 1.3 (see p. 16). Although early schemata used by Chase (1978) and Lovelock (1983) have been refined considerably, as in Tynan (1997), some relational dimensions have been retained in current categorization of services, with minor modifications. Concepts of customization versus standardization and the idea of differentiating on the basis of the type of relationship envisaged have been adapted by recent authors, notably Palmer (2004) and Kasper, Van Heldsingen and de Vries, (2002) with only minor changes. More recently, Gabbott and Hogg (2003) suggested

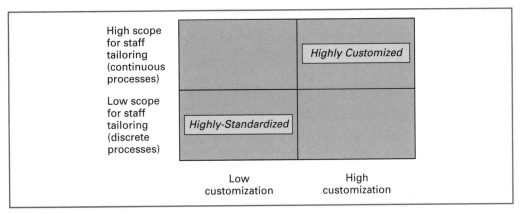

FIGURE 4.3 Potential Service Configuration Patterns
Source: Lovelock (1983).

Task 4.2

Visit your local leisure centre/health club. Get a brochure and look at their facilities. Then look at their website entry.

■ Identify the standardized elements they offer.

■ When using the centre, what scope do employees have to tailor activities and shape relationships with their customer groups?

■ In what way can the management of the leisure centre or health club further develop customization in the service process online?

five key elements within a service encounter: temporal duration, physical proximity, participation, degree of emotional/cognitive involvement and degree of customization. Thus, some continuity can be traced from relationship dimensions in classic services thinking to the present day.

Qualities of Services and Relationship Elements

Dating back to the 1970s, services have been described as having underlying qualities: search; experience; and credence-based. Goods with high search qualities involve categories of goods where knowledge can be gained prior to consumption through an information search and therefore some judgement can be made before consumption (e.g. furniture). Goods high in experience qualities do not permit this, as it is difficult to make any judgement prior to actually experiencing the product or service (restaurant meal). Darby and Karni (1973) extend this distinction in the work of Nelson (1973) to include credence-based goods, i.e. goods which are difficult to evaluate, even after consumption. Zeithaml (1981) supports this view, noting many services high in credence qualities where customers have limited knowledge and derive confidence from the credence of the service provision (credibility, expertise, etc. for example legal services). She further argues that, due to the nature of services – intangibility, inseparability and variability – they are more difficult to evaluate beforehand. Therefore, most services are high in experience or in credence qualities.

> INSIGHT: "In sum, the inseparability, non-standardization, and intangibility of services lead them to possess few search qualities and many experience qualities. Credence qualities also dominate in many services, especially *those provided by professionals and specialists*" (Zeithaml, 1981: 41, emphasis added).

Figure 4.4 shows three services, ranging from amazon.com with search qualities to a holiday with experience qualities, to lawyers, with strong credence qualities. It shows the level of prior knowledge by customers, ways in which each service may be evaluated, the interaction level and points of comparison for each service. These three categories are clearly relevant to service relationships. In the search-based service the interaction is limited to remote options, as a strong customer relationship may not be developed as the service can, arguably, be easily substituted. The experience-based service will have a greater level of interaction with customers than a search-based one. Clearly, leisure services such as music concerts depend on the actual experience of the performance and holidays are difficult to judge until they have been experienced. Therefore, the way the service is delivered and the behaviour of the service personnel are important to the relationship building. The credence-based service has the most complex level of relationship building, but it will depend on many implicit factors and indicators, because the customer will find it hard to evaluate the outcome or the expertise of the service provider: thus, the lawyer's behaviour, their personality, the processes of the office and the kinds of emotions which they might generate with the customers (respect, intimidation, deference, distrust) will feature as part of how successful the customer–lawyer interactions become.

Whether services can really be differentiated according to search, experience and credence-based qualities is an evolving issue. The implied suggestion that in search-based services we

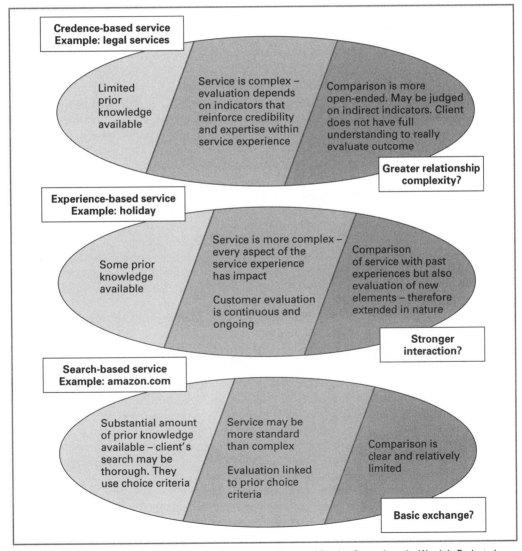

FIGURE 4.4 Illustration of the Qualities of Services and How the Nature of Service Determines the Way it is Evaluated

Source: Developed by author (Broderick), based on work of Darby and Karni (1973).

Task 4.3

Of the three services identified above: legal services, holiday and amazon.com. – which service is more intangible? Taking each service, which elements would you regard as tangible and which intangible?

Service	Tangible Elements	Intangible Elements
Corporate Legal Service		
Holiday		
Amazon.com		

might experience less loyalty than in a more complex service, where we have to invest more resources, is not accurate if we consider the online service. As multimedia, more realtime responses and digital manipulation become integral elements in service experiences, this permits a more extensive range of behaviours online and generates service experiences at more than one level.

A good example of this is the online car warehouse, Motorpoint.co.uk. At this website customers can check online the availability of both new and second-hand cars of the make and model they are interested in. They can also, though the links to financial services, get an indicative quote on a car loan, with specified repayment periods (a sub-menu permits them to make choices on the level of borrowing, the duration of the loan periods, etc.). Insurance quotes can also be obtained through another menu link. In this way, the car warehouse operates directly with customers through additional content. It enables an integrated experience that combines visual models, searching capability, mix and match quoting of prices, easy access to related services and simulated quotes for the vehicle on the road, fully insured and taxed (with self-selected features).

Evolving Trust-building in Service Relationships

This artificial simulation and visualization with its real-time effects has shifted customer perceptions of most services and has affected the way we build trust in services. Inseparability was seen as traditionally important, as it affects service location and delivery formats. Services were potentially differentiated according to levels of consumption and production flexibility. This is still true of many leisure facilities such as gyms, museums and theme parks – they are location dependent – you have to go to the location to avail of the services. But it is less true of many other services, notably financial, legal and other professional services.

This type of customer-consumption flexibility is now standard for many services. Global communications, easier international communication and mobile, Internet and wireless connections have reduced dependence on location-dependent consumption and production in some service formats. Unlike the case of the hair salon, physical closeness of clients to financial service firms is no longer as urgent, with many financial services handled through remote contact. We, as consumers want to access our bank in several different ways (by telephone, by email, online,

> INSIGHT: Five years ago Barclays Bank developed an advertising campaign based on the 'Big Bank' idea and the main theme was that Barclays were so versatile that you could do your banking in any way you wished, the bank services would be available. The advertisement featured two well-known actors: one as a businessman travelling in a taxi being able to access his bank services with a lot of personal attention by bank personnel. The second was accessing his bank online in his pyjamas in his hotel room in the early hours of the morning with a view of skyscrapers in the background.

through automated machines, by modem if we are abroad, though broadband links, by calling into the bank in the high street). Thus, we want our bank services to be completely inseparable – the production of the service is as flexible as our consumption of it and is made available at the time we want to access it (24–7). This expectation is pervasive.

Even museums, sports events and location-specific services can now be experienced virtually to some degree. Live feed pictures, webcams, digital taster exerpts, and simulations of these places are now available online. You can click to get online live feed with visuals of Wimbledon tennis matches while sitting in a hotel room in Singapore preparing for a business convention.

> INSIGHT: CHELSEA FLOWER SHOW
>
> When we look at service events, it is now possible to revisit a service experience through some creative Internet websites. Since 2002, keen gardeners do not need to make the trek to London physically to visit the Chelsea Flower Show. Individuals can make a virtual visit online through a website that allows the visitor to see all the garden and flower exhibits by making their own virtual journey in an online website representation of the actual exhibits at the show. This enables the event to be more accessible to a greater number of people and allows many people to revisit the experience a number of times during the week – each day the public can cast a vote on their favourite garden in the different categories and each day there are possibilities of interaction through email, bulletin messages, listening in to interviews with prize-winning exhibitors, while feedback can be obtained from television presenters online. Such creative service developments online offer an opportunity to prolong the service experience, broaden the exposure of the event and meet additional demand for a popular annual event.

Customer reliance on own ability – changing degrees of trust in services

At a further level, it may be that the degree of trust being experienced is changing. If a good measure of information residing traditionally with government services, with service intermediaries and with professional firms is now accessible to customers in other ways, through sophisticated informative media, then credence in these service providers diminishes.

Certain strongly credence-based services are now consumed online (logging in to the NHS; logging in to legal services; conducting investment decisions via the Internet). Given that websites are anonymous, and particular expertise may be less apparent, it has to be acknowledged that the credence factor, as traditionally viewed, may be lessened. Perhaps clients are substituting other cues as indicators. For example, online health encounter contrasts with more traditional credence-based service formats, e.g. hospital surgery, where there may be a broader range of well-defined "professional" service scripts (e.g. surgeon, nurse, operating room nursing staff, day nurse, physical therapist), which build/reinforce credence qualities.

Perhaps, unlike our parents, we do not necessarily want a closer relationship with any bank personnel. A metaphor to use might be "degrees of separation". The film that featured Will Smith was based on the idea that, between any two people who meet, there are only six degrees of separation. Some linkages can be traced: through family, past meetings, neighbours, networks of friends – and each link in the chain is one degree of separation. As customers, we live comfortably with varying degrees of separation. With our banks and many other services, online or offline, we may be quite comfortable with service relationships at two or three degrees of separation.

At an individual level, the lifetime customer is not necessarily the reality of how modern service consumers make choices, and particularly not online. All our social networks suggest, among other elements, adaptability and timeliness. This goes back to social penetration theory in which present beneficial interactions determine the likelihood and depth of future service encounters (Simmel, 1908/1950; Altman and Taylor, 1973). There is an implicit link between the appropriateness of the behaviour adopted currently and the likelihood of success in future social encounters. We accrue new relationships and new networks as we move though different stages of our lives. Some are enduring, some interchange, some are consecutive, some transitory. Service relationships would typically reflect some of the same characteristics – enduring, interchangeable, consecutive, transitory.

Task 4.4

Looking at how you purchase the following services, do you feel that you need specialist advice on the purchase?
- Buying a digital or satellite TV viewing package
- Choosing a mobile phone provider

■ Identify where you might search for information prior to buying.

■ How important is choosing one well-known service provider to you?

With the growth in competitive service choices available in many sectors such as finance, estate agency and retailing, it is possible to fixate on the need for customer retention. A body of work has already identified the importance and complexity of RM (Dwyer *et al.*, 1987: Christopher *et al.*, 1991; Grönroos, 1994: Morgan and Hunt, 1994) and this complexity needs to be recognized and adequately considered in the new marketspace. The duration, level and intensity of relationship to be developed with service customers could more specifically encompass the degree of online interactivity envisaged with different customer groups. This is undoubtedly important for b2b customers.

Focus on Service Interaction

The above section has focused on relational dimensions that have emerged in the 1970s and 1980s. Taking this a stage further, other classic services ideas have focused strongly on the interactive domain of services.

Stages of consumption in services

The importance of the interaction elements throughout the service encounter was noted by Fisk (1981), in his discussion of the three phases of a service encounter, ranging from pre-consumption, during consumption and post-consumption. Potential factors might influence each stage. In pre-consumption, internal elements related to the customer are their level of experience and the perceived risk they see in the service. External, firm-produced factors can also affect the pre-consumption – these might be the level of information available, the reputation of the service firm, competitive offerings, etc. In the same way, multiple factors might affect a client during consumption and these will vary according to the service. Examples might be the service personnel and the processes of delivery. Similarly, there are follow-up elements in every service experience that will lead to post-consumption evaluation of satisfaction.

In Fisk's (1981) approach the bottom line is that there is the potential to retain or to lose customers at any stage of the service experience – a classic concept in more recent Relationship Marketing thinking, both in customer retention arguments (Rust and Zahorik, 1993), and in customer loyalty ideas (Dwyer *et al.*, 1987; Reichheld, 1993). Many of these factors are process- or people-related, may be behavioural in nature and will affect the service relationship within the experience through the level of positive or negative interaction that is experienced.

A good example of how service companies are giving a lot of attention to each stage of consumption is in the competitiveness of inflight service innovations in business-class airline services. The positive service experience that can be created in business airline services is closely linked with interactions both within the service encounter and internally within the service provision team.

MINI-CASE: EMIRATES AIRLINE – BOOK YOUR FLIGHT AND YOUR BED

British Airways was the first to introduce lie-flat seats in business class in Club World. The seat pitch and the distance between the seats are carefully measured to ensure greater comfort and many seats now convert into fully flat beds. Since then, the same design has been incorporated into seat design by other airlines. Malaysian Airlines are now installing the third generation of sleeper seats in first and business class. Virgin has introduced double beds in upper class on some Boeing 747-400s. Dubai Emirates airline has taken it a stage further and set up first-class suites on board long-range Airbus A340-500 aircraft. The cabins have privacy screens and leather seats which can give you a massage and convert into a flat bed. You are allocated a sleep suit and there is a small built-in vanity table with mirror and a dining table. Air France has an Espace Premiere where first-class seats now convert into 2-metre-long beds with mattresses. You get a duvet, pillow and wool blanket to make you comfortable.

Source

Financial Times, 15 May 2006.

Questions

1 Identify the key factors at each stage of consumption.

2 Taking a first-class passenger, travelling from London to Dubai on an Emirates airline, trace the elements in the Pre-, During and Post-Consumption phases of their service experience.

3 Identify factors that would act in a positive way for relationship building at each stage of consumption in this service.

4 Are there factors that could encourage the customer not to continue with the service?

One key idea to emerge is the cultivation of increasingly customized and "managed" interactions. Airlines such as British Airways are seeking to strike a balance between privacy of passengers and also personal attention to passengers when they want it. It is the ultimate in personal comfort for frequent travellers, and follows on from pre-booking priority with no waiting, selective facilities for first and business-class passengers at departing airport lounges as well as special arrangements for luggage transfers and courier transport links at destination airports. A key challenge is creating added value in customer interactions that offers something personal to customers and builds the relationship. See some areas for creating value are suggested in Figure 4.5.

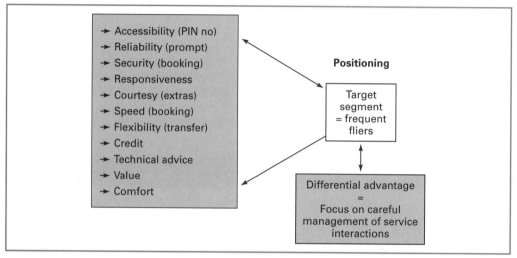

FIGURE 4.5 Airline Service Creating Extra Value

Service process and Relationship Marketing – service blueprint

The most used service process analysis is the service blueprint, which can take on an operational bias in service mapping and flowcharting but can also represent a micro-process and offer a structured means for developing good service interaction in service delivery. A blueprint (Shostack, 1984; Hoffman and Bateson, 2002) represents a service delivery process for a typical client as they experience service, and sets down some expected pattern of events.

Processes included in the blueprint by Shostack (1977) are

- the backstage area (which is internal);
- the frontstage area (where service operations are visible to customers);
- the interactive area (where service providers and customers interact directly).

The interactive area is separated from the frontstage areas by the *line of interaction*, while the frontstage area is separated from the backstage areas by the *line of visibility*. The blueprint traces the main tasks or service actions that are taken in each domain within that service process. The separation of frontstage from backstage activities reflects the way, for instance, a computer retail outlet will have shopfloor activities and backroom activities: both need to be managed effectively and integrated well to achieve successful service delivery. In different service formats the scope for developing a relationship within the actual service encounter varies a lot. In Figure 4.6, we see a typical service blueprint for a restaurant. When looking at the areas where extra value can be generated for a restaurant service, much depends on the onstage set of activities – all that is visible to the customer.

For people-based services such as restaurants and hairdressing salons, the interactions in the visible area are critical to whether the customer feels comfortable, feels that staff are responsive and that they are being looked after. The interactions they have with different staff (reception, hair washer, hair stylist, manager) create the atmosphere in which the relationship will thrive or otherwise. Also, all onstage interactions – staff with other customers, discussions between staff, and exchanges between customers are all interactive inputs and can create value (see mini-case, p. 94).

A more detailed consideration of this idea of visible and invisible elements arose in the work of Fisk and Grove (1996), who developed a drama metaphor for services, and in Solomon *et al.* (1985) in which the professional role of the service provider was analysed. Both developed clear ideas on the importance of role development.

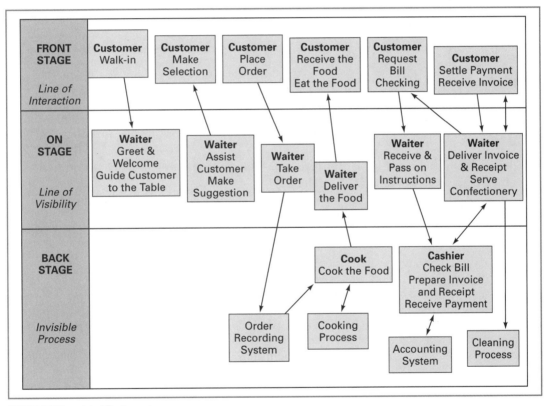

FIGURE 4.6 Blueprint of Restaurant

Focus on Service Behaviour – Critical to Relationships

Interpersonal dimensions in service quality

In the 1980s a number of authors in services marketing began to look at the issue of customer service and service quality. Predominant in this is SERVQUAL, which is a measurement instrument that was developed to gather data on how customers evaluated services. The basis of this

MINI-CASE: £6.4 BILLION SPENT IN UK ON EATING OUT IN PUBS

In Britain, £28 billion was spent in 2005 on eating out. This figure, estimated in a study carried out by Mintel, shows an increase of £2 billion on 2004 and a 25 per cent increase since 2000. Pubs were the most popular places to eat, accounting for 6.4 billion of the total and this was a 30 per cent increase over 2004. "Pubs have become more family-friendly and are offering a wider selection of healthier food and soft drinks, making them more appealing for people who don't want to drink alcohol", says Chris Haskins, in an interview for The *Independent on Sunday*, October 2005.

A marketing analyst of Britivic, Lisa Hogg, expected the trend to rise, stating "It's about lifestyle. People don't have the time (to cook) it's not just to do with disposable income". The trend for eating out, according to Nigel Popham, a leisure analyst at Teather and Greenwood, has been affected by demographic change as well as the improved offerings by pubs and restaurants. He expects that the proportion of food consumed outside the home will move much closer to the US level of 50 per cent.

Source

Independent on Sunday, 19 October 2005.

Questions

1 Based on the blueprint set out in Figure 4.6, what are the critical points in the service process for customers who have a pub meal?

2 Where can added value be generated in the interactive domain of the blueprint?

3 Are there areas where activities can foster loyalty?

kind of measurement are key dimensions that are believed to be key indicators of service quality. In SERVQUAL service quality encompasses five key dimensions: tangibles, reliability, responsiveness, empathy and assurance (Parasuraman *et al.*, 1985, 1988). Incorporated into a 22-item scale which was developed from customer and manager focus groups, service quality outcomes are derived from a comparison of service expectations and perceived service. Similar but different measurement approaches have also emerged – some are variations on the original five dimensions, others focus on actual service performance, rather than expectations (e.g. SERVPERF by Cronin and Taylor, 1994).

An alternative view of service quality, shown in Figure 4.7, places emphasis not just on outcomes, but also on process aspects in service quality evaluation.

Two key elements of service quality are reflected in functional quality and technical quality as outlined by Grönroos (1988). Technical quality refers to features that are outcomes of the service, i.e. what the client receives from the service (this might be professional knowledge, standard of equipment, etc.). Functional quality relates to how the service is delivered, i.e. how the process is experienced (this might be attitudes of staff, or smoothness of process). In people-based services, these two elements of service quality depend strongly on the customer interface within the service encounter. Thus, relational factors are explicitly important in good service performance.

Technical and functional aspects of service quality are not the only factors of importance. Grönroos (1988) focuses on the idea that perceived service quality is determined not just by the

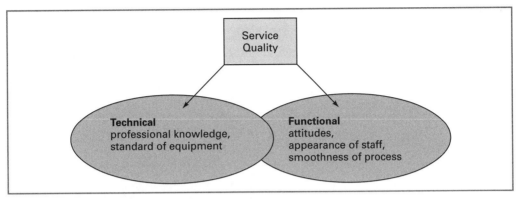

FIGURE 4.7 Key Elements in Service Quality
Source: Grönroos (1990a).

customer's experience of service quality, but also by the nature and activities of the marketing function within the organization and how these activities affect customer expectations. In the Nordic school of thought on service quality (Grönroos, 1990a; Gummesson, 1993) different key dimensions are important. Grönroos (1988) identified six:

- Professionalism and skills
- Attitudes and behaviour
- Accessibility and flexibility
- Reliability and trustworthiness
- Recovery
- Reputation and credibility

Both approaches (Parasuraman *et al.* and Grönroos) can be seen if we look at a typical service encounter in a supermarket. Looking at the blueprint for the supermarket visit in Figure 4.8 (p. 98), there is clearly a mix of technical and functional aspects within the process. In addition, there could be unexpected elements such as the manager dealing with a complaint, the delicatessen counter running out of particular products or a cashier dealing with a technical, say pin number machine, problem. Key steps in the blueprint depend on many elements of SERVQUAL, which are largely the responsibility of particular service personnel. For example, it is important for the counter staff to be courteous, have an appropriate appearance, show interest and give assurance in dealing with a customer query.

    If we look at service quality dimensions of both SERVQUAL and the Grönroos model in Table 4.4 (p. 96) we see that in service quality thinking, there is a strong focus on people, on behaviour and an emphasis on interactive factors, and what Lehtinen and Lehtinen (1991) saw as the quality of relationship – scope and duration.

Increased focus on service behaviour

A natural evolution in services marketing in the late 1980s and 1990s has been a movement towards exploring in more detail the service encounter itself. It is during interactions between client and service provider that functional quality is transferred. At a basic level, as part of the development of relationships with customers, promises are made to the client about the service

TABLE 4.4 Focus on Interaction and Behaviour in Service Quality Approaches

Grönroos (1990a) Model Dimensions	Parasuraman *et al.* (1985) Model Dimensions
■ Professionalism and skills ■ Attitudes and behaviour ■ Accessibility and flexibility ■ Reliability and trustworthiness ■ Recovery ■ Reputation and credibility	■ Tangibles ■ Reliability ■ Responsiveness ■ Empathy ■ Assurance

Task 4.5

Do some desk research and locate a recent report on consumer attitudes/perceptions towards the following services in your country:

Banking   Airlines   Grocery Retailers

■ Select findings about how customers perceive the online services offered by two different companies in ONE of the above sectors. List what the customers perceived as problematic about one or more firms.

■ Identify any reasons for switching services (if noted in findings). Were any concerns expressed about elements in Figure 4.8?

■ Suggest necessary investment that the companies should take to improve their relationships with customers.

Note:

In the UK you might search for Which? reports, Consumer Advice Bureau reports, Ombudsman reports, as well as checking Keynote and Mintel databases.

outcomes and way it is delivered (Grönroos, 1990a). In return, the client may offer commitment to the service relationship (further use). The maintenance of the relationship will, according to Grönroos (1990a), depend on both parties keeping promises across time periods. This is most evident in business-to-business contexts, such as corporate insurance markets, where the planning and development of client relationships has to be long term (see Chapter case, p. 101).

This more detailed focus on the service encounter was demonstrated in work on the internal service encounter (Matsson, 1994) in which he looked at how service personnel treated internal clients in organizations. A related development was the focus on client and service provider behaviour; with studies on the dynamics of how service behaviours develop in interactions, for example, Solomon *et al.*'s (1985) analysis of people-based services. This was evident across different kinds of studies in the 1990s. There was:

■ an increased emphasis placed on interactive elements within service relationships (Berry, 1983; Grönroos, 1990b; Shemwell *et al.*, 1998);

■ a greater focus on dyadic dimensions of the service experience and , further exploration of personalization elements in services (Chandon *et al.*, 1996; Mittal and Lassar, 1996).

One implication to arise from these studies was the importance of behavioural elements in the service encounter. What dimensions of service encounters are most relevant?

Interaction and moments of truth

Interaction is the basis of successful encounters. Customer satisfaction and a good service experience are ultimately based on the interactions between the customer and the service provider which are called *critical incidents* or *moments of truth.* Edvardsson and Roos (2001) identified a framework of describing and analysing critical incidents in a *model of critical incidents in a relational context* by taking into account all possible relationships within their study. In services, successive critical interactions are sometimes regarded as "moments of truth" (Normann, 1983; Grönroos, 1990b) and organizations need to maximize the potential to create or reinforce positive service quality perceptions within such interactions. This idea was famously developed by Jan Carlsson in the late 1980s in his analysis of SAS airlines and how the firm learnt to improve their service delivery and develop service excellence.

Edvardsson and Roos (2000) argue that there is a need to understand the context of "critical" in a critical incident. One way to consider this is to identify elements in an encounter with a client that are critical to positive further interaction. They also suggest categorizing the source for any critical incident according to their origin. Basic categories applied are:

- Service factors
- Acts (interaction between service provider and customer)
- Routines (procedures applied to customers)
- Strategies/policies
- Physical structures (space, lighting, design)

Critical incidents also differ over time and between customers, as well as the level of acceptance of built-in features within the service process by customers. Edvardsson and Roos (2001) further suggest that the future of customer relationships is determined by the evaluation of critical incidents.

Task 4.6

Look at the extended blueprint in Figure 4.8. Identify the critical points. Identify the personnel that are responsible for that task.

- A number of critical incidents are identified. In what way has the supermarket dealt with the customer enquiry or concern? Break down each incident into two elements – acts and routines.
- Why is the behaviour of the checkout assistant important?
- What role does training and internal culture play in making the service experience positive for customers?

In the Aegon case at the end of the chapter, the CEO identified the knowledge and experience throughout the value chain as a unique advantage. The question that arises is: as these corporate relationships develop, are some service behaviours more prominent as service encounters evolve?

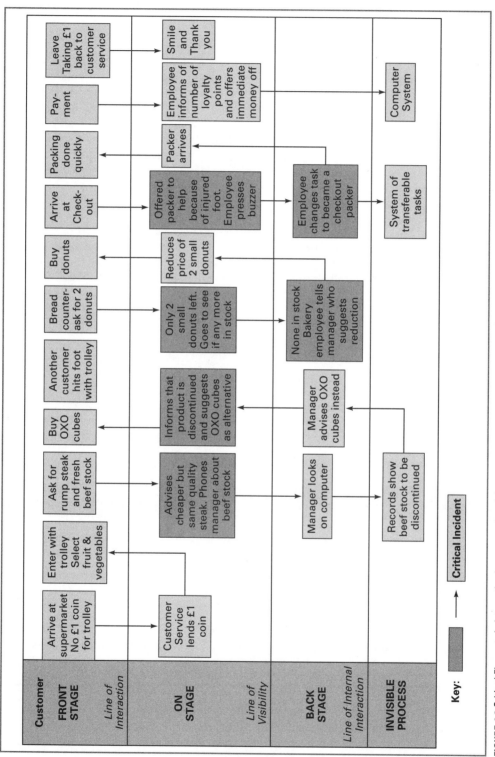

FIGURE 4.8 Critical Elements in Interaction in supermarket.visit

Source: Broderick, author.

Focus on Service Personnel as Relationship Builders

Role of service personnel, service recovery and relationship management

Gremler, Bitner and Evans (1994) identified the key role of frontline employees in service excellence. They identified and analysed incidents and circumstances and evaluated the employee responses and behaviours to those service incidents. They argued that certain behaviours such as employee spontaneity can be very good at solving critical events. They furthermore linked this to actions that might follow on from service failure to retrieve the situation and recover the customer. Significant work on service recovery has been carried out since the mid-1980s in services marketing. This work identifies some of the strategies that firms can adopt to rebuild good relationships with customers. Key actions that are considered are:

- management of service encounter failures;
- development of complaint management systems in service companies;
- developing recovery actions such as compensation and intervention;

This has led to a recognition of the value of good service recovery strategies to developing customer loyalty and retention.

Task 4.7

Consider the last time you had a poor service experience with one of the following:

- A local train operator
- Your network provider for a mobile phone
- A local restaurant
- Your bank

- What was the source of your frustration with the service?
- Identify what actions the service provider could have taken to recover the service and rebuild your loyalty.

Good service is determined to a significant degree by service personnel and how well they filter and reinforce the organizational image – frequently, they are carried out by service personnel from non-marketing areas, such as counter staff. Gummesson (1993), in describing these personnel as "part-time marketers", argues that every component of a service needs to be treated as a potential marketing opportunity; therefore, there is a strong need to foster a service culture which encourages good service and customer orientation. This involves encouraging employees to understand their part in the marketing process and the impact that they have on relationship building.

Bettencourt and Gwinner (1996) explored the potential for customization of the service experience – in particular, the scope for customization of frontline employees. In some service environments, customer retention can only be developed through more personalized service offerings. For instance, the ongoing, continuous interactions which occur throughout a consultation with a doctor will incorporate some personalization aspects. What occurs in the service encounter over time gives some *cumulative* evaluation of the quality within service relationships, identified as important by Rust and Oliver (1994: 2). Good focus on "personalized" dimensions has been seen as important in past studies (Mittal and Lassar, 1996). The performance of the front line can encourage loyalty by personalizing elements of service delivery. This thinking demonstrates the way services thinking has focused consistently on critical elements within relationship management.

Chapter Summary

In this chapter we have traced the way in which relationship focus has emerged in core services marketing ideas. While early authors in services marketing focused on relational dimensions implicitly in their research, later authors such as Grönroos (1990a) have written in a mainstream way about relationship elements, strength and duration.

Customer interactions were a definable area of theory development, with the focus on service process, the application of pre-, during and post-consumption phases, and the visible elements of the service blueprint. An important area of services marketing that links strongly to relationship development was the service quality thinking of the 1980s. The dimensions of service quality are multiple and many focus strongly on interpersonal factors. Achieving service excellence is one key to relationship strength.

Focus on specific service behaviours emerged in the 1990s, with areas such as critical incident analysis, and the management of moments of truth emerging as important. The key value of service personnel in customer retention and relationship building with customers and the value of good service recovery actions were highlighted in the final section. Personalization and customization were regarded as critical factors in successful relationship development.

In conclusion, service marketing has contributed significantly to our conception of active relationship development. Within that contribution the focus has been on specific processes, interactions and behaviours, which shape the service relationships that are developed with customers. The next chapter will consider some of the important dimensions relating to people and to trust that are central to RM.

Review Questions

1 In what ways does the customer perception of quality influence the strength of the relationship they might have with their bank?

2 Is it more difficult to develop an enduring relationship with customers in a credence-based service or a search-based service?

3 What can marketers learn from a service blueprint when seeking to improve service behaviour of employees and encourage customer loyalty?

Further Reading

Bolton, R.N. and J.H. Drew (1991) "A Multistage Model of Customers' Assessments of Service Quality and Value", *Journal of Consumer Research*, vol. 17, no. 4, pp. 375–384.

Fisk, R.P., S.W. Brown and M.J. Bitner (1993) "Tracking the Evolution of the Services Marketing Literature", *Journal of Retailing*, vol. 69 (Spring), 61–103.

Flanagan, J.C. (1954) "The Critical Incident Technique", *Psychological Bulletin*, vol. 51, July, p. 327.

Surprenant, C.F. and M.R. Solomon (1987) "Predictability and Personalization in the Service Encounter", *Journal of Marketing*, vol. 51, April, pp. 86–96.

END OF CHAPTER CASE AND KEY QUESTIONS

Aegon Insurance: Gaining Commitment of Corporate Clients

Aegon is one of the world's largest insurers. The UK part of the business employs 4500 workers and it has £47 billion assets under administration in the UK alone. "The UK has a real need for good solutions, for reliable and well-executed, credible ways of dealing with real issues – it has an insurance industry that is largely built on old models. There is real opportunity for a brand to change the UK market for long-term savings and that's what we're aiming at", says Otto Thoresen, Chief Executive of Aegon UK. Thoresen took over in January 2005 and split the core life and pensions business into separate operations to better service the needs of corporate clients. The company moved to a wider-ranging mix of higher-margin products, such as individual annuities.

The next step in Thoresen's plan is to make Aegon UK a more viable proposition for companies seeking corporate pensions solutions. He also wants to woo the high-street banks, which are now permitted to sell financial products of other providers. To build interest, he sees a need to meet with key decision-makers. To get into boardrooms and sell corporate pensions products, Thoresen says that he needs to use and illustrate the group's global financial might, using the Aegon name directly.

Identifying the importance of commitment, he comments:

Companies making big, long-term commitments to providers of services need to know that you're going to be around long term. They want to know that you have got access to resources to maintain a high-quality proposition and access to the global capability and insight into what can be learnt form other markets ... We have quite a distinctive position – we operate in all parts of the value chain, in delivery of long-term financial solutions to customers from asset management, manufacturing and distribution of life and pensions products as well as distributing business solutions. What customers want is to share their asset risks. If you go back 20 years, with-profits was the accepted way of doing things, but these days with-profits are not transparent enough for customers to have confidence in the process. What we have to look at are alternatives.

Source

The Times, 15 May 2006

Questions

1 Looking at the range of Aegon financial products, how would you describe their services for corporate clients – search-based, experience-based or credence-based services?

2 Taking the dimensions of the Grönroos model in Figure 4.7, distinguish the technical and the functional quality elements for Aegon when dealing with corporate pensions solutions.

3 In what way can dimensions such as assurance, responsiveness, reliability and empathy be developed in their relationships with prospective high-street bank clients?

References

Altman I. and D. Taylor (1973) *Social Penetration: The Development of Interpersonal Relationships*, New York: Holt, Rinehart and Winston Inc.

Berry, L.L. (1983) "Relationship Marketing", in L.L. Berry *et al.* (eds), *Emerging Perspectives of Services Marketing*, Chicago: American Marketing Association.

Bettencourt, L. and K. Gwinner (1996) "Customization of the Service Experience: The Role of the Frontline Employee", *International Journal in Services Industry Management*, vol. 7, no. 2, pp. 2–20.

Chandon, J., P. Leo and J. Philippe (1996) "Service Encounter Dimension – A Dyadic Perspective: Measuring Dimensions of the Service Encounter as Perceived by Customer and Personnel", *International Journal of Service Industry Management*, vol. 8, no. 1, pp. 65–86.

Chase, R. (1978) "Where Does the Customer Fit in a Service Operation?", *Harvard Business Review*, Nov.–Dec., pp. 137–142.

Christopher, M., A. Payne and D. Ballantyne (1991) *"Relationship Marketing: Bringing Quality, Customer Service, and Marketing Together"*, Oxford: Butterworth-Heinemann.

Cronin, J. and S. Taylor (1994) "SERVPERF Versus SERVQUAL: Reconciling Performance-based and Perceptions-minus-expectations Measurements of Service Quality", *Journal of Marketing*, vol. 58, no. 1, pp. 125–131.

Darby M. and E. Karni (1973) "Free Competition and the Optimal Amount of Fraud", *Journal of Law and Economics*, vol. 16, April, pp. 67–86.

Dwyer, F.R., P.H. Schurr and S. Oh (1987) "Developing Buyer–Seller Relationships", *Journal of Marketing*, vol. 51, April, pp. 11–27.

Edvardsson, B. and I. Roos (2001) "Critical Incident techniques", *International Journal of Service Industry Management*, vol. 12, no. 3, p. 251.

Fisk, R. (1981) "Towards a Consumption/Evaluation Process Model for Services", in J.H. Donnelly and R. George (eds), *Marketing Services*, Chicago: American Marketing Association Proceedings.

Fisk, R. and S. Grove (1996) "Applications of Impression Marketing and the Drama Metaphor in Marketing, An Introduction", *European Journal of Marketing*, vol. 30, no. 9, pp. 6–12.

Gabbott, M. and G. Hogg (2003) *Consumers and Services*, Chichester, England: John Wiley and Son.

Gremler, D.D., M.J. Bitner and K.R. Evans (1994) "The Internal Service Encounter", *International Journal of Service Industry Management*, vol. 5, no. 2, pp. 34–56.

Grönroos, C. (1988) "Service Quality: The Six Criteria of Good Service Quality", *Review of Business*, vol. 9, no. 3, pp. 10–13.

Grönroos, C. (1990a) "Relationship Approach to Marketing in Service Contexts: The Marketing and Organizational Interface", *Journal of Business Research*, vol. 20, pp. 3–11.

Grönroos, C. (1990b) *Service Management and Marketing, Managing the Moments of Truth in Service Competition*, Lexington, MA: Free Press/Lexington Books.

Grönroos, C. (1994) "Quo Vadis Marketing? Toward a Relationship Marketing Paradigm", *Journal of Marketing Management*, vol. 10, no. 5, pp. 374–384.

Gummesson, E. (1993) *Quality Management in Service Organizations*, St. Johns University, NY: International Service Quality Association.

Hoffman, D. and J. Bateson (2002) *Essentials of Services Marketing: Concept, Strategies and Cases*, Orlando, FL: Dryden Press.

Kasper, H., P. van Heldsingen and W. de Vries (2002) *Services Marketing Management: An International Perspective*, Chichester, England: John Wiley and Sons.

Kotler, P. and G. Armstrong (1991) *Principles of Marketing*, 5th edn, Englewood Cliffs, NJ: Prentice-Hall.

Kotler, P., V. Wong, J. Saunders and G. Armstrong (2005) *Priniciples of Marketing*, 4th European edn, Harlow: Pearson Prentice Hall.

Lehtinen, U. and J.R. Lehtinen (1991) "Two Approaches to Service Quality", *The Services Industry Journal*, vol. 11 (July), 287–303.

Lovelock, C. (1983) "Classifying Services to Gain Strategic Marketing Insights", *Journal of Marketing*, vol. 47, Summer, pp. 9–20.

Lovelock, C., B. Lewis and S. Vandermerwe (2004) *Services Marketing: European Perspectives*, 3rd edn, London: Prentice-Hall.

Matsson, J. (1994) "Improving Service Quality in Person-to-person Encounters: Integrating Findings from a Multidisciplinary Review", *The Service Industries Journal*, vol. 14, no. 1, pp. 45–61.

Mittal, B. and W.M. Lassar (1996) "The Role of Personalization in Service Encounters", *Journal of Retailing*, vol. 72, no. 1, pp. 95–109.

Morgan, R.D. and S. Hunt (1994) "The Commitment-Trust Theory on Relationship Marketing", *Journal of Marketing*, vol. 58, July, pp. 20–38.

Nelson, P. (1973) "Advertising as Information", *Journal of Political Economy*, vol. 181, July–August, pp. 729–754.

Normann, R. (1983) "Service Management", Malmo: Liber in J. Mattson (1994) "Improving service quality in person-to-person encounters", *The Service Industries Journal*, vol. 14, January.

Palmer, A. (2004) *Principles of Services Marketing*, 3rd edn, Maidenhead, UK: McGraw-Hill.

Parasuraman, A., V. Zeithaml and L.L. Berry (1985) "A Conceptual Model of Service Quality and its Implications for Future Research", *Journal of Marketing*, no. 49, Fall, pp. 41–50.

Parasuraman, A., L.L. Berry, and V.A. Zeithaml (1988) "SERVQUAL: A Multiple-Item Scale for Measuring Consumer Perceptions of Service Quality", *Journal of Retailing*, vol. 64 (Spring), pp. 12–37.

Perez-Rivera, M.M. (1994) "A Systematic Classification of Services to Gain Strategies in Services Marketing", *Developments in Marketing Science*, Vol. 27, Nashville: Academy of Marketing Science, pp. 386–390.

Rust, R.T. and R.L. Oliver (1994) *Service Quality: New Directions in Theory and Practice*, California: Sage Publications.

Shemwell, D., U. Yavas and K. Bilgin (1998) "Customer-service Provider Relationships: An Empirical Test of a Model of Service Quality, Satisfaction and Relationship-oriented Outcomes", *International Journal of Service Industry Management*, vol. 9, no. 2, pp. 155–168.

Shostack, L. (1977) "Breaking Free from Product Marketing", *Journal of Marketing*, vol. 41, April, pp. 73–80.

Shostack, L. (1984) "Designing Services that Deliver", *Harvard Business Review*, Jan.–Feb. pp. 133–139.

Simmel, G. (1908/1950) "Types of Social Relationships by Degree of Reciprocal Knowledge of the Participants", in K. Wolff (ed. and trans.) *The Sociology of Georg Simmel*, New York: Free Press, pp. 317–329.

Solomon, M., C. Surprenant, J. Czepiel and E. Gutman (1985) "A Role Theory Perspective on Dyadic Interactions; The Service Encounter", *Journal of Marketing*, vol. 49, Winter, pp. 99–111.

Thomas, D. (1978) "Strategy is Different in Service Businesses", *Harvard Business Review*, vol. 6, July–August, pp. 153–165.

Vandermerwe, S. (1997) "Increasing Returns: Competing for Customers in the Global Market", *Journal of World Business*, Winter, pp. 333–350.

Zeithaml, V. (1981) "How Consumer Evaluation Processes Differ Between Goods and Services", in J.H. Donnelly and W.R. George (eds), *Marketing of Services*, Chicago: American Marketing Association, pp. 39–47.

05

Interpersonal Relationships and Trust

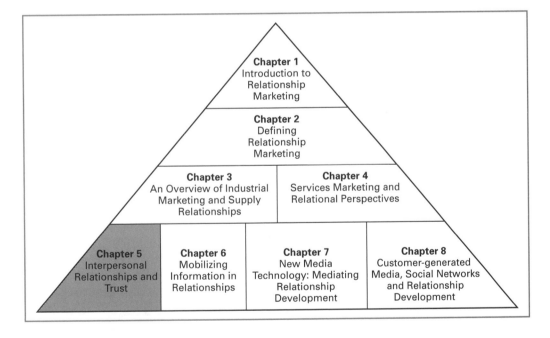

❖ LEARNING OBJECTIVES

After studying this chapter you should be able to:

1 **build** on the previous chapter (services marketing and relational perspectives) and **identify** and **understand** the differing roles and contributions of people in commercial relationships

2 **evaluate** how people affect relationship mediators

3 **understand** that RM comprises both internal and external relationships

4 **appreciate** the implications of differing RM strategies on HRM-based strategies

Chapter Contents

Introduction

Historically, the focus of marketing was concentrated on external marketing activities. However, this traditional approach has largely been superseded with a realization of the key role that the organization's employees play in influencing customer satisfaction through their interaction and relationships with customers. Consequently, there has been increasing recognition of the contribution employees make to successful RM and, in particular, the relational mediators of commitment, trust, relationship satisfaction and relationship quality (Palmatier *et al.*, 2006). Recognizing this, RM has been "broadened" to include relationships internal to the organization with its employees as well as those external with its customers (see Figure 5.1). In reality, it is very difficult to consider in isolation the separate components surrounding the interfaces between employees, customers and the organization because of how interrelated and complex they are.

Task 5.1

How does the classification of relationships in Fig. 5.1 apply to a fast food chain?

When considering all these interfaces, it is perhaps appropriate to classify them into two general areas. The first comprises the "hard" interfaces such as its systems, strategy and structure, and is relatively easy to define, control and measure (Athos, 1981). Examples of these include IT

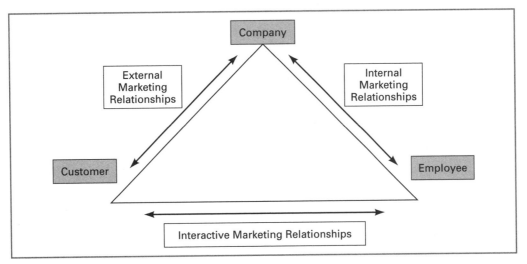

FIGURE 5.1 The Relational Marketing Triangle

systems, organizational hierarchies and quality control issues (e.g. the number of minutes taken to serve each customer). The "softer" issues encompass aspects related to employee attributes such as management style and shared values. These aspects are more difficult to define, control and measure and primarily revolve around "people" issues. These softer issues, in turn, determine the "atmosphere" in which interactions between the various participants take place. The atmosphere may encompass factors such as the closeness of the participants, mutual expectations and the state of any conflicts or co-operation between the parties involved. To highlight this, compare and contrast an interaction with a call centre with a regular trip to a familiar dentist.

For example, there may be passive acceptance where a partner in the relationship accepts or adheres to another's specific requests or policies. On the other hand, there may be a more proactive atmosphere of co-operation in which partners work together to achieve mutual goals. There will always be disagreements or "conflict" in relational exchange. Indeed, such conflict prevents stagnation, stimulates interest and provides a medium through which problems can be aired and solutions arrived at. However, it is the nature of their resolution that contributes towards the atmosphere of relationships. For example, where there is a poor relationship between an organization and its employees, this may be reflected in the interactions the employee has with the customer.

The purpose of this chapter is to explore and evaluate these "softer" people issues which influence the atmosphere in which such relationships may take place and which are "relational mediators" (Palmatier *et al.*, 2006). The chapter is structured as follows: in the first half there is an exploration of these issues related to interactions between the customer and the employee (Interactive Marketing Relationships). The second part of the chapter moves the emphasis towards the organization and its internal relationships.

The Customer–Employee Relationship and Relational Mediators

As highlighted in the previous chapter, the importance of employees as relationship builders with customers has long been recognized. Every time a customer (business or consumer) comes into contact with an organization whether face to face, or by phone, email or letter, interaction occurs (Shostack, 1984). From the customer's perspective, a relationship may develop as a result of these interactions. These interactions may range from two individuals in a b2c context, to complex networks across business departments and hierarchical levels consisting of technical, marketing and senior management personnel in a b2b context (e.g. the auditors of blue chip companies) These personal contacts may fulfil a number of roles including providing information, selling and negotiation, technical specification, social friendships or "bonding" and even "ego enhancement".

Task 5.2

What do organizations hope to achieve through taking customers or potential customers to corporate hospitality events such as Wimbledon (tennis) or Twickenham (rugby)?

Research suggests there is a connection between relationship development and the roles of personal contact. For example, information exchange is prominent at the start of a relationship, negotiation becomes prominent as the first order is placed and then, as the relationship develops, other contact roles are activated such as social bonding and ego enhancement.

As a result, each interaction may contribute to the customer's overall satisfaction (Bolton and Drew, 1992). Thus, each interaction presents the possibility of influencing perceptions of quality and ultimately satisfaction with the entire relationship. To quote Turnbull "Parties are able to seek out and evaluate information about the competence and credibility of the other party which may lead to mutual trust, respect and personal friendship" (1979: 81). Personal contacts between organizations lowers perceived risks and decreases uncertainty as far as the two parties are concerned.

In markets where there is the opportunity for relationship development between the customer and the organization, the organization has the opportunity to include additional value adding attributes to the core product or service. This may create a total service offering to the customer that evolves as the relationship develops (Grönroos, 1997). What should be included in this "holistic offering" is crucial to creating and maintaining customer relationship quality. As highlighted in the previous chapter, the nature of the holistic offering and the likely extent to which a relationship will develop will depend on the nature of the product and its contexts and the level of customer participation.

Relationship quality is interpreted by some researchers as a multi-dimensional construct that "captures the many different facets of the exchange relationship" and therefore "its structure and underlying dimensions vary across empirical studies" (Palmatier et al., 2006: 139). Other researchers combine trust, commitment and satisfaction into a single latent construct of relationship quality (e.g. Crosby et al., 1990; see Table 5.1).

More recent research demonstrates that trust, commitment and satisfaction may be separated out (see Figure 5.2) and that these may interact differently for different types of customers based on their prior experience (e.g. Lin and Ding, 2005), effectively acting as relationship mediators. These are now discussed in more detail.

TABLE 5.1 Relational Mediators

Construct	Definition	Common Aliases
Trust	Confidence in an exchange partner's reliability and integrity	Trustworthiness, credibility, benevolence and honesty
Commitment	An enduring desire to maintain a valued relationship	Affective, behavioural, obligation and normative commitment
Relationship Satisfaction	Customer's affective or emotional state toward the relationship, typically evaluated over the history of the exchange	Satisfaction with the relationship but not overall satisfaction
Relationship Quality	Overall assessment of the strength of the relationship conceptualized as a composite capturing the different but related facets of a relationship	Relationship closeness and strength

Source: Based on Palmatier *et al.*, 2006.

Task 5.3

How might these relational mediators differ in priority when considering a customer's trip to the dentist with a trip to their hairdresser?

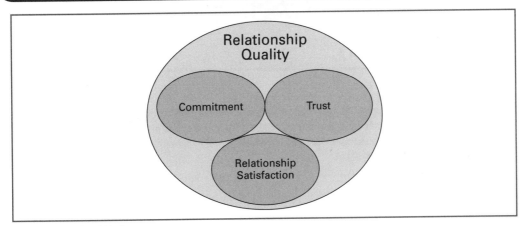

FIGURE 5.2 Relational Mediators

Trust

Trust is an important concept in understanding expectations for co-operation and planning in a relational context and as such is included in many relationship models. Berry (1995) suggests that Relationship Marketing "is built on the foundation of trust" (p. 242) and many authors cite it as being an important variable in terms of its effect on relationship outcomes (e.g. Crosby *et al.*, 1990).

Trust is particularly important in the formation of service-based relationships because of the intangible nature of some services. As discussed previously, many services are difficult to evaluate prior to purchasing and some remain difficult to evaluate even after they have been performed.

> INSIGHT: *Trust* is when "one party has confidence in an exchange partner's reliability and integrity" Morgan and Hunt (1994: 23).

Even in b2b contexts, many aspects of agreements between buying and selling organizations are not fully formalized or based on legal criteria. It may not be possible to cover all contingencies in a formal contract for sustained co-operation, but if parties trust each other it may be unnecessary to cover all contingencies. As a result, trust has been studied widely in social exchange literature in terms of organizational behaviour (e.g. Barney, 1990), communications (e.g. Hovland *et al.*, 1953) delivering promises (e.g. Rotter, 1967; Schurr and Ozanne, 1985) and confidence (Moorman *et al.*, 1993).

Morgan and Hunt (1994) identified a number of precursors (or antecedents) for the development of trust (see Figure 5.3). These are shared values (discussed later in the chapter), good communication and not behaving opportunistically at your partners expense (i.e. putting your own self-interest before that of your partners). A number of outcomes of trust between partners are suggested such as reduced uncertainty, greater co-operation and the recognition that there will always be differences between parties, yet disputes can be solved amicably (functional or constructive conflict). They also suggest that trust influences commitment insofar as, without trust, there can be no commitment.

Task 5.4

Do you trust your bank? Justify your answer!

> INSIGHT: *Commitment* is when "An exchange partner believes that an ongoing relationship with another is so important as to warrant maximum efforts at maintaining it; that is, the committed party believes the relationship is worth working at to ensure that it endures indefinitely". Morgan and Hunt (1994: 23).

Commitment

Commitment is widely viewed as one of *the* defining variables of RM and is therefore the most common variable used in buyer-seller relationship studies (Wilson, 1995). Many regard it as the key feature in a relationship that actually differentiates that relationship from other forms of business transactions. Without commitment it would be merely repeat purchases where loyalty may be purely behaviourial rather than involving any conscious effort. Barnes (1994) emphasizes this point by stating that repeat business alone may not be product loyalty but merely a result of product availability.

Morgan and Hunt (1994) also identified a number of precursors for the development of commitment. These are the costs of terminating the relationship (having to spend time and effort seeking out new partners, for example), the benefits of the relationship to both parties and once again, shared values.

A number of outcomes of commitment between partners are also suggested. There is greater acquiescence and less likelihood of one party leaving the relationship and a higher degree of co-operation between the parties.

Relational metaphors

As stated above, many factors have been suggested for the development of relationships which differentiate them from being purely transactional and behavioural based. Duck (1991) identified several elements including caring, loyalty, support, placing priority on others, interest and honesty, giving help when needed and working through disagreements. Argyle and Henderson (1985) suggest respecting privacy, looking the other person in their eye, keeping confidences and not criticizing publicly.

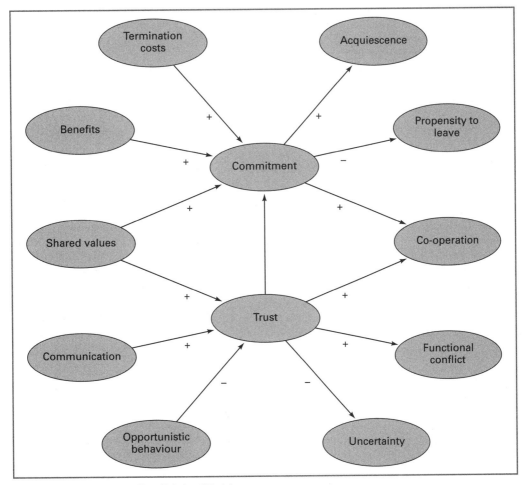

FIGURE 5.3 The Commitment–Trust Relational Model
Source: based on Morgan and Hunt (1994).

Some of these have been learned from social psychology, which has resulted in many of the metaphors proposed for successful business relationships being related to marriage and personal relationship life cycles. Examples of these include Wilson and Mummalaneni (1986; courtship, bonding and forsaking others); Dwyer *et al.* (1987; awareness, exploration, expansion, commitment and dissolution) and Tynan (1997; polygamy, prostitution, stalking, rape and seduction).

More recently Johnston and Hausman (2006) have used the metaphor of the extended family and friends (singlehood, honeymoon, couplehood, additions to the relationship, adulthood, possibly dissolution) in an attempt to encapsulate the complexities of personal dyadic relationships and how they may be affected by relationships with others.

What becomes apparent from examining these studies is the role that affect and emotion may have in determining relational satisfaction. Indeed, Palmatier *et al.* (2006) define relationship satisfaction as a customer's affective or emotional state towards a relationship. For these reasons, affect and emotion are now discussed in more detail.

Relationship satisfaction

There has always been relationship building between buyer and seller incorporating an element of social bonding. For example, one only has to look at the existence of corporate hospitality to recognize this. Where there is a high degree of personal contact, "social exchange" (Ford, 1980) will occur and may develop into "social bonding".

Mummalaneni and Wilson (1991) found that buyers and sellers who have a "strong personal relationship" are more committed to maintaining a relationship. The situation is made more complex within some markets because of the difficulty customers have in evaluating the quality of the service they receive. To quote Wilson (1995: 335) "Relationships develop in a natural way over time as buyers and sellers develop trust and friendships supported by quality products and services".

INSIGHT: *Social bonding* is "the degree of mutual personal friendship and liking shared by buyer and seller" (Wilson, 1995: 339).

As a relationship develops, based on an increased number of positive assessments arising out of individual encounters, a process of bonding takes place. This signifies the transformation in the nature of the relationship from what Mummalaneni and Wilson (1991) term a "formal role" to a "close personal role" which is ultimately reflected in the parties' degree of commitment to the relationship. So why is commitment viewed with such enthusiasm by RM researchers? Like personal relationships, in business relationships Morgan and Hunt (1994) suggest it is important to differentiate between superficial and shallow relationships and deeper relationships. They suggest that what should be central to understanding Relationship Marketing is whatever distinguishes productive, effective, relational interaction from those that are unproductive and essentially superficial

INSIGHT: *Affect* is "An umbrella for a set of more specific mental processes including emotions, moods and possible attitudes" (Bagozzi et al., 1999: 184).

Emotional interaction between individuals in a business context is critical, primarily because it is difficult for competitors to imitate and therefore may provide a source of competitive advantage (e.g. Barnes and Howlett, 1998). Within tangible product-based markets such as cars, it has long been recognized that there is a cognitive (thinking) and affective (feeling) component to customer satisfaction and that any positive or negative emotions felt are the result of (dis)satisfaction with the product (Westbrook, 1987). In other words, if you are (dis)pleased with the product you are (un)happy. However, within a service context, affect may be generated during the provision of the service rather than after it.

Research by Barnes and Howlett (1998) identified an affective dimension to service provision which stresses the importance "of how customers are made to feel in their dealings with their provider" (p. 21).

> INSIGHT: *Emotion* is "a mental state with a specific referent and is therefore evoked by a specific target such as a person, object or event" (Johnson and Stewart, 2006: 5).

MINI-CASE: HOTEL EMPLOYEE OF THE YEAR

After travelling in Australia and Thailand, Freyja Thirlaway landed back in the North East and walked straight into a job she loves. The 26-year-old, from Byker, Newcastle, swapped backpacking for the glamorous surroundings of Malmaison Hotel on the Quayside 11 months ago and has never looked back. As a receptionist at the hotel, Freyja welcomes everyone, from family holidaymakers to businessmen, with a friendly smile. Freyja said: "This is the first hotel job I've had, as before I went travelling, I was working as a clothing shop assistant. Travelling in Australia and Thailand has actually been really helpful and I think we've got a lot to learn from the Australians in terms of customer service."

Freyja was nominated by Malmaison regular Antony Jones, from Surrey, who stays at the hotel on business trips to the North East. Antony said: "Every time I have stayed at Malmaison the welcome received from Freyja, the efficiency of the check-in, the desire to fix the small details and, most importantly, the ability to handle problems makes her a real ambassador for her hotel group and definitely for the North East." The 26-year-old's dream job is as a tourism and development officer, but for now she is happy at Malmaison and enjoys telling visitors all about the attractions in her home town.

Freyja, who studied leisure and tourism at Newcastle College, added: "At the hotel we've always got the maps out telling people where is good to go and visit. I always loved customer service so it was a natural progression and once you've been travelling you're open to things, "I had an idea for my career and I was thinking about the hotel industry. It's great working at Malmaison as we are all of the same age on reception. We always talk about our dream of opening a bed and breakfast in the south of France, "I honestly love coming to work and everybody's personalities behind the desk are different, which makes it a great place to be."

Source

The *Newcastle Evening Chronicle*,
13 July 2005

Questions

1 Customers have different emotional needs. How might these differ between a stay at a hotel and a trip to the dentist?

2 How might the service provider manage these?

This is especially the case where there is a high degree of interaction between the customer and the provider (usually an employee) and they may become the focal point of the service as far as the customer is concerned. Thus, consumer affective reactions to the service provider may become very important in determining the intention to continue a relationship (see the mini-case, Hotel Employee of the Year).

As discussed previously, this becomes critical where the consumer may be unable to gauge the quality of the core service they are receiving. For example, with some services such as financial advice, dentistry or law, performance assessments about the quality of the financial advice, dentist treatment or legal advice are difficult to make because the consumer is not qualified to make them.

According to Alford and Sherrell (1996), in such circumstances, consumers will often use three sources of information to evaluate satisfaction with a relationship (see Figure 5.4):

- General affect, that represents the consumer's opinion of that particular category of service provider, which is usually based on direct or indirect experiences in the past. (So, for example, they (dis)like lawyers, accountants, etc. in general)
- The consumer's affective reaction to the individual service provider
- How they think the service should be delivered (expectations) and the consistency with which the service process is performed

The labour intensiveness of such services makes the traditional distinction between affect for the product and affect for the person difficult. Affect is thus evoked through interaction during the service interaction and is instantaneous.

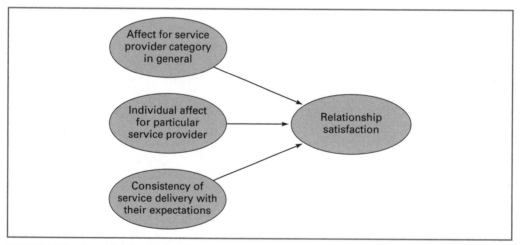

FIGURE 5.4 Affect-based Relationship Satisfaction Model
Source: based on Alford and Sherrell (1996).

MINI-CASE: DAVID LLOYD LEISURE CENTRES AND THEIR CUSTOMER RETENTION CLASSES

The market for leisure centres and swimming pools has enjoyed an unprecedented period of growth during the past decade, prompted by considerable investment in new provision, funded largely by the National Lottery and by private companies developing their own leisure centres. With 60 clubs in the UK, Whitbread-owned David Lloyd is one of the UK's largest racquets, health and fitness club brands with over 340 000 members. By April 2007 Whitbread, the owner of Premier Travel and the Costa cafes chain, was deciding whether to sell its David Lloyd centres after a two-year restructuring was nearing completion. Operating profits had risen by 12.3 per cent to £46.4 million on the previous year, prompting several unsolicited approaches to buy with the price of some offers rumoured to be as high as £1 billion. The bidders were thought to include David Lloyd's rivals Esporta and LA Fitness as well as the UK property investor Robert Tchenguiz.

David Lloyd has focused on delivering to its members the widest available racquets, health and fitness facilities and expertise. The centres offer a range of facilities that cater for individual and family members alike. Collectively these include: 5000 employees of whom 250 are qualified tennis coaches and 500 fitness instructors; 550 tennis courts; 100 badminton courts; 79 squash courts; 90 swimming pools and 52 000 square meters of gym space containing over 9000 exercise machines.

Although gym facilities remain the primary attraction for new members, fitness classes have grown in importance in recent years as a key means of customer retention. Such classes are wide and diverse and include: aerobics; circuit training; yoga; dance fitness; pilates; boxercise; legs, bums and tums; step aerobics; aqua aerobics; studio cycling; body pump; spinning; ab-blast/ab-attack and t'ai chi. Encouraging members to participate in such classes is not only seen as a method of adding variety to their exercise regime and making them more likely to persist with their fitness programme and so renew their membership, but also as a way of reducing gym usage to create space there for new members starting off.

A primary focus recently has been to develop a better understanding of its members' behaviours and attitudes. This has included a LTV analysis (lifetime value analysis) model that develops a risk profile indicating when members in certain categories are at maximum risk of cancelling their membership. The analysis shows that, by increasing members' usage of the facilities by one visit a week, there is a corresponding but dramatic decrease in the likelihood of the member cancelling their membership. The result of this has been that David Lloyd maintains membership retention rates well ahead of the industry average.

Sources

"Crunch date nears for David Lloyd sale", Hotten, R., *The Daily Telegraph*, 25 April 2007.

"A tried and tested solution that integrates prospecting, membership and EPoS modules: Not 'just' a membership package for David Lloyd". A Torex Retail Case study available at <www.torexretail.com/english/download/casestudy/david-lloyd>
David Lloyd website at <www.davidlloydleisure.co.uk/aboutus>

Question

How might the model in Figure 5.4 be applied to a relationship between a David Lloyd Leisure centre and a club member?

Employees and Relational Quality

The importance of the concept of the "part-time marketer" (Gummesson, 1981) and the need within the company to foster a service culture which encourages good service and customer orientation has also been emphasized elsewhere. It should be stressed that this concept refers to non-marketing personnel employed by the organization and focuses on encouraging all employees to understand their part in the marketing process and the impact that they have on both functional and technical quality perceptions. While many organizations take a departmental or functional approach to marketing, whereby specialized marketers are employed within a marketing department and are engaged in marketing activities, Christopher *et al.* (2002) take this a step further and suggest the categories of contactors, modifiers, influencers and isolateds (see Table 5.2).

TABLE 5.2 A Classification of Marketers and their Roles and Responsibilities

	Involved with Marketing	**Not Directly Involved with Marketing**
	Contactors Involved in conventional marketing activities such as sales	**Modifiers** Employees that are "customer facing" and may, for example, be involved in the delivery of a service. This may include receptionists, waitresses, bars staff, etc.
Frequent or periodic contact with customers	*Knowledge and Skills Requirements* Usually experienced and qualified marketers	*Knowledge and Skills Requirements* Understanding of organizational mission and marketing strategy and their role within that. They should have an understanding of and be trained in the importance of developing customer relationships
	Influencers May be part of the marketing department but do not have a "customer facing role". The term influencers is used because of their fundamental role in shaping and influencing marketing effort	**Isolateds** No "customer facing role" and little involvement with traditional marketing practices
Infrequent or no customer contact	*Knowledge and Skills requirements* Often specialist skills related to some kind of marketing. Examples of this may include market analyst, market researcher and product developer, etc.	*Knowledge and Skills requirements* Often specialist skills in a non-marketing role such as HRM or accountancy. Appreciation of their role required in satisfying overall strategic marketing objectives

Source: based on Christopher *et al.* (2002).

As highlighted by Christopher *et al.* (2002), this suggests that employees may, to varying degrees, form a critical input in determining the extent of value added in service quality and ultimate relational satisfaction. Indeed, a number of studies have highlighted the link between service quality, employee satisfaction and customer retention. Principal among these are studies by Reichheld and Sasser (1990) and more recent studies by Schlesinger and Heskett (1991; see Figure 5.5).

When jobs are well paid, interesting and variable, employee satisfaction is higher and this leads to lower employee turnover. Employees attain a higher level of experience and possibly get to know the customers on an individual level. The level of service quality improves, and relationships between customers and employees are strengthened. Customers remain loyal, there is less expenditure on recruitment and training and profit margins improve. In Figure 5.5 the diagram of the cycle of success portrays this with two concentric but interactive cycles. One involves factors revolving around employee satisfaction and the other revolves around issues related to customer satisfaction and the links between them (see the mini-case on p. 118).

Many organizations now recognize that the quality of relationships a company has with its employees largely determines how employees may interact with customers. A variety of terms

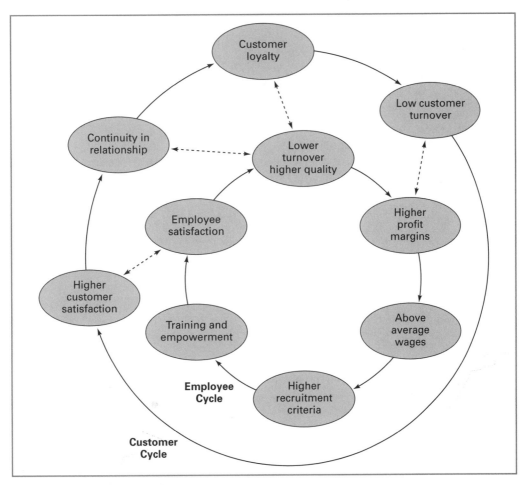

FIGURE 5.5 The Cycle of Relational Success
Source: based on Schlesinger and Heskett (1991).

MINI-CASE: TNT EXPRESS WORLDWIDE – CASCADING BENEFITS TO THE CUSTOMER

As part of a company-wide strategy to increase profitability, TNT Express Worldwide focused on improving its frontline customer service skills. By training all 120 members of the customer service workforce, TNT has made excellent progress, increasing customer satisfaction and customer retention, as well as improving year-on-year profitability since the programme was introduced.

Based on an existing customer care programme, an external training consultancy designed a five-day facilitators' workshop for TNT. This was devised for the national customer service manager and the European customer service manager. Before the workshop, both managers spent six to eight weeks collecting and surveying specific data from a sample of customers and other employees. The workshop programme involved five modules:

■ Total customer focus

■ Listening to the voice of the customer

■ Opportunities to delight

■ Customer service skills and

■ Service recovery

Alongside each module, the managers learned facilitation skills so that they could cascade their knowledge to other managers who, in turn, could pass it to frontline staff.

The first part of the cascade programme involved two five-day workshops for 20 customer service managers and supervisors. The programme mirrored the content of the original workshop, including facilitation skills. Finally, managers and supervisors cascaded their new skills and knowledge to the remaining 100 frontline staff in a further 10 three-day residential workshops. Participants were assessed through skill-practice exercises and feedback was evaluated through 15-point questionnaires. Customer satisfaction surveys had also been made before and after the workshops, to provide an indication of success.

The evaluation showed that individuals were able to transfer their learning directly to their jobs and benefit from clear, action-oriented objectives linked to each of the five modules in the training. Frontline staff now have more empowerment in dealing with customers, which has helped to increase their commitment and motivation. By holding the workshops residentially, the company has benefited from improved teamwork and camaraderie between colleagues and management. Customer satisfaction surveys show positive improvements, and customer retention has exceeded TNT's expectations. Finally, the customer service function has met its targets for contributing to profitability.

Source

'Celebrating Winners' Success', <www.nationaltrainingawards.com>

Question

How does TNT skill development relate to the Cycle of Relational Success (see Figure 5.5)?

have been used to describe this process of interaction between organizations and their employees. Examples include:

■ Internal partnership development

- Internal relationship building
- Internal focus
- Internal marketing
- Internal Relationship Marketing

For the purpose of consistency it will be called Internal Relationship Marketing (IRM).

Internal Relationship Marketing

Differing interpretations and elements of IRM have developed with different contexts and with differing perspectives. On the one hand, it may be perceived as an enabling tool for the implementation of strategic plans. The traditional marketing concepts of segmentation, targeting and positioning are used internally to "sell" management requirements (Jobber, 2004). On the other hand, it may be viewed as an organization-wide philosophical approach that transcends departments and functions and is informed by its values. A review of the literature identifies a number of themes related to IRM (e.g. Varey and Lewis, 1999). These may be categorized as follows.

Employee motivation and satisfaction

This builds on the work of Berry (1995) and views internal marketing as staff recruitment, motivation and retention and develops the premise that satisfied employees are more motivated and therefore more productive.

Customer orientation and satisfaction

Grönroos (1990) views internal marketing as a means of developing customer-orientated behaviour.

Inter-functional co-ordination and integration

One of the key elements of a marketing-orientated approach is inter-departmental co-operation (e.g. the accounting function co-operating with the production function, the production function co-operating with the marketing function, and so on) and internal marketing is used as a tool to ensure all marketing efforts are aligned (Narver and Slater, 1990).

Strategic implementation

Piercy (2002) views internal marketing as part of the strategic planning process whereby it is used as a tool to communicate strategic implementation and to get employees to "buy-in" to the strategic plan.

Employees as customers

This is based on the recognition of employees being customers with their own relative sets of needs and wants. Berry first used the phrase "internal marketing" as early as 1980 and defined it as "the means of applying the philosophy and practice of marketing to people who serve external customers so that (i) the best possible people can be employed and retained and (ii) they will do the best possible work".

Varey and Lewis (1999) are critical of the previous approaches to IRM mentioned insofar as it is portrayed as a management tool of employee persuasion. They take a more social approach defining internal marketing as "an integrative process within a system for fostering positive working relationships in a developmental way and in a climate of cooperation and achievement" (Varey and Lewis, 1999: 941).

Little and Mirandi (2003) suggest that all these approaches are not necessarily mutually exclusive but may be viewed as two opposite ends of a continuum. At one end is a transaction-based approach to internal marketing, whereas at the other is a relationship-based approach (see Figure 5.6).

Essentially, the nature of IRM is determined by the nature of the market being served and more specifically the potential service configuration patterns (see Chapter 4). These impact in a number of areas.

Skills

As highlighted previously in the chapter, some services providers require relatively low levels of skills (e.g. fast food) while others may require years of education and training (e.g. an orthopaedic surgeon)

Employee recruitment and retention

Related to the above, Little and Marandi (2003) draw some interesting parallels between customer–suppliers and management–employee relationships in relation to aspects such as perceived level of risk, uncertainty of outcome, etc. The higher the level of perceived level of risk of employing someone, the more extensive the information search (or in this case, the selection process) conducted by the employer. For example, compare and contrast the hiring of bar staff with that of airline pilots.

Shared values, culture and climate

Crucial to the success of the IRM philosophy within any organization is a set of shared values that is understood and shared by all the employees at all levels within the organization. It is widely recognized that values are fundamental to the shaping of organizational culture (e.g., Enz, 1988) and as such have an important role to play in relationship development and behaviour. The importance of shared values between organizations and individuals is highlighted by Morgan and Hunt (1994). Shared values is the only variable that they view as being a direct precursor of both relationship commitment and trust.

Related to the concept of shared values, Wilson (1995) suggest that mutual goals influence performance satisfaction which, in turn, influences the level of commitment to the relationship. They view shared values as a similar but broader concept (see Figure. 5.7).

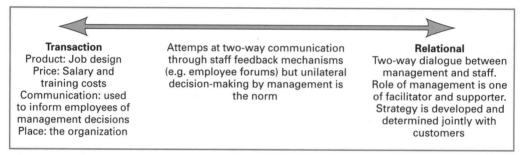

Transaction	Attemps at two-way communication	**Relational**
Product: Job design	through staff feedback mechanisms	Two-way dialogue between
Price: Salary and	(e.g. employee forums) but unilateral	management and staff.
training costs	decision-making by management is	Role of management is one
Communication: used	the norm	of facilitator and supporter.
to inform employees of		Strategy is developed and
management decisions		determined jointly with
Place: the organization		customers

FIGURE 5.6 The Internal Marketing Transaction-Relationship Continuum
Source: based on Little and Marandi (2003).

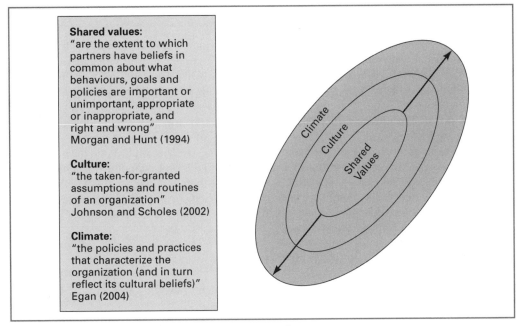

Shared values:
"are the extent to which partners have beliefs in common about what behaviours, goals and policies are important or unimportant, appropriate or inappropriate, and right and wrong"
Morgan and Hunt (1994)

Culture:
"the taken-for-granted assumptions and routines of an organization"
Johnson and Scholes (2002)

Climate:
"the policies and practices that characterize the organization (and in turn reflect its cultural beliefs)"
Egan (2004)

FIGURE 5.7 The Relationship Between Shared Values, Culture and Climate

At its conceptual best, the individual's personal value system should be aligned with the organization's. This is crucial, as the climate and the culture of the organization are determined by the employees' perception of the organization and, more critically, how they are valued by that organization. Johnson and Scholes (2002) suggest this will incorporate elements such as the organization's ethical stance related to issues such as the sourcing of raw materials, the use of labour in the manufacturing process, wages and selling and marketing.

INSIGHT: A *Mission Statement* is a "generalised statement of the overriding purpose of the organisation" (Johnson and Scholes, 2002: 421).

Obviously, for shared values to be understood, they must be clearly defined and communicated throughout the organization. The starting point for this for most organizations is the mission statement.

Empowerment versus control

As discussed in the previous chapter, the extent of empowerment that is devolved to employees is largely determined by the nature of the service provided. For example, a service production line context will require considerably more control and less empowerment than a professional service context. Even within the same organization, differing levels of empowerment may exist. For example, if one considers GPs' surgeries, the degree of empowerment given to the receptionist may be considerably different to the degree of control retained by the doctor.

Leadership style

The leadership and management style used to support the relational strategy which the organization is implementing should be appropriate. This will encompass areas such as reporting hierarchies, degrees of flexibility, the extent of the devolvement of decision-making, etc.

Chapter Summary

This chapter has explored the roles of people within commercial relationships. It began by highlighting the different types of internal and external relationships that exist between employees, customers and management and how these will vary depending on the type of context and the level of customer participation. The chapter proceeded by exploring some of the people dimensions of relationships such as trust, commitment and social bonding and how these may affect the quality of relationships between customers and employees. Subsequently, the role of IRM was explored.

The last five chapters have identified some of the key perspectives on RM and have discussed what can be seen as the key dimensions that are valuable to our understanding of client–provider relationships. We now take a critical look at some of these themes and place them in the context of what currently seems the dominant legacy of RM. Then, in the following three chapters, Chapters 6 to 8, we consider the way in which changes in markets are challenging us to consider the application of some core RM ideas.

Review Questions

1 Is an employer's internal relationships with its employees as important as external relationships with its customers? Justify your answer.

2 How might employees be used as a barrier to competition? Give examples to justify your answer.

3 What are the key ethical issues that employees should consider when developing relationships with customers?

Further Reading

Morgan, R.M. and S.D. Hunt (1994) "The Commitment–Trust Theory of Relationship Marketing", *Journal of Marketing*, vol. 58, July, pp. 20–38.

Narver, J.C. and S.F. Slater (1990) "The Effect of a Market Orientation on Business Profitability", *Journal of Marketing*, October, pp. 20–35.

Palmatier, R., R. Dant, D. Grewal and K. Evans (2006) "Factors Influencing the Effectiveness of Relationship Marketing: A Meta Analysis", *Journal of Marketing*, vol. 70, October, pp. 136–153.

Reicheld, F. and W.E. Sasser (1990) "Zero Defections: Quality Comes to Services", *Harvard Business Review*, September–October, pp. 105–111.

British Airways' Heathrow flights grounded by dispute at Gate Gourmet

A dispute over restructuring plans at Gate Gourmet, the catering supplier to British Airways (BA) at Heathrow airport, resulted in unofficial strike action in August 2005 with BA ground staff at Heathrow taking "sympathy" action. The walkout by BA staff led to the cancellation of hundreds of flights and stranded 100 000 passengers. The disruption was estimated to have cost the company up to GBP 40 million, with further damage to its reputation. This was the third consecutive summer that BA passengers had experienced severe disruptions due to industrial action and many who had remained loyal to BA in the past were switching airlines.

Industrial relations at BA

The second half of the 1980s saw the firm's financial position improve as a result of favourable market conditions. Between 1984 and 1990, the number of employees working for BA rose from around 35 000 to around 50 000. However, industrial disputes and occasionally, industrial action, remained a feature of industrial relations at BA. There was at least one dispute every year between 1982 and 1990. In the early 1990s the airline environment changed markedly. In particular, deregulation opened up competition within Europe, added to which was a general market downturn due to recession and the first Gulf war. With no option of government subsidies, BA pushed ahead with aggressive cost-cutting. The balance between a value-added, high-quality strategy and a cost-cutting approach shifted towards the latter in the early 1990s. The pressure on business units to deliver improved performance helped erode the BA corporate ethos of an open management style and changes were secured more by threats of selling off or franchizing operations than through consultation and negotiation. Between 1990 and 1993 some 5400 jobs (10 per cent of the workforce) were lost. There was evidence of low employee morale, and industrial disputes were a persistent feature with at least one bargaining group in dispute every year in the early 1990s.

In 1996 the company announced record pre-tax profits of GBP 474 million and, with the prospect of an alliance with American Airlines, the outlook seemed good. In a bid to increase profitability further, management embarked on a move to cut costs by GBP 1 billion within three years in what became known as the Business Efficiency Programme (BEP).

Inevitably management also sought to reduce labour costs. The most notable example was an attempt to restructure allowances and pay scales for cabin crew. This prompted a strike in the summer of 1997. British Airways management adopted an extremely tough position in the dispute, closing the Heathrow office of the main cabin crew union and threatening to sack strikers and even sue them for breach of contract. The company's confrontational stance was seen as counter-productive, however. It appeared to be bullying, and turned moderate staff opinion against the company. Although only 300 cabin crew joined the three-day strike in July, more than 2000 went on sick leave. This resulted in longer-term disruptions through August. The cost of the strike was estimated at GBP 125 million. The effects on staff morale, service and company reputation (further damaged by the simultaneous introduction of a new baggage-handling system which led to record levels of lost baggage) could not be quantified.

The Gate Gourmet dispute

Gate Gourmet is one of the world's largest providers of in-flight meals, operating in 29 countries with a total workforce of 22 000. The company has not made a profit since 2000 due to falling revenues in the face of increased cost competition in the airline sector and rising oil prices, which have squeezed catering services and budgets. The UK firm lost GBP 22 million in 2004 and was due to make a bigger loss in 2005.

On 5 August 2005 BA offered to mediate and this was scheduled for 12 August. However, the dispute came to a head on 10 August when the company took on 130 seasonal staff who were employed on lower rates of pay. Workers interpreted this as a threat to their jobs, since the company was considering redundancies. One shift refused to return to work while their representatives sought talks with management and were sacked.

Implications for BA

The next day, around 1000 baggage handlers and loading staff at Heathrow refused to work. This was to express their support for the sacked Gate Gourmet workers. Sir Rod Eddington, BA's chief executive, condemned the unofficial action as 'outrageous' and 'a body blow that defies belief'. Meanwhile, BA was compelled to intervene directly in the Gate Gourmet dispute, not least because it remained dependent on the company to source the heavy volume of meals it required at its Heathrow hub. With the management of Gate Gourmet threatening to take the company into administration, and further solidarity action from its own staff a possibility, BA agreed to renegotiate its contract.

Questions

1 To what extent do you think BA's problems are the result of poor IRM?

2 With increased pressure in many organizations to balance value-added, high-quality strategies with a cost-cutting approach, how relevant are models such as the Cycle of Relational Success (see Figure 5.5) in today's market?

References

Alford, B. and D. Sherrell (1996) "The Role of Affect in Consumer Satisfaction of Credence-based Services", *Journal of Business Research*, vol. 37, pp. 71–84.

Argyle, M. and M. Henderson (1985) *Anatomy of Relationships*, London: Heinemann.

Athos, A. (1981) *The Art of Japanese Management*, New York: Simon and Schuster.

Bagozzi, R.P., M. Gopinath and P. Nyer (1999) "The Role of Emotions in Marketing", *Journal of Marketing Management*, vol. 10, pp. 561–70.

Barnes, J. (1994) "Close to the Customer: But is it Really a Relationship?", *Journal of Marketing Management*, vol. 10, pp. 561–570.

Barnes, J. and D. Howlett (1998) "Predictors of Equity in Relationships between Financial Service Providers and Retail Customer", *International Journal of Bank Marketing*, vol. 16, no. 1, pp. 15–23.

Barney, J. (1990) "The Debate Between Traditional Management Theory and Organisational Economics", *Academy of Management Review*, vol. 15, no. 3, pp. 382–394.

Berry, L.L. (1995) "Relationship Marketing of Services – Growing Interest, Emerging Perspectives", *Journal of the Academy of Marketing Science*, vol. 23, no. 4, pp. 236–245.

Bitner, M.J. (1995) "Building Service Relationships: It's All About Promises", *Journal of the Academy of Marketing Science*, vol. 23, no. 4, pp. 246–251.

Bolton, R. and J. Drew (1992) "Migrating the Effect of Service Encounters", *Marketing Letters*, vol. 3, pp. 57–70.

Christopher, M., A. Payne and D. Ballantyne (2002) *Relationship Marketing: Creating Stakeholder Value*, Oxford: Butterworth Heinemann.

Crosby, L., K. Evans and D. Cowles (1990) "Relationship Quality in Services Selling: An Interpersonal Influence Perspective", *Journal of Marketing*, vol. 54, no. 3, pp. 68–81.

Duck, S. (1991) *Understanding Relationships*, New York: Guildford Press.

Dwyer, F., P. Schurr and S. Oh (1987) "Developing Buyer–Seller Relationships", *Journal of Marketing Management*, vol. 51, no. 2, pp. 11–27.

Enz, C. (1988) "The Role of Value Congruity in Intraorganizational Power", *Administrative Science Quarterly*, vol. 33, pp. 284–304.

Ford, D. (1980) "The Development of Buyer–Seller Relationships in Industrial Markets", *European Journal of Marketing*, vol. 14, pp. 339–354.

Grönroos, C. (1990) "The Marketing Strategy Continuum: Towards a Marketing Concept for the 1990s", *Management Decision*, vol. 29, no. 1, p. 9.

Grönroos, C. (1997) "Value-driven Relational Marketing: From Products to Resources and Competencies", *Journal of Marketing Management*, vol. 13, pp. 407–419.

Gummesson, E. (1981) "The Marketing of Professional Services – 25 Propositions", in Donnelly and George, *Marketing of Services*, Chicago Il: American Marketing Association, pp. 108–112.

Hart, S. and M. Hogg (1998) "Relationship Marketing in Corporate Legal Services", *The Service Industries Journal*, vol. 18, no. 3, pp. 55–69.

Hovland, C., L. Janis and H. Kelly (1953) *Communications and Persuasion*, New Haven CT: Yale University.

Jobber, D. (2004) *Principles and Practice of Marketing*, London: McGraw-Hill.

Johnson, A. and D. Stewart (2006) "A Reappraisal of the Role of Emotion in Consumer Behaviour: Traditional and Contemporary Approaches", in N. Malhortra (ed.) *Review of Marketing Research*, New York: M.E. Sharpe.

Johnston, J. and A. Hausman (2006) "Expanding the Marriage Metaphor in Understanding Long Term Business Relationships", *Journal of Business and Industrial Marketing*, vol. 21, no. 7, pp. 446–52.

Johnson, G. and K. Scholes (2002) *Exploring Corporate Strategy*, Harlow: Financial Times/Prentice Hall.

Kotler, P. (1994) *Marketing Management: Analysis, Planning and Implementation*, Englewood Cliffs, NJ: Prentice-Hall, p. 470.

Lin, C.P. and C.G. Ding (2005) "Opening the Black Box: Assessing the Mediating Mechanism of Relationship Quality, and the Moderating Effects of Prior Experience in ISP Service, *International Journal of Service Industry Management*, vol. 16, no. 1, pp. 55–80.

Little, E. and E. Marandi (2003) *Relationship Marketing Management*, London: Thomson Press.

Moorman, C., R. Deshpande and G. Zaltman (1993) "Factors affecting Trust in Market Research Relationships", *Journal of Marketing* (January), pp. 81–101.

Morgan, R.M. and S.D. Hunt (1994) "The Commitment–Trust Theory of Relationship Marketing", *Journal of Marketing Management,* vol. 58, July, pp. 20–38.

Mummalaneni, V. and T. Wilson (1991) "The Influence of a Close Personal Relationship Between a Buyer and Seller on the Continued Stability of their Role Relationship", Working paper 4–1991. The Institute for the Study of Business Markets, Pennsylvania State University, University Park.

Narver, J.C. and S.F. Slater (1990) "The Effect of a Market Orientation on Business Profitability", *Journal of Marketing,* October, pp. 20–35.

Palmatier, R., R. Dant, D. Grewal and K. Evans (2006) "Factors Influencing the Effectiveness of Relationship Marketing: A Meta Analysis", *Journal of Marketing,* vol. 70, October, pp. 136–153.

Peters, T. and R. Waterman (1985) *In Search of Excellence,* London: Harper Collins Business.

Piercy, N. (2002) *Market-Led Strategic Change: Transforming the Process of Going to Market,* Oxford: Butterworth-Heinemann.

Reichheld, F.F. and W.E. Sasser (1990) "Zero Defections: Quality comes to Services", *Harvard Business Review,* September–October, pp. 105–111.

Rotter, J. (1967) "A New Scale for the Measurement of Interpersonal Trust", *Journal of Personality and Social Psychology,* vol. 35, no. 4, pp. 651–656.

Schlesinger, L, and J. Heskett (1991) "Breaking the Cycle of Failure in Services", *Sloan Management Review,* vol. 31 (Spring), pp. 17–28.

Schurr, P.H. and J.L. Ozanne (1985) "Influences on Exchange Processes: Buyers' Preconceptions of a Seller's Trustworthiness and Bargaining Toughness", *Journal of Consumer Research,* vol. 11, pp. 939–953.

Shostack, L.G. (1977) "Breaking Free from Product Marketing", *Journal of Marketing,* vol. 41, no. 2, pp. 73–80.

Shostack, L.G. (1984) "Designing Services that Deliver", *Harvard Business Review,* vol. 62, no. 1, pp. 133–139.

Turnbull, P. (1979) "Roles of Personal Contacts in Industrial Export Markets", *Scandinavian Journal of Management,* pp. 325–337.

Tynan, C. (1997) "A Review of the Marriage Analogy in Relationship Marketing", *Journal of Marketing Management,* vol. 13, no. 7, pp. 695–703.

Varey, R.J. and B.R. Lewis (1999) "A Broadened Conception of Internal Marketing", *European Journal of Marketing,* vol. 33, nos. 9–10, pp. 926–944.

Westbrook, R.A. (1987) "Product/Consumption-Based Affective Responses and Post-purchase Processes", *Journal of Marketing Research,* vol. 24, pp. 258–270.

Wilson, D. (1995) "An Integrated Model of Buyer–Seller Relationships", *Journal of the Academy of Marketing Science,* vol. 23, no. 4, pp. 335–345.

Wilson, D.T. and V. Mummalaneni (1986) "Bonding and Commitment in Supplier Relationships: A Preliminary Conceptualisation", *Industrial Marketing and Purchasing,* vol. 1, pp. 58–66.

Zeithaml, V. and J. Bitner (2003) *Services Marketing: Integrating Customer Focus Across the Firm,* New York: McGraw-Hill.

Mid-Part Review: Critical Focus on Relationship Marketing

The previous chapters have identified some well-established themes of RM and captured critical theoretical elements which have subsequently been adopted as core dimensions of RM strategies.

Two questions arise:

- How do we interpret these strands of thinking and what frameworks are predominant today?

- Which elements of RM have been adopted strongly in the 2000s and what is the current legacy of this?

Evidence of Customer Orientation

Taking the first question, we can look at this from different viewpoints and identify many recent trends that suggest a greater importance of one framework, one set of ideas over another. The value of one framework over another is sometimes about relevance to sectors. If we look at current trends in buyer-to-buyer markets, some very sophisticated reciprocal customer relationship arrangements have come to the fore. Allied to benefits of customization for important clients, this is evident in reverse linkages where organizations mutually buy from each other; it is also evident in dedicated supplier development programmes that span online and offline modes of communication. Significant supply relationships and networks within sectors are now operating very efficiently through intranet supply hubs to which member organizations belong, a structure which offers priority status and access to rapid real-time ordering and delivery arrangements. An interesting example is the reverse engineering seen in the relationship between Sony and its supply partners in the development of their organic light-emitting diodes. These developments are a clear application of the relationship development and ongoing relationship management concepts that flowed from the industrial marketing research. (See Sony case in Chapter 3.)

In corporate and professional relationship markets, the Industrial Marketing and Purchasing group (IMP) model continues to be an underlying platform, albeit implicitly, in the close cultivation of corporate clients through an extension of corporate relationships into the social domain. Golf tournaments, joint firm activities, are all now part of the wooing of relevant and influential clients. Corporate organizations have paid £1 million over a ten year period to have the use of a corporate space at the new Wembley football arena. Completed in Spring 2007, a significant level of promised, upfront corporate hospitality spend proved an important source of investment funds and will remain a strong future revenue generator for the new stadium. The goodwill generated by the attendance of a select client group at the first FA Cup Final at the new arena in May 2007 becomes a mediating element in the interaction atmosphere that is created within the corporate relationship.

Corporate hospitality is not just about maintaining brand reputation and presenting a window onto corporate values, its premise is very much based on the IMP model of improving the atmosphere of the interactions and tying in the client to a closer relationship by encouraging them to get to know and care about the people that they may deal with on Monday morning.

If we examine public services on the other hand, we see many relationship management processes that originate from the services marketing literature: strong procedures to manage service quality, service delivery and service recovery as part of the management of patients in health services. Clear evidence of this has emerged since the mid-2000s, where UK healthcare is now referring patients to European hospitals, partly in order to cut waiting lists and reflect responsiveness but equally because of the special expertise that some European hospitals have in certain medical fields. In effect, due to heightened customer expectations of care, a pseudo-partnership model is emerging.

Looking at business to consumer markets, customer retention arguments have taken centre stage in the theoretical discussions of RM. Reichheld (1993) suggested that investment in current customers generates greater profits for firms. They quantified this with some figures and this idea became a very optimistic barometer for many firms to evaluate and improve (and in some cases, create from scratch), a customer retention policy.

In some service firms, this translated into significant investment in service recovery programmes, with the development of improved complaints procedures, exit interviews with dissatisfied customers and redress for poor service in the form of compensation. A very clear legacy of this was the current 28-day, no-quibble returns policy that most high-street fashion clothing stores operate. In tandem with this, policies to encourage repeat use of services and repeat purchase of products became the norm.

An area of tremendous investment related to customer retention studies (Reichheld 1993; Rust and Zahorik, 1993) at firm level has been the development of CRM. As noted in the Preface, this book does not deal with CRM in depth as it seeks to focus more on the classical and original perspectives of RM. Customer relationship marketing has its main premise in profitable customer retention and has made a valuable contribution to client management. Customer relationship marketing and e-CRM have both a strategic and an operational role in customer management, but they are not the sum of better relationships with clients. In some firms CRM has been adopted as a set of firm activities to emerge from the drive for better customer retention and indeed it can act as an enabler to the relationship-building activities of firms.

Therefore, we can conclude that RM ideas have led to significant changes in organizational processes since the early 1990s. While some of these are in the self-interest of the organization and their profitability, they have also encouraged greater consideration of client satisfaction and an increased level of customer orientation in industrial, public service and business-to-consumer markets.

How do we Characterize the Dominant Legacy of RM in Current Markets?

As briefly argued in the Preface, RM concepts have been to some extent reduced from their original classical conceptualization of relationship development as characterized by high customer service, strong customer orientation and an implicit value change that recognized mutuality of trust and reciprocal benefits as cornerstones of sustainable client relationships. This characterization, for some firms, particularly in commoditized markets, may be the high ground of RM that was always difficult to achieve.

What is perhaps problematic about the current legacy of RM is that what has become main-stream for the 2000s is an abstraction from the original concepts with some narrow interpretations of the original theories. The evidence for this narrower interpretation of RM and how its legacy is currently translated is threefold:

■ Inordinate focus on functional customer management (database driven) and equation of such management tools with effective RM

■ Overuse of behavioural loyalty programmes and belief that these programmes equal RM

■ Over-simplification and reification of transaction vs relationship

Databased Customer Management Focus – Restrictive in Terms of RM

There is a counter-intuitive aspect to many database-driven customer management schemes. Ultimately, these tools treat customers not as individuals, but as units of potential revenue with limited acknowledgement of what works in human interaction. The philosophy is that customers can be managed if sufficient communication and incentives are targeted at them by organizations. This runs counter to the antecedents of trust in Morgan and Hunt (1994), is contrary to the conception of a client relationship as evolving in an interactive atmosphere or environment (as in the IMP model) and fails to really grasp the Grönroos (1990) focus on reciprocal interactions and high customer service.

Many of the operational elements of these programmes are simply management processes that tend to be outsourced, remotely located and driven by telephone, Internet, email or mobile text-based communications that originate with the organization. Significant firm resources are allocated to moving desired client groups through some ladder of loyalty and to achieving a level of customer commitment. It is often approached in a minimum resource allocation mode where much corporate effort is measured in transaction cost, and the customer targets are based on widely accepted but somewhat untested ideas on switching behaviour.

In commoditized markets, the search for customer apostles is fierce and never-ending. This has always been true. But the approach taken by some firms using large data-based programmes is framed through short-term incentives and a successive roll-out of online and offline direct marketing approaches to tempt customers away from competitors or to encourage existing clients to buy more from your firm.

These activities are now seen to represent the creation of a loyal customer database (which is, by definition, temporary). This is questionable in terms of the real market value of that loyalty – which may be behavioural only. A case in point is the mobile phone market where users are now *expecting* incentives to be showered upon them, resulting in constant comparison of the present provider with another on the basis of short-term aspects of the service.

Valuable and important as database-driven marketing is to firms in highly competitive markets, in their client management philosophy the thinking is quite restrictive – by force of how they are implemented, they exclude some of the more complex elements in the formation of trust, loyalty and commitment that are essential to enduring relationship development. In addition, associated with database-driven approaches, are some untested narrow classifications of how customers will become loyal through data-mining, and can therefore be retained for further profits.

Concepts of mutual trust, of enduring customer loyalty and of strong relationship commitment development that characterize a classical relationship-oriented approach in marketing sit poorly in these target-driven programmes. When placed in the context of long-term, flexible and enduring relationships with many stakeholders, some of the current operationalization of these data-driven techniques have fundamental limitations in real marketing orientation.

Overuse of Behavioural Loyalty Programmes as Epitome of RM

One area of marketing investment that currently dominates in the client development activities of business to consumer firms is a strong focus on the development of loyalty programmes for customers. As noted above, the focus on customer retention in the 1990s led to a particular interest in concepts of loyalty and how to implement programmes to encourage store loyalty, brand loyalty and organizational loyalty. Academic thinking has generated quite robust theoretical refinements on the definition and antecedents and mediators of loyalty (Dick and Bassu, 1994; Dwyer, Schurr and Oh, 1987). However, the actual use of strategies to generate increased customer loyalty in business to consumer markets such as grocery and clothing retailing seems to have been narrowly focused on behavioural loyalty programmes. We know that Tesco Clubcard is now a widespread incentive scheme, used in the expectation that customers will stay with the provider because they can redeem points on their card. Yet this kind of scheme is a very limited interpretation of how to improve customer retention and excludes some more substantive concepts of loyalty, trust, and commitment. Indeed, to equate loyalty programmes with RM *per se* is to misinterpret the original contributions of both Christopher, Payne and Ballantyne (1991) and the nano-relationship concepts of Gummesson (1993).

Reduction to a Dominant Simplistic Representation

In some current commentary, RM has been reduced to a simplistic rendering of the concept into a transactional vs relationship presentation of marketing exchange. Originally a useful preliminary conceptualization, it has now become an almost factual reporting of a stage of evolution in marketing thought – the transactional basis of exchange before RM thinking and the relationship mode of exchange after RM emerged. The representation of a continuum of transactional marketing activities at one end and of relational marketing activities at another has somehow become reified. In reality both transactional and relational elements exist in every classical marketing exchange (Bagozzi, 1975).

While we can see the inaccuracy of the transactional versus relational in this view, it is true that RM has consistently been set out as a new mode of thinking about customers. Similar to the product life cycle concept, it works reasonably as a conceptual device to represent potential differences in orientation of firm activities but has a devaluing halo effect if used as some real tool for management.

Has the Philosophy Behind RM Become Tired and Tainted?

Looking at the dominance of database-driven customer management programmes and the widespread adoption of loyalty points schemes in some business-to-consumer sectors, there is a worry for marketers about the philosophy behind them. It could be argued that the way some of these programmes to generate customer apostles of the firm are implemented is synonymous with the original selling orientation of businesses.

The focus of these efforts is to treat marketing as simply a programme to be designed and implemented with selected groups, to treat customers largely as opportunities for cross-selling your own services/products and to believe that, if you have more loyal customers or "customer apostles" this year than your competitors, you are successful in the market. It is less about real innovation of product/service; or sustainability of marketing position over time or the building of reciprocal trust and enduring competence with customers.

In one sense, by association with the dominance of narrowly focused loyalty points schemes and the emergence of efficient but anonymous provider-led customer management pro-grammes, RM ideas have become tired and predictable. It might be argued that the value in the complex and significant past research into the components of RM has been tainted by these developments.

RM needs to recapture some of its high ground and to orient some of this functional pro-gramme-based thinking back into a business philosophy that reflects the real complexity of relationship-building. This is particularly critical because of the way markets are evolving as much socially as economically.

Mobility and Co-production

Markets are now characterized by significant mobility and flexibility.

- *Mobility* in terms of the rapid developments in consumer contexts brought about by the massification of broadband and other digital communications technologies, which underpin the idea that anyone can be accessible 24/7/365/worldwide. Furthermore, there are now very few barriers to consumer imagination and consumption of products and services irrespective of their exclusivity, availability or accessibility. The consumer has become empowered in ways that they themselves are not yet fully cognisant of.

- *Flexibility* in terms of the increasingly dynamic way in which an organization can operate and structure itself to reflect its market opportunities – the versatile organ-ization now captures and harnesses its information-based competences in order to evolve.

This is emerging in more fragmented, varied and yet economically viable models of business, in rapid start-up, lean and partnership investment modes and in an increasing importance of social dimensions, which are permeating all classical marketing relationships.

For example, these ideas are played out every day through the recognition that personalities can transcend their traditional niche and generate different revenue streams – sportsmen and women readily become business entrepreneurs and media influencers, drawing on their social capital and strong social networks.

Much consumption has become an aspirational life pattern for the "average consumer" and is expressed in the modern blogosphere, where there is little objective difference between the identity an individual portrays and their adopted role as a consumer. Many consumer decisions are now mediated through almost real-time social reporting of their choice of brands, consump-tion of products and services and reflection upon their consumer experiences in an *immediate* and almost *intermediate* mode. From the consumer perspective, a business is not a mysterious or formal concept – almost anyone can imagine being a part of a business and being a successful entrepreneur. Their interactions and relationships with organizations are part of an extended social experience that expresses and reinforces what they would like to co-produce.

In the next three chapters we explore some of the ways the increasing complexities of information-driven markets and "networked" consumers are demanding new thinking about relationship building.

References

Bagozzi, R.P. (1975) "Marketing as exchange", *Journal of Marketing*, vol. 39 (October), pp. 32–9.

Ballantyne, D. (2003) "A relationship mediated theory of internal marketing", *European Journal of Marketing*, vol. 37, no. 9, pp. 1242–1260.

Christopher, M., A. Payne and D. Ballantyne (1991) *Relationship Marketing: Bringing Quality, Customer Service and Marketing Together*, Oxford: Butterworth Heinemann.

Dick, A. and K. Bassu (1994) "Customer loyalty: toward an integrated conceptual framework", *Journal of Academy of Marketing Science*, vol. 22, no. 22, pp. 99–113.

Dwyer, F., P. Schurr and S. Oh (1987) "Developing buyer–seller relationships", *Journal of Marketing*, vol. 51, April, pp. 11–27.

Gummesson, E. (1993) *Quality Management in Service Organizations*, St John's University, NY: International Service Quality Association.

Reichheld, F. (1993) "Loyalty-based management", *Harvard Business Review*, March–April, pp. 64–73.

Rust, R. and L. Zahorik (1993) "Customer satisfaction; customer retention and market share", *Journal of Retailing*, vol. 69, no. 2, pp. 193–215.

06

Mobilizing Information in Relationships

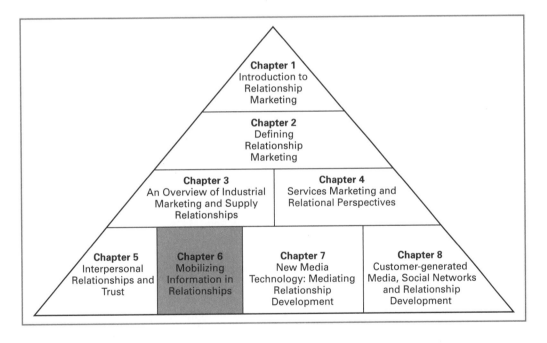

After studying this chapter you should be able to:

1 **understand** how information is used and mobilized in marketing relationships

2 **explain** the nature and roles of information and knowledge, and learning and expertise in managing relationships at organizational and individual levels

3 **assess** how information and knowledge management is influencing the development of marketing and industrial relationships

Chapter Contents

Introduction

An area that has received growing attention in RM is how information about relationships, their development, progress and proclivities are managed. Relationships, as highlighted in Chapter 1, are long-term focused and, as a consequence, there is an accumulation of data, information and knowledge held by individuals and organizations which is used to facilitate exchanges for greater competitive advantage. Nevertheless, RM is notoriously difficult to do well, often because of failings in understanding between organizations, how they learn about each other and their market contexts, and especially how information is handled in ways that ensure longevity. This is not surprising: people are complex, learning continuously; their knowledge, which relates to experience and expertise, is difficult to transfer and information is rarely complete or perfect, except perhaps with the benefit of hindsight!

As a strategic resource to individuals, let alone organizations, the management of information is multi-faceted. In previous chapters the exchange of information between organizations has been highlighted as fundamental to relationship success. For example, the development of trust and commitment in relationships is predicated upon communication and information exchange between the parties. Consider how a customer feels when restaurant waiting staff fail to pass the correct information about preference for a steak to the chef. Consider also what happens with a relationship between a garage and car owner when an apprentice engineer fails to maintain the vehicle properly. In the first case, the customer may complain and never visit the restaurant again. In the latter case, depending on the type of relationship the customer has with the garage manager or owner, the relationship may be damaged although may continue if the bond is strong enough, or the apprentice contrite and showing evidence of improved skills.

This chapter explores the nature of information and knowledge management and its role in RM at individual, organization and inter-organizational levels.

Mobilizing Information for Competitive Advantage

A competitive advantage is what makes an organization different from its competitors – it is often determined to be the organization's core competence, what they are especially good at in the market. In commoditized markets the differential is mainly the people working for the organization – their knowledge and skills in reading the market and meeting the needs of customers, negotiating the best supplies and managing finance and operational assets in order to achieve efficiencies are the most important asset an organization has. The ability effectively to manage marketing activities and processes which ensure competitive advantage for organizations in meeting customer needs is one such example of the importance of people's knowledge and skills. For example, BMW cars differentiate from the competition not only through their technically advanced car designs but also by offering a premium range of services that support the needs of their customers, from technical advice and personalized build specification at the point of purchase to financing, fast servicing and accident repair. The customer's experience in purchasing a new BMW car is managed to a high degree by a number of individuals in the showroom – the salesman, the receptionist, support salesmen, financial advisor, service support staff. When the customer walks through the door of the car showroom, they are greeted by name and conversed with by a range of employees as if they are long-time friends.

From BMW's perspective this is good customer management but it requires a level of information and knowledge management – about the customer's name, their purchasing intentions and preferences and any other relevant personal information. This is held in a customer database, is accessible to all staff, and helps them to communicate with the customer and, hopefully, maintain the relationship so that the customer will return in future. Contrast this to a small and local repair garage. The mechanic has an equal, if not better, understanding of a customer's needs, perhaps built up over a period of a few years, and yet he has no sophisticated customer database with which to manage his customer information and knowledge of how specifically to support the customer in order to maintain the relationship.

In terms of theory, the literature on knowledge management draws on different multi-disciplinary threads: economics, sociology, strategy (Quinn *et al.*, 1998; Demsetz, 1991; Grant, 1996; du Toit, 2003). Relationship Marketing and knowledge management have been linked by a number of authors (Ballantyne, 2004; Tzokas and Saren, 2004; Ballantyne and Varey, 2006). Both concepts require trust, commitment, knowledge sharing and information exchange through dialogue between individuals in order for efforts to be of benefit to the organization. Such efforts are underpinned by processes that are often technologically supported. Fundamentally, both RM and knowledge management contribute to organizational effectiveness by extending the "product offer" to markets: RM does this by enabling the development of stronger relationships with customers and others within a network of relationships (Gummesson, 1999). Knowledge management does so by enhancing learning within individuals and across the firm (Chaston *et al.*, 2000). This is explored further in the next section.

In the meantime, it is evident from the car example above that knowledge about customers is a significant resource to the organization. Yet the example also highlights that other forms of knowledge may be important to the exchange with customers – knowledge about products and services offered by the organization, about others within the organization, their roles, expertise and potential value to the customer; also knowledge about how to order cars using the systems and processes in place, as well as how to maintain vehicles and repair them. Thus, knowledge management for RM is about how information and knowledge is captured, stored, used, understood, interpreted, adapted and mobilized – that is, transferred to others and used as the basis for new ideas.

Close interaction with other individuals, including customers and potential customers, results in knowledge creation about customers' needs and wants, about the products and services they use and prefer as well as about their view of the market context and how it is changing. When this knowledge is used to inform decisions, at individual, product and service and customer levels as well as between the organization and its supply partners, this is knowledge being mobilized into new actions.

Information and knowledge management in a marketing context derives from the resource-based view of the firm (Hunt and Morgan, 1995). A term now used to describe knowledge as an organizational resource, similarly to the term "financial capital", is that of "intellectual capital". This term emphasizes the strategic value of knowledge to the organization (Stewart, 2001), which is perhaps a difficult concept to understand because knowledge in this sense is difficult to separate from its "owner" (person), who is likely to be a strategic resource for a great many reasons! Factors that have stimulated interest in knowledge and its management include the following (Huczynski and Buchanan, 2001):

- The growth of the service economy, which emphasizes the importance of sophisticated knowledge within the organization, especially in a marketing context where knowledge of customers is often fundamental to their retention

- Knowledge as an organizational resource, similar to a "raw" material, that can be collected, owned and used for competitive advantage

- The importance of retaining those expert staff within the organization, such as the mechanic mentioned above, without whom knowledge of key customers may be lost (although important, this aspect is outside the scope of this text)

- The role of new technologies in managing knowledge, such as sophisticated database and information management systems (discussed further in Chapters 7 and 8)

- The lifecycle of knowledge – how it influences innovation, creativity, flexibility – and its impact on competitive positioning

The importance of effective information and knowledge management is summarized in Figure 6.1. The diagram illustrates that raw data, which should be viewed as an important organizational asset, provides insight into how the organization should progress itself. The result of this is knowledge that enables the organization to build customer relationships and develop its strategic thinking. Strategy is what leads the organization to be profitable, maximizing the benefit from its clearly identified competitive advantage in the marketplace. For example, data about customer purchases made using a loyalty card enable a retailer to generate a better understanding of the customer's purchase behaviour, enabling it to target individuals with appropriate offers. This, in turn, enables the retailer to focus on its strategic development of product lines sold and also being developed for future in conjunction with its key suppliers.

Constraints upon mobilizing knowledge within organizations arise from the formalities and processes around exchanges of information. Clearly, where there are few or no opportunities for sharing information, there is also likely to be limited mobilization of knowledge, and this has important implications for ensuring the longevity of relationships. Ballantyne (2003) has identified three idealized situations that may facilitate exchanges of knowledge:

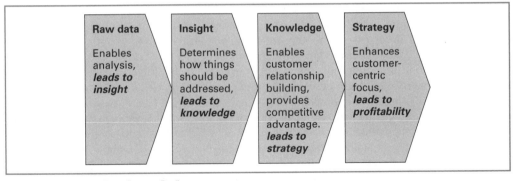

FIGURE 6.1 Knowledge: From Data to Profit
Based on Evans *et al.* (2004); © Peppers and Rogers Group 2002.

1 *Hierarchical exchanges* where managers facilitate the process through levels within the organization, such as by briefing team colleagues about key customers

2 *Inter-functional exchanges*, such as value chains, where knowledge is fed through the organization based on identified customer needs (albeit that the customer may be unaware of the processes), and each component in the value chain makes explicit their contribution to meeting the customers' needs

3 *Network exchanges* which are voluntary, spontaneous, may be driven by social purpose and may also be an attempt to formalize and extend the reach of hierarchical exchanges

These are discussed further later in this chapter.

Task 6.1

Which of Ballantyne's three idealized situations best describes how you might share knowledge in a work context? Contrast this to how you currently share knowledge while studying for your degree.

Ballantyne makes the important point that no one of these approaches is likely to work in all situations, even within one organization, because of the different actors and dynamics involved, making the process of effective relationship management complex at best! Nonetheless, it is important for knowledge to be transferred and for it to form the basis of innovation in order for an organization to remain competitive. Exchanges of information and knowledge may lead to some new insight which may ultimately enhance some market or relationship development.

The next section explores the concept of organizational learning and its importance in maintaining relationships.

Organizational Learning

Mobilizing information and knowledge inside the organization, as described in the previous section, is about organizational learning – the ability of members to pass knowledge and "wisdom" (expertise) on to others in order to promote business continuity, especially where key stakeholders are external to the organization's boundaries, such as in marketing relationships. Of course, business is never merely about continuity, but also involves adapting to maximize opportunities in a dynamic business environment, influenced by new competitors, new members of the organization, new customers, new processes, new technologies and new knowledge. Organizational learning has been described by Argyris and Schön (1974) as being "single-loop" and "double-loop". These two approaches are visualized in Figure 6.2.

Single-loop learning is recognized as the kind of organizational learning which results from experience, where experience is reflected upon for a period of time and used as the basis for other experiences (the generalization and testing phases of the model). Double-loop learning is where the experience results in a significant change in thinking (paradigm shift), leading to new ways of knowing and new understanding. It is the double-loop process that leads organizational members to create, innovate and develop processes, practices, products and services in order to maximize the opportunities offered by the organization's business environment and competitive position. It is, in practice, a challenging idea because, in effect, it requires the organization to manage change continually. Indeed, it is the double-loop process that enables an organization to mobilize its experience in relationship management to new relational contexts, whereas the single-loop process is most likely to represent development of understanding within a relationship.

The idea of learning which leads to change or adaptation has also been referred to as the "knowing cycle" (Choo, 1998) where new understanding is mobilized by the organization further in adaptive behaviours (see Figure 6.3).

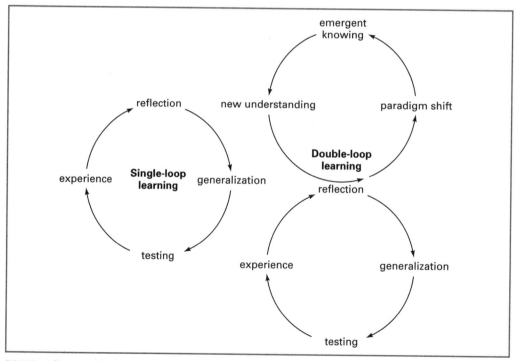

FIGURE 6.2 Single and Double-loop Learning
Source: Hawkins (1997).

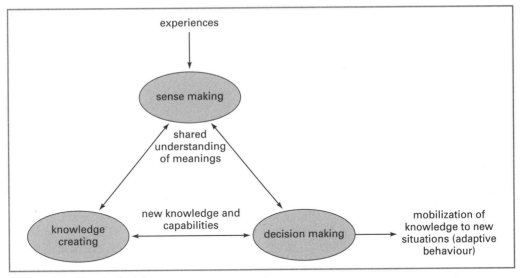

FIGURE 6.3 The "Knowing Cycle"
Source: based on Choo (1998).

Thus, from experiences and reflection, leading to sense-making by organizational members, new knowledge is created which facilitates decision-making (strategy development) leading to adaptive behaviour.

As well as at organizational levels, individuals will engage in learning cycles in order to solve a particular problem, be that personal development, or resolution of some business problem (Poell *et al.*, 2000). It is, however, hard to separate knowledge sharing and exchange from individual input (see the Nucor mini-case).

MINI-CASE: THE KNOWLEDGE MACHINE AT NUCOR STEEL

Nucor operates in an undifferentiated, tangible and commoditized market of steel production in the US. This market sector has declined since the early 1970s and yet Nucor Steel seems to have been successful, showing an annual growth rate of 17 per cent since start-up in 1968. Such growth is attributed to three distinctive strategic competencies: plant construction and "start-up know-how"; manufacturing expertise; and their utilization of new technologies to beat the competition. How so?

Nucor's employees are actively encouraged to take an interest in the business's operations and growth. Employees are incentivized through remuneration packages and continuous on-the-job development, including training and job sharing. Salary bonuses are paid out on the basis of production output at a quality standard. This results in efforts to improve performance through process innovation – and a certain tolerance of failure. Their approach to knowledge acquisition means that expertise among the workforce is particularly high, enabling staff to discuss detailed implementation issues with suppliers for more rapid adoption of new technologies than competitors. Retention of knowledge is equally high because staff are committed to the business, resulting in low staff turnover.

Not only does this imply a high level of individual involvement in the business but also in dealings with suppliers and customers. Internally, Nucor staff are actively encouraged to share opportunities and practices in order to promote strong performance. This is achieved through development of interpersonal relationships – everyone knows everyone else! When problems arise, individuals with specific expertise are re-assigned to help out. Thus, expert knowledge is managed through phases of acquisition, retention and mobilization.

Source

Based on A.K. Gupta and V. Govindarajan (2000).

Questions

1 **Comment on which of single- or double-loop learning cycles is most evident in this case. Justify your answer.**

2 **Describe how information and knowledge are mobilized at Nucor Steel.**

3 **Explain why a tolerance of failure might be important for organizational learning.**

These ideas are important to our understanding of how an organization becomes a "learning organization" (Senge, 1990), which is subtly different to organizational learning! Senge argued that an organization should learn at all its levels in order to be sustainably competitive. He identified the five learning disciplines which state that one should have realistically achievable goals, assumptions should be challenged, there should be commitment to a shared vision and teamwork should be a fundamental mechanism for development (Huczynski and Buchanan, 2001). This requires considerable interaction among the organization's members which enables greater understanding of interdependencies among members and encompasses feedback in a "systems thinking" approach.

Noble *et al.* (2002) argue that an organization's ability to process knowledge, that is, mobilize it, is directly related to its ability to absorb new knowledge: that is to reflect upon and interpret it. Poell *et al.* (2000) suggest that a learning "elite" is created in a division between individuals who continually engage with learning and those who are less enthusiastic. Thus, it can be argued that those individuals within an organizational context who are acting at the cutting edge of developing and maintaining marketing relationships are likely to be best placed to mobilize their knowledge into developing and maintaining new relationships.

Task 6.2

Discuss how a learning culture can be developed in an organization so that relationships with customers may be retained over the longer term.

Individual Learning

Much of the discussion so far has emphasized the role of information and knowledge management at organizational levels, yet it is the individual learning that occurs which really shapes knowledge creation, as commented on by Chauvel and Despres' (2002: 218): "individuals are the fundamental reality of organizations ... individuals accomplish work in groups that confer an identity, physical and psychological resources, organizational power, a sensemaking ground".

This is also highlighted by Liedtka *et al.* (1997). These authors identify a learning cycle which links personal and market development together by leveraging expertise to solve complex problems (see Figure 6.4), such as may be presented in relationship identification, establishment, development and management.

Therefore, the role of the individual is fundamental in knowledge management (see the hotel mini-case study, p. 142).

As is evident from the discussion in this chapter, knowledge itself is far from an easy concept to understand. In many literary works, knowledge is discussed in two broad domains: theoretical knowledge which is *academic*, relating to how learning reflects the processes of knowledge acquisition; and where knowledge, once acquired, is applied to *professional* practice, such as in the management of organizations and relationships with stakeholders – that is, knowing what something is and knowing how to do something.

> INSIGHT: *Knowledge* is "an understanding gained through experience" (Awad and Ghaziri, 2004: 33).

Consider also, for example, Polanyi's comment "we know more than we can tell" (1966: 4). This refers to "tacit knowledge", which is the type of knowledge that is difficult to describe, otherwise known as "skill", "competency", or "know-how". By contrast, "explicit knowledge" is that which can be taught, explained and described. Knowledge also has implicit properties (Nonaka, 1991), which Li and Gao (2003) suggest is the expertise held by a group of individuals, e.g. craftsmen (Badaracco, 1991), specialists, scientists. There are, however, many different ways of understanding what knowledge is and means, depending on where it has derived from, which includes Western and Eastern traditions of learning, although this is outside the scope of this chapter.

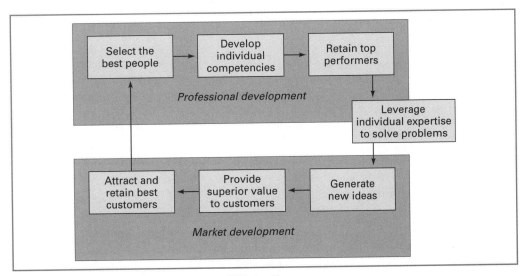

FIGURE 6.4 A Learning Cycle Linking Knowledge and Relationships
Source: Liedtka *et al.* (1997).

MINI-CASE: THE OLD VICARAGE HOTEL – LEARNING IN A SMALL SERVICE ORGANIZATION

In a small business it is not always explicit competence of staff that brings in business; it can equally be the result of interacting well with customers. The specialist nature of knowledge is not always a source of competitive advantage in small firms. Many successful small businesses have limited "specialist" or "technical" expertise but may adapt well to new circumstances.

Consider the case of The Old Vicarage Hotel. This is a small, privately owned, luxury country house hotel situated in the northern part of the UK, known by its customers for fine food and wine and hospitable atmosphere. The organization is typical of a small business – there are no departments, duties are shared among owner-managers and their staff and also extended to members of the community in which the business operates.

Within the hotel the exchange of knowledge is a facilitated rather than formally directed process. Each morning, one of the owner-managers will cook a full breakfast for all the staff. Over breakfast, the staff engage in open and extensive discussion about the forthcoming day's, week's and month's duties, incoming and outgoing customers, menus, recipes, local supply sources, interesting events and activities in a tacit exchange. The dining table is located on one side of the office and, through the course of each day, sees many visitors, cups of coffee and exchanges.

A notable feature is how the staff use diverse sources for learning and are largely self-educating, rather than formally educated, using professional publications (Masterchefs of Great Britain) and experimentation. The business is not only knowledge intensive for individuals, but experience and a need for quick learning is important. Individual learning is important and takes place incrementally. It is achieved by the way individual paths interconnect.

Staff can identify periods when they have been more active learners and where they had been more active in the network incorporating contact with suppliers and customers. They will actively engage competitors, suppliers and even other customers in exchanges regarding trends and custom. Thus, the organization learns from individuals who may be only tentatively linked to the core business but who, nonetheless, form a central and recognized part of the service experience.

Source

Based on Harwood and Broderick (2004).

Questions

1 Discuss the importance of social bonding between employers and their staff in managing information and knowledge.

2 Reflect upon the organizational culture that the case highlights and compare it to an organization with which you are familiar (or use the Internet to find the employee policy for a large company such as Honda).

3 Make recommendations to the employers on how they can ensure information and knowledge about customers is mobilized to staff across the hotel.

Knowledge is acquired by a process of learning, which has been seen as (Marton and Saljo, 1997):

- an incremental increase in knowledge;
- the ability to memorize;
- the use of information, facts, techniques;
- the ability to abstract some meaning;
- the ability to interpret in order to better understand a portion of reality.

Evidently, the result of learning is the ability to perform some task, which may require facts, an understanding of how something relates to another thing and some guiding principles on the use of the knowledge (Awad and Ghaziri, 2004).

Task 6.3

Consider which form of learning are you using with this textbook – and why.

To complicate things further, individual learning is also considered to take place in three distinctive "domains" (Bloom, 1956):

1 The *cognitive* domain is about knowledge.
2 The *conative* domain is about physical actions and *doing*.
3 The *affective* domain is about feelings and relating to oneself.

These are interlinked in some way as learning takes place. In recognizing these domains, however, it becomes easier to see how the capture of raw data (as highlighted in Figure 6.1) is insufficient to build marketing relationships that create competitive advantage or turn the data into marketing actions.

INSIGHT: "… don't rely on databases, encyclopedias, and libraries if you don't have 'librarians' who can help you navigate through all this stuff and find what you want." (Stewart, 2006).

Clearly, for greatest success, it is important for individuals not only to have knowledge but to be experts in their field (Hackley, 1999). Individuals, after all, are an organization's greatest asset, especially in a service-based market. Expertise also has a number of distinct components, which Atherton (2002) identifies as being the following:

- *Competence*, which is the ability to carry out a set of skills.
- *Contextualization*, which is about knowing *when* to do *what*. It encompasses the skill of flexibility, and the ability to differentiate and act appropriately in different contexts or situations.
- *Contingency*, which is about coping with a situation when things go wrong. Thus, it necessitates great depth of understanding of a situation.
- *Creativity*, which is the ability to apply learned skills in new and unfamiliar ways.

These may all be considered as particularly important to developing and managing marketing relationships.

These points are also noteworthy, because in a modern business context individuals, as the fundamental reality of an organization, are increasingly seen as being "knowledge workers". This term arose from the impact of technological advancements and was originally used to describe what workers know, rather than what they can do. Recently, the term has been associated with all workers who hold specialist knowledge which is of value to an organization (Huczynski and Buchanan, 2001). For example, anyone with knowledge of customers and suppliers' people, preferences, needs and wants, processes, networks of relationships and business intentions might be considered to be key to the continuation of a marketing relationship. In consequence, an individual's personal ability to learn, and become expert, is important from both the organization's perspective, as a valuable resource, and the individual's, whose prospects depend on employment.

> INSIGHT: "Knowledge management is about the conversion of tacit knowledge to explicit knowledge in order that others may learn from experts. It turns personal learning into organizational learning" (Huczynski and Buchanan, 2001).

It is evident that from an organizational perspective the challenge is the articulation of tacit knowledge in order to enhance competitive advantage (Ambrosini, 1995). Gupta and Govindarajan (2000) argue that for organizations to sustain competitiveness, they must be effective at two tasks in knowledge management: to create and acquire new knowledge and to share and mobilize that knowledge throughout the organization. Furthermore, in a Relationship Marketing context, this includes the partner organizations through collaborative processes. This is discussed further in the next section.

Implications of Information and Knowledge Management for Marketing Relationships: Inter-organizational Learning

Knowledge management is often discussed in terms of information management, and there is much literature about the management of knowledge by artificial (non-human) means, such as through various technologies. Indeed, the terms "knowledge" and "information" are often used interchangeably, as highlighted throughout the earlier sections of this chapter. Kakabadse *et al.* (2003), for example, highlight a "chain of knowledge flow" from data to information, realization, action/reflection to wisdom, which rather reflects the levels beyond competence to expertise. In other literature, knowledge management and information management have been clearly separated. The former relates to organizational learning and the latter to the application of technology to store, retrieve, process, use and re-use knowledge (Huczynski and Buchanan, 2001).

By its very nature, RM is concerned with people, processes and the interactions between and within organizations in a market context that are somehow interdependent upon one another. The notion of a relationship implies a level of understanding, which may be deep, between and among the parties. This necessitates the generation of knowledge which is appropriate to the context. Yet a range of market contexts have been highlighted throughout this text which not only includes dyadic partnership-type relationships but also networked relationships, where many partners collaborate for market success. This type of relationship is particularly important in an industrial marketing context – for example, in supplier associations – and yet the nature of knowledge management across such networks is not well understood (Morgan, 2004).

Kakabadse *et al.* (2003) have, however, identified a number of different modes of knowledge management which help to explain the differences between approaches to managing knowledge, including a network-based model, a cognitive-based model and a community model (see Table 6.1).

The *cognitive model* is about the exploitation of knowledge for competitive advantage, predominantly at the operational level within organizations. Knowledge management is seen as a formal process, typically supported by technologies, and is about the manipulation of information from a variety of sources. Knowledge is treated as an organizational asset. A typical approach to this has been identified through Nonaka and Takeuchi's (1995) work, based on engineering practices at Honda cars (see Figure 6.5).

TABLE 6.1 Three Modes of Knowledge Management

	Cognitive model	**Network model**	**Community model**
Treatment of knowledge	Objectively defined as concepts and facts	External to the adopter in explicit and implicit forms	Constructed socially and based on experience
Dominant metaphor	Memory	Network	Community
Focus	Knowledge capture and storage	Knowledge acquisition	Knowledge creation and application
Primary aim	Codify and capture explicit knowledge and information for exploitation	Competitive advantage	Promote knowledge sharing
Critical lever	Technology	Boundary spanning	Commitment and trust
Primary outcomes	Standardization, routinization and recycling of knowledge	Awareness of external development	Application of new knowledge

Source: adapted from Kakabadse *et al.* (2003).

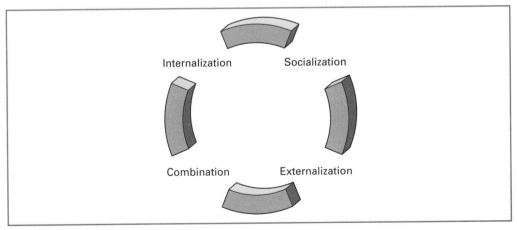

FIGURE 6.5 Nonaka and Takeuchi's Knowledge Conversion Process
Source: based on Nonaka and Takeuchi (1995).

Nonaka and Takeuchi's (1995) model articulates a process for organizational learning by *internalizing* knowledge. This must be subsequently mobilized for further learning into new and different contexts – for example, to solve problems in marketing relationships and maximize new opportunities. The four sequential stages of knowledge management are as follows:

- *Socialization* – where colleagues working together share tacit information about practices and develop skills as a consequence. This is learned *behaviour*, typically through observation and shared experiences, rather than taught *per se* (Choo, 1998).

- *Externalization* – colleagues develop a language around their behaviours through use of metaphors and models which result in dialogue and, eventually, explicit exchanges through reflection. The information is often passed on to others through a storytelling approach during which general ideas and principles are shared.

- *Combination* – knowledge is formally combined with other knowledge and disseminated through explicit means, such as reports, emails, etc., and upon receipt is recombined by the knowledge receiver. A data warehouse is a typical repository for this knowledge.

- *Internalization* – learning by doing, repeatedly, until the explicit aspects of the knowledge are absorbed and become tacit. Once tacit, in effect, the learner becomes teacher and so the process continues with each cycle spreading the knowledge further and wider across the organizational context.

The *network model* is more complex and considers the flow of information horizontally across an organization and beyond its boundaries into a broader network, of, say, suppliers, customers, competitors and other stakeholders. Gummesson (1999: 168) said "to be successful in the future economy, we need network organizations based on knowledge from many contributing sources, and from which tacit and embedded knowledge can be made accessible". Networks are loose connections between individuals who share a common language and/or problem-solving environment. In such a setting, organizational members have social as well as economic drivers for their exchanges of information. Individuals will seek out opportunities to learn (about things they know they do not know, or things they think they know!) as well as to influence others. The argument advanced by du Toit (2003) is that learning is achieved through knowledge which is socially constructed from the interaction between individuals within an organization, as they seek to make sense of phenomena. In turn, behaviour is influenced by others within the network of relationships.

Task 6.4

Who (individuals and organizations) influences how you learn? Describe how and why you are influenced.

Morgan (2004) identifies that, in a small firm context, knowledge is effectively managed, although its optimization is less well understood. In this context, it is, however, through a plethora of networking activities that managers solve particular business and marketing problems (Blankson and Stokes, 2002). In a larger organization, a flow of information is enhanced by Internet-based technologies – typical actors within networks tend to be active daily (Kakabadse *et al.*, 2003) in their exchanges in attempts to "control" the flow of information.

A similar approach is the *community-based model*. This is where knowledge resides within a community of practice, where members are bound together by common values. This may be based on participation within the community, such as marketers sharing ideas about product-management issues, and assumes a level of expertise held by each participant. Knowledge is shared in order to solve problems, and therefore retained within the community by common understanding. It is predicated on the idea that knowledge cannot really be separated from the knower (Heron, 1996; Kakabadse *et al.*, 2003).

Chapter Summary

This chapter has considered how individuals and organizations learn, manage and mobilize information and knowledge. Knowledge is defined as being an understanding gained through experience, which is influenced by the ability to learn. Three models of knowledge management were reviewed (cognitive, community and network models), where management is considered to be more and less formal and technology dependent. Approaches to mobilizing knowledge across and between organizational members were discussed, particularly through hierarchical, inter-functional and network means. Finally, expertise within organizations was identified as a valuable asset which has the capability of influencing market developments.

The next chapter takes some of the ideas discussed here further by exploring in depth the ways information-based competition and emerging technologies are creating significant new communication opportunities and are requiring firms to invest in new areas to improve their multimedia interactions with customers.

Review Questions

1 Describe how information is used and mobilized in marketing relationships.

2 What is an expert? Provide examples to support your answer.

3 How is information and knowledge management influencing change in industrial markets?

Further Reading

Journal of Knowledge Management – a source of articles about knowledge in use and its management across a variety of contexts.

http://en.wikipedia.org/wiki/Epistemology – a useful, web-based resource that reviews and discusses in some depth the nature, origins and scope of knowledge.

END OF CHAPTER CASE AND KEY QUESTIONS

The great British outdoor market

A complex network of relationships between sportspeople, including mountaineers, skiers, fell runners and cyclists, fabrics manufacturers, retailers, and the general outdoors consumer, has supported the growth of a massive industry in UK outdoor clothing and sports gear over a period of 60 years, since the Second World War. Brands such as Karrimor, Berghaus and Mountain Equipment are now internationally known for their durability, weatherproof comfort and style. What is surprising about this network is that it was built not around the immediate vicinity of major mountains, such as those in Europe or the Himalayas, but in the UK.

Changes in the market arose from post-war economic growth, resulting in increased leisure time, better communications, wider availability of the automobile and a new focus on marketing activities. This was underpinned by new product development in the materials sector, including nylon and other similar plastics-based products, which set the scene for innovation in outdoor clothing and gear.

Initially, the owners of the small firms, being enthusiasts at various levels in their sports, developed new products suitable for adventure sports through their extensive network of personal friends and family members. The entrepreneurs' networks were based on experience and were conducted through social contact. This level of contact meant that products were produced with great craftsmanship, reflecting a deep understanding of the needs of, for example, climbers at high altitudes. It also resulted in commercial benefits from expedition photographs that could be used to promote products to a wider audience, through advertising and catalogues.

Eventually, however, these innovative entrepreneurs extended networks beyond their immediate environment in order to generate information and expertise which allowed for mutual learning to take place among the community of sportspeople. Such networks involved more contractual arrangements and strategic alliances, such as that between Karrimor and BM Coatings (rucksacks) and Berghaus and Gore-Tex (clothing), which enabled sharing of knowledge and innovation as well as commercial advantages through distribution and licensing arrangements. Retailers became a focus for exchange of key information about the products between customers and manufacturers. Customers were also the source of inspiration for further product development.

The media too played a role as the sportspeople, successful in their endeavours to conquer high peaks, became the marketers' celebrity endorsers. Individuals, such as Chris Bonington, became household names, and their relationships with manufacturers an important consideration in the exchange of knowledge about product performance. However, the untimely deaths of two climbers, who were friends and technical advisors to Karrimor, changed the focus of exchange at this company. Instead of individuals, Karrimor began to use a "think tank" of people including guides, photographers, travellers, skiers and journalists, all of whom brought in new knowledge to the company, enabling them to improve their products and grow in the market yet further.

Indeed, across the sector, the wider the network became, the more radical were the innovations and the higher the market growth. Now, however, a new phase is being entered, where the result of globalization means that few products are manufactured in the UK and lead times for new products are reduced. This is seen within the sector as a threat to the exchange of knowledge and information between those who design and those who test new products.

Source

Based on Parsons and Rose (2004).

Questions

1 Describe how information and knowledge is being exchanged and transferred between the stakeholders in this market.

2 Discuss which of the three modes of Kakabadse *et al.*'s knowledge management models best fits this market. Give examples to support your answer.

3 Explain why reduced lead times, brought about because of globalization, may be seen as a threat to product innovation in this market.

References

Ambrosini, V. (1995) 'Researching tacit knowledge: an empirical methodology', Cranfield School of Management, paper presented at the British Academy of Management Annual Conference, Sheffield, 11–13 September.

Argyris, C. and D. Schön (1974) *Theory in Practice: Increasing Professional Effectiveness*, Reading: Jossey-Bass.

Atherton, J. (2002) Doceo [On-line] UK: Available: http://www.doceo.co.uk/. Accessed: 23 April 2006.

Awad, E.M. and H.M. Ghaziri (2004) *Knowledge Management*, intern edn, New Jersey: Prentice Hall.

Badaracco, J.L. (1991) *The Knowledge Link*, Boston: Harvard Business School Press.

Ballantyne, D. (2000) "Internal Relationship Marketing: A Strategy for Knowledge Renewal", *International Journal of Bank Marketing*, vol. 18, no. 6, pp. 274–286.

Ballantyne, D. (2003) "A relationship Mediated Theory of Internal Marketing", *European Journal of Marketing*, vol. 37, no. 9, pp. 1242–1260.

Ballantyne, D. (2004) "Relationship Specific Knowledge", *Journal of Business and Industrial Marketing*, vol. 19, no. 2, pp. 114–123.

Ballantyne D. and R. Varey (2006) "Creating Value-in-use Through Marketing Interaction: the Exchange Logic of Relating, Communicating and Knowing", *Marketing Theory*, vol. 6, no. 3, pp. 335–348.

Blankson, C. and D. Stokes (2002) "Marketing Practices in the UK Small Business Sector", *Marketing Intelligence and Planning*, vol. 20, no. 1, pp. 49–61.

Bloom, B.S. (ed.) (1956) *Taxonomy of Educational Objectives the Classification of Educational Goals – Handbook 1: Cognitive Domain*, New York: McKay.

Chaston I., B. Badger and E. Sadler-Smith (2000) "Organizational Learning Style and Competences: A Comparative Investigation of Relationship and Transactionally Orientated Small UK Manufacturing Firms", *European Journal of Marketing*, vol. 34, nos 5/6, pp. 625–642.

Chauvel, D. and C. Despres (2002) "A Review of Survey Research in Knowledge Management: 1997–2001", *Journal of Knowledge Management*, vol. 6, no. 3, pp. 207–223.

Choo, C.W. (1998) *The Knowing Organization*, Oxford: Oxford University Press.

Demsetz, H. (1991) "The Theory of the Firm Revisited", in O.E. Williamson and S.G. Winter (eds) *The Nature of the Firm: Origins, Evolution and Development*, New York: Oxford University Press, pp. 159–178.

du Toit, A. (2003) 'Knowledge: A Sense Making Process Shared Through Narrative', *The Journal of Knowledge Management*, vol. 7, no. 3, pp. 27–37.

Evans M., L. O'Malley, and M. Patterson (2004) *Exploring Direct and Customer Relationship Marketing*, 2nd edn, London: Thomson Learning.

Grant, R.M. (1996) "Toward a Knowledge-Based Theory of the Firm", *Strategic Management Journal*, Winter: Special Issue, vol. 17, pp. 109–122.

Gummesson, E. (1999) *Total Relationship Management*, London: Butterworth-Heinemann.

Gupta, A.K. and V. Govindarajan (2000) "Knowledge Management's Social Dimension: Lessons from Nucor Steel", *Sloan Management Review*, Fall, pp. 71–80.

Hackley, C. (1999) "Tacit Knowledge and the Epistemology of Expertise in Strategic marketing management", *European Journal of Marketing*, vol. 33, nos 7/8, pp. 720–735.

Harwood, T.G. and A.J. Broderick (2004) "The Tangled Knowledge Web of a Small Service Firm", Proceedings of International Colloquium in Relationship Marketing, Hamilton, New Zealand, 4–6 December.

Hawkins, P. (1997) "Organizational Culture: Sailing Between Evangelism and Complexity", *Human Relations*, vol. 50, no. 4, pp. 417–440.

Heron, J. (1996) *Co-operative Enquiry: Research into the Human Condition*, London: Sage.

Huczynski, A. and D. Buchanan (2001) *Organizational Behaviour*, 4th edn, London: Financial Times Prentice Hall.

Hunt, D. and R. Morgan (1995) "The Comparative Advantage Theory of Competition", *Journal of Marketing*, vol. 59, no. 2, pp. 1–15.

Kakabadse, N.K., A. Kakabadse and A. Kouzmin (2003) "Reviewing the Knowledge Management Literature: Towards a Taxonomy", *Journal of Knowledge Management*, vol. 7, no. 4, pp. 75–91.

Li, M. and F. Gao (2003) "Why Nonaka Highlights Tacit Knowledge: A Critical Review", *Journal of Knowledge Management*, vol. 7, no. 4, pp. 6–14.

Liedtka, J.M., M.E. Haskins, J.W. Rosenblum and J. Weber (1997) "The Generative Cycle: Linking Knowledge and Relationships", *Sloan Management Review*, Fall, pp. 47–58.

Marton, F. and R. Saljo (1997) "Approaches to Learning", in F. Marton, E. Hounsell and N.J. Entwistle (eds) *The Experience of Learning: Implications for Teaching and Studying in Higher Education*, 2nd edn, Edinburgh: Scottish Academic Press.

Morgan, R.E. (2004) "Market-based Organisational Learning – Theoretical Reflections and Conceptual Insights", *Journal of Marketing Management*, vol. 20, pp. 67–103.

Noble, C.H., R.K. Sinha and A. Kumar (2002) "Market Orientation and Alternative Strategic Orientations: A Longitudinal Assessment of Performance Implications", *Journal of Marketing*, vol. 66, no. 4, pp. 25–39.

Nonaka I. (1991) "Knowledge-creating Company", *Harvard Business Review*, vol. 69, no. 6, pp. 96–104.

Nonaka, I. and H. Takeuchi (1995) *The Knowledge-creating Company: How Japanese Companies Create the Dynamics of Innovation*, London: Oxford University Press.

Parsons, M.C. and M.B. Rose (2004) "Communities of Knowledge: Entrepreneurship, Innovation and Networks in the British Outdoor Trade, 1960–90", *Business History*, vol. 46, no. 4, pp. 609–669.

Peppers, D. and B. Rogers (2002) online, available http://www.peppersandrogers.com

Poell, R.F., G.E. Chivers, F.J. van der Krogt and D.A. Wildemeersch (2000) "Learning-network Theory: Organizing the Dynamic Relationships Between Learning and Work", *Management Learning*, vol. 31, no. 1, pp. 25–50.

Polanyi, M. (1966) *The Tacit Dimension*, New York: Doubleday and Co.

Quinn, J.B., P. Anderson and S. Finkelstein (1998) "Managing Professional Intellect", *Harvard Business Review on Knowledge Management*, Harvard Business School Press, pp. 181–205.

Senge, P. (1990) *The Fifth Discipline: The Art and Practice of the Learning Organization*, New York: Doubleday Currency.

Stewart, T.A. (2001) *The Wealth of Knowledge: Intellectual Capital and the 21st Century Organization*, New York: Currency.

Stewart, T.A. (2006) "Knowledge is Today's Capital: An Interview", on-line, available http://www.managementfirst.com/knowledge_management/interviews/stewart.php, accessed 24 November 2006.

Tzokas, N. and M. Saren, (2004) "Competitive Advantage, Knowledge and Relationship Marketing: Where, What and How?", *Journal of Business and Industrial Marketing*, vol. 19, no. 2, pp. 124–135.

CHAPTER

07

New Media Technology: Mediating Relationship Development

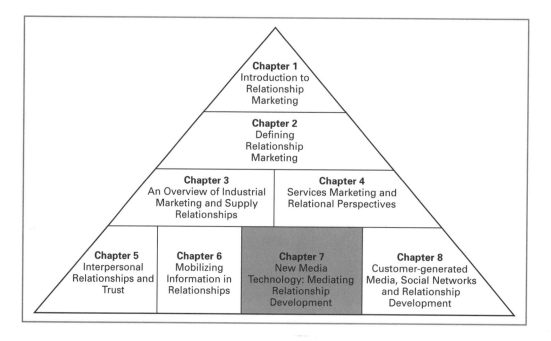

❖ LEARNING OBJECTIVES

At the end of this chapter, you should be able to:

1 **outline** the implications of information-based competition and its effect on online product innovation

2 **examine** levels of interactivity and the use of websites as evidence of company commitment to customers

3 **identify** elements of personalization and customization in relationship development online

4 **understand** the challenges within search engine marketing for brand relationship development

Chapter Contents

Introduction

Three characteristics exemplify contemporary product and service environments – flexibility, mobility and interactivity. These characteristics are evident in multiple formats of delivery; rapid start-up and transfer of resource possibilities for organizations; the use of mobile communication channels and the emergence of electronic, networked, real-time local and global service interactions. Since the mid-1990s markets have experienced accelerated change, evident in more fluid concepts of marketplace such as the move from single transactions to "marketspaces" as outlined some years ago by Vandermerwe (1997).

In the previous chapter, the importance to businesses of dynamic knowledge structures and knowledge mobilization were clearly highlighted. Where this is currently evident across products and services is in technological change within new media. New media developments are influencing our ideas of relationship development significantly. It is not possible to cover all areas where new technology is both permitting a greater versatility in client-technology-firm solutions and generating a different form of client relationship. This chapter explores selected areas where the impact of new media on the development of customer relationships is now visible. It identifies four strategic implications for marketers:

1 The need to adapt to information-based competition and incorporate intelligent processes when seeking to develop online relationships

2 The need to create dynamic websites that are adequate in intellectual content and functionality and show commitment to customers

3 The requirement to plan for optimum level of online customization and to acknowledge increased customer role in online environments

4 The recognition of the increasing importance of search engine marketing (SEM) and how it influences relationship development and customer retention

Information-based Competition: Strategic Awareness and Level of Interactivity

Technological developments have encouraged greater strategic awareness of information-driven structure(s). One of the key developments, acknowledged as important in the emergence of the digital environment is the changing role of information (Rayport and Sviokla, 1994; Sterne, 1999). Leverick et al. (1997) see information management as a strong competitive asset in virtual environments; yet Dutta and Segev (1999) suggest that few firms were taking advantage of these possibilities. More recently, Chaffey et al. (2003) have highlighted the need for a similar strategic focus.

Weiber and Kollman (1998), in analysing the digital environment some years ago, indicated the change in the role of information, notably the movement from being a support for traditional business practices to becoming an independent function of production and consumption, and suggested the need for two markets – marketplace (traditional format) and marketspace (virtual format).

What does the virtual format mean for relationship development?

In online environments where resource availability (i.e. access to information and possibilities to manipulate it) may no longer be a significant constraint to customers, information-related aspects are, arguably, becoming an important means of value creation. Customers now expect to search for information about any purchase or consumption; they expect it to be available at a click, and they want to be knowledgeable and informed. This gives them a sense of empowerment as they select products and services. Information in the digital environment, is, of course, both medium and content, as Aldrich (1999) summed up in his identification of "digital containers" (hardware and software conduits for important information exchange) and "content" (actual product) for digital containers. For customers the hardware has to work effectively and the software needs to be stimulating for them to develop trust in the supplier. Online, the key is interactivity.

> INSIGHT: "Digital communications enable customers to direct the time and duration of communication contact with organizations, and also the content, through instantaneous feedback arising from interactivity" (Broderick, 2003).

Linked to the interactive experience are two dimensions – time and interactive capability. Creating a time advantage in the manipulation of information and in the integration of digital possibilities makes the real-time nature of competition a feature of new media. If we consider an example here, we can choose the furniture retailer, IKEA. We have seen this company in an earlier chapter; now we can consider their online activities. IKEA have a very successful offline store format, which is unique in the degree of personal choice and interactivity that customers can have with the product range. The act of seeing the product, choosing the product, selecting the product from the shelving, then taking it home and assembling it gives a real involvement for customers who visit an IKEA store. If we then look at IKEA online, they have sought to recreate this level of engagement in a different way.

Task 7.1

Visit the IKEA website (Ikea.com). Note the options that are available to you on the website. Imagine you are furnishing a bedroom and checking the IKEA product range – beds, wardrobes for clothes, drawers, bedside lamps, floor rugs, duvets, curtains.

■ Go through the menu options needed to get information on this. Identify what the website allows you to see online.

■ In what way does it permit you to select different products or combinations?

■ What are to the limits to the website in terms of making a choice?

■ What would you do in-store on a visit to IKEA that is different to what you can do online?

■ In what ways can IKEA generate repeat visits to their site and encourage further interest from you?

Although the IKEA website has some limitations, it is nonetheless a powerful adaptation of content to maximize the level of customer empowerment. If we examined the IKEA online experience and used a service blueprint, as discussed in Chapter 4, it would be important to incorporate the time factor – to consider how time for customers can be experienced as a competitive advantage, where there is automatic execution of service elements in real time and where interface with background hub activities (these might be links that enabled you to view the relevant parts of the IKEA product catalogue online) are effective.

The other key aspect of new media is how interactivity can be technically manipulated. Managing information flows effectively and enabling new forms of customer interaction on the website are critical. Gamet (1996) suggested that the experienced physical environment itself plays an instrumental role. User satisfaction is dependent on website features such as speed to download, content and design, interactivity, navigation and security (Jayawrdhena and Foley, 2000; Jiang, 2000). Managing information possibilities, real-time processes and the interactivity of customers and technology in remote service formats creates challenges.

INSIGHT: "What the virtual environment requires is that we not only make the benefits within service offerings more intelligent: we also culturally absorb the technological medium into service organization and delivery" (Broderick, 2003).

"Intelligent" service products are now clearly demanded by customers, whether asking about an emergency health problem on the NHS website, whether renegotiating their account charges with the bank or relaxing and listening to a movie through real.com. It is the intelligence of the service offering (its real-time attributes; its availability and adaptability; its interactive links and its capacity for customization) that will be determinant and may drive the online strategy.

Intelligent processes to encourage successful customer retention

When we consider how products and services actively *vary* online, we see that the level of relationship to be developed with service customers is complex and needs to specifically encompass the degree of online interactivity envisaged with different customer groups. There could also be *consideration of the product/service elements as part of a networked offering* of online and offline elements and a look at the integration effect of online and offline marketing activities on service product consumption. The configuration of online services has broadened to offer more "mix and match" options to customers – where menus can be streamlined to simultaneously offer a full service or just one separable element. This is evident in a property website such as Right Move – which is powerful enough to list a significant proportion (over 70 per cent) of all properties listed for sale in the UK (RightMove.com). The client can examine house prices for their street and their neighbourhood, can then leave the site *or* they can go though a range of more complex options, such as contacting a local estate agent, getting detailed information on the process of house buying, checking the local area for maps or schools, checking local planning and amenities, or the names of potential conveyancers.

Websites that can integrate and extend the customer experience through enriched informational features and opportunities for customer creativity are important to maintaining customer interest (as is borne out by studies by Wang *et al.*, 2000 and Shih, 1998). In terms of generating intelligent online products, processes and increasing customer creativity options, some areas to consider might be the following:

- The interactivity level of different service products
- The extent of informational "realtime" inputs that are part of the service
- The time aspect in terms of intervention and response
- The "additional" content aspect of the service offering

Encouraging Dynamism of Websites – Online Showrooms of Companies' Commitment to Customers

There is, however, not just a need for companies to create dynamic websites that are adequate in intellectual content and functionality – there is an equal need to show commitment to customers though the website. We are aware of the increasing sophistication of websites, no longer as mere sources of basic information with a contact point, but as the centrepoint of enquiry and of dialogue about companies products and services.

What we are now witnessing is significant investment in the substance of what websites contain – this is being achieved through sophisticated channelling of users to their chosen question or area of interest, and through clever site construction and important links to substantive databases. Websites today can be as intellectually rich or content rich as the company feels is relevant for its stakeholder and customer groups.

Broader content is the focus of many website upgrades. Backbone Media's Turcotte (2004) noted that company spending in the US generally falls in the following ranges for website upgrades:

✍ INSIGHT:

- Small businesses ($500 000 to $2 million in annual revenue) typically spend $8000 to $20 000 for a redesign and $10 000 to $30 000 annually for search engine optimization, depending on the competitiveness of the marketplace.
- Small to medium-sized businesses ($5 million to $20 million) spend from $20 000 to $80 000 for redesign and $30 000 to $80 000 annually for search engine marketing.
- Mid-sized businesses ($20 million to $200 million) earmark $30 000 to $60 000 for upgrades and $80 000 to $200 000 annually for search engine marketing.
- Corporations over $100 million often spend hundreds of thousands for an upgrade and hundreds of thousands annually for search engine optimization and advertising.

Turcotte (2004).

These are significant investments in website development. What is driving this and how does it relate to customers? Two interesting examples are Hewlett Packard and ETL Semko, Intertek.

MINI-CASE: HEWLETT PACKARD AND INTERTEK – MAJOR UPGRADES TO WEBSITE TO DRIVE CUSTOMER RELATIONSHIPS

Hewlett Packard

Hewlett Packard (HP) recently completed a major upgrade to its main site with particular emphasis on beefing up its private business-to-business section. The section now offers a library of 4000 white papers and case studies, plus improved search navigation features and customized product information for individual accounts to help large customers find what they need quickly.

Stephanie Acker-Moy, HP's vice president of Internet and marketing services, explained: "We conducted extensive customer research to get feedback on the sites. Based on that feedback, we identified three key priorities: more robust and relevant content, better navigation and site design, and improved global capabilities", said Moy. Those areas became the focus of a six-month upgrade project. Moy said: "It all goes back to the war for the customer and our expectation that these site upgrades will drive stronger customer relationships. The payoff is customer loyalty."

Intertek ETL Semko

An expanded resource library was also a key component of the new website built from scratch this spring by Intertek's *ETL Semko* division, which tests and certifies electrical, HVAC, semiconductor, and building materials. This is part of the original Thomas Edison company with $120 million turnover. By expanding the site to 700 pages and boosting the search and navigation capabilities, the site has become an invaluable resource for engineers who need to know the certification requirements for new products under development, explained Mike Parker, manager of global Internet Marketing. He explained that the website was rebuilt on a modest consulting budget, supplemented by intensive effort from an in-house team involving 120 people for varying amounts of time. The three-month reconstruction featured a large increase in content to help product designers with certification requirements and a three-faceted search engine to help them find what they are looking for by keyword, category, and parametric look-up. Parker saw the website redevelopment as very important in maintaining their reputation and credibility to enhance their customer relationships. " We deal with an intellectually driven audience that needs to get its products in and out of testing as soon as possible," Parker said. "If we can demonstrate via our content that we have the expertise they need, we will get their business."

Source

Derringer, P., (2004), "Under The Hood: More Web Sites Valuing Good Content", *American Executive Magazine*, October 2004.

Questions

These are major investments by both companies in time and money to get an optimum website presence.

1 What did each company envisage as the core payback for this effort?

This case highlights the earlier arguments that competition in many industries now depends on generating clear intelligent content online.

2 What was the nature of the 'intelligent' content in the case of HP and Intertek?

3 How did each company anticipate that customers would interface with the additional content on the website?

4 In your opinion, how would these developments encourage loyalty?

Turcotte (2004) suggests that website development is less about flash effects than focusing on relevant content. He outlines the importance of identifying the content management tools used to streamline site construction, and allowing updates to be faster, cheaper and initiated directly by in-house staff closest to the formation. He also outlines the trend for websites to be more software-based, to allow for user identification and tracking. This is one example of the evolution in greater customer focus and more possibilities for client interactivity.

This ties in with developments in online customer management, e-CRM (as noted by Feinberg and Kadam, 2002) in the drive for websites to be more ROI accountable. Companies are paying close attention to the visitor-to-sales ratio. With measurable results in hand, companies are willing to spend money to improve their sites.

> ᏩᏋ INSIGHT: Building trust online with core clients:
>
> Schwartz Communications (US PR firm) on revamp of their website : "We wanted a showcase for our current 120 clients and the results we achieved for them ... It's a trophy case for us" (2005).

This is just one illustration of the new media influence on the way companies are modifying the market arena in which they hope to build relationships with their most valued customers. It is the drive to make websites scenes of further engagement, vehicles for realtime discussion with customers and arenas for customers or suppliers to meet.

Identifying Areas of Potential Personalization and Customization

Daniel (1999) predicted that by facilitating customer's comparisons of purchase alternatives, electronic networks such as the Internet would shift power from the supplier to the buyer via the value of customer information. Currently, in online services such as travel, the Internet is not only a service-delivery channel but also includes a high level of customer participation in the service delivery process, as noted by Chandler and Hyatt (2003). One critical element is the extensive nature of virtual customer participation and how this influences the scope of relationship development with providers. Defining the degree of customer input into the delivery of the product or service is a challenge for marketers – where can they customize efficiently?

Task 7.2

Visit Thorntons online (Thorntons.co.uk). Thorntons are manufacturers of hand-made chocolates and are visible at many UK and European airports.

- Looking at the range of products offered online, with which range of products can Thorntons customize efficiently?

- What level of personalization does Thorntons offer online?

- Identify the main customer groups for Thorntons. Looking at the menu option, Our Services, what main customer group is targeted?

- Can you suggest any additions to their site that would enable Thorntons to generate greater loyalty?

In services, the service provider might ask where service-development cycles online can be more streamlined. How can an online service designer judge the level of relationship to be developed with online customers? In online travel services it could specifically encompass the degree of interactivity envisaged with different customer groups. For instance, for adventure holidays, clients may want to see some of the adventure evidence before they select the holiday elements. This may involve increased graphics and photographs of past trips, simulation of activities through video links and the opportunity to hear from past customers through blogs. For individual families the online information and selection options of greatest interest might be facilities available at certain destinations (family-friendly services), the accommodation choices, the side options of children's activities, etc. Families will ideally want some leeway to choose within these areas – extremely attractive would be any menu, graphic features or additional links of the online website that give customers the chance to mix and match these together in an integrated holiday that the family can envisage beforehand. In future, authors (Jiang, 2000), predict that firms can engage in quite personally oriented, one-to-one marketing though Internet channels.

> INSIGHT: "The Internet is not only a service delivery channel but also includes a level of customer participation in the service delivery process. In the virtual environment, customers are, in effect, now managing their own marketspace" (Broderick, author).

Aldrich (1999) identified "additional" content as crucial to value added intelligent products. For travel services, this might involve looking creatively at the traditional three P's – People, Process; Physical evidence (online environment) – to incorporate more streamlined and interactive informational elements for keeping clients interested in the website. The People element might be the possibility of talking to service providers in real time, or having a time-delayed videolink with local third parties who can give specific, practical advice from the desired location itself, or interaction possibilities with other customers in that location. The Process elements may involve some level of customization that permits a customer to sign on where they left off from their last research through a Pin number. By previously registering choices and interests in certain of the activities or holiday features, they get updates via email on new deals or new activities available. The Physical Environment features are any tangible features (e.g. though text messages, online brochures, online destination photos, online blogs) that can make the prospective holiday more real to customers as they are selecting their holiday elements (an application of this is discussed in the mini-case, p. 169).

Acknowledging Increased Customer Role – Implications

When it comes to evaluation and customer retention in the virtual environment, it is no longer just the service provider behaviour and actions that are important. The customer's own participation and management of the service encounter are also critical elements in their evaluation of satisfaction. Peattie and Peters (1997) suggested that some customer manipulation occurs, in which the decision as to what will be seen or followed through is in the hands of the customer. Chandler and Hyatt, (2003) also highlight the importance of customer-centred service design. Specific management implications arise in:

- greater scope for client intervention in micro-service processes;
- degree of participation and self-determination that clients will have in the overall service experience.

One area where there are immediate implications is how the virtual environment mediates service perceptions. Once a service process is jointly produced online, shared understanding of the service process and recognizing different points of activation of the service setting become important. In looking at how customers perceive and relate to service organizations, we need to consider how customers perceive and relate to the medium, the virtual environment itself. An illustration of customer engagement with the online environment can be seen in online banking. In a recent study of online Internet banking, customer perceptions of service quality in the online environment were examined through participant observation online and offline (Broderick and Vachirapornpuk, 2002). What emerged was that the customer role in online banking can expand significantly as they engage with the service, and this influences how they view the service experience (see Figure 7.1).

Overall, the Customer Role Expansion Model in Figure 7.1 suggests that customer participation operates not just in starting the service experience in Internet banking, leading to interaction with the service setting and to engaging in various service encounters, but also frequently completes the process and acts as a filter to the service attitudes which have been formed. For instance, R_2 might be follow-up intervention to contact service providers via email. R_4 could be giving advice to other customers about how to complete a transaction.

Implications of expanded customer role for customer retention

Online customers are, to some extent, judging multidimensional elements – the website medium, the service product content, the organizational interface and their own capability. When problems occur, customer responses are frequently to intervene and be proactive. This parallels Kellog *et al.*'s (1997) argument that customers, when faced with an impending service failure may repeat information exchange or intervene. As they work harder at the service scripts and become more active in seeking a script that resolves their problem or answers their query, they may become more critical of the total service experience and feel less "related" to events and the service provider due to less interaction. Some of this evaluation is emergent and occurring in real time, reflecting their own sense of competence. This demonstrates a need for service providers to create more clarity in the service interface. This is not confined to Internet banking services but is also

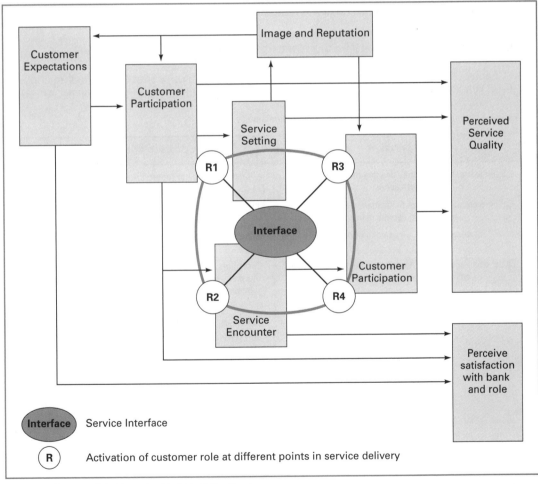

FIGURE 7.1 Customer Role Expansion Model in Online Services
Source: Broderick and Vachirapornpuk (2002).

applicable to management of other Internet offerings (see Table 7.1 below, where key implications of the potential gap between customer expectations and management thinking are apparent).

A better configuration of the service interface could be a real differentiating feature to permit better brand relationships to develop with banks. Devlin and Azhar (2004) identified that UK banks had poor brand uniqueness and limited service differentiation. Disclosures in the press (*Financial Times*, March 2007) about UK banks and their unjustified level of charges for unauthorized overdrafts has created a level of distrust of some of the main banks. The culture of UK banks now reflects a strong sales orientation, rather than customer orientation. Strong cross-selling strategies are being implemented. This is, arguably, a short-term strategy that may lead to medium-term customer disillusionment and encourage switching.

One area that remains unexploited in banking and in many other businesses with online capabilities is the potential for better relationship-building online. Service providers need to consider their service as a set of product/service elements that are part of a networked offering and *look at the integration effect of all online and offline activities* on product or service consumption. If online service encounters can successfully reinforce and link with traditional channels in a time-effective manner, they can be an important strategic source of value creation within customer relationships. Some of this relates to new sources of trust that are emerging for customers.

Evolving Cues for Trust and Sources for Trust

In Chapter 5 we have seen the importance of trust as a mediator of successful client relationships. What is the impact of new media for trust building with customers in services? At one

TABLE 7. 1 Implications for Managing Interfaces within Online Services

Company view	Customer view
Service organizations may imagine the Internet as a remote service	Customers do not regard the Internet as a remote service
There are opportunities to maintain a standardized approach in service delivery	Customers expect a lot of straightforward, honest and timely communication, strong interactivity
Systems are easy to use and understand	Customers will have different learning curves. Service script may be unclear
FAQs, email address online and the call centre deal well with customer follow up problems	Customers intervene but do not know who to contact if there are problems. They expect good interfacing with backstage activities and adequate support. This is usually not available through call centres
Dedicated online staff are the best approach. Keep it separate from offline	Customers want to know who and where to follow up if they have some further questions or clarification. They feel frustration when a bank staff in a high street branch is unable to do anything
	If really unhappy, customers switch
Necessary investments for better customer retention	

- Online education of customers about their Internet roles and the appropriate service script for dealing with problems
- Clear processes and adequate support for dealing with problems or extending transactions
- Configuring better interfaces (see centre of diagram) between backstage and frontstage activities; between online and offline
- Clear offline route for follow-up transactions

Source: Broderick, author.

level, we need to identify cues for trust. Client expectations of an effective business relationship can be relatively simple and some cues for trust remain transparently the same:

- A good company reputation and image
- Identifiable brand values
- The experience of competence and reliability
- Evidence of some service provider care
- A sense of reassurance when using the service

Other cues are perhaps less certain when using new media and we need to adapt to the influence of mobile and online interactions. They may include:

- Portability of value
- Potential for flexibility of use with other media
- Amenability of use to other service elements being supplied elsewhere (online or offline)
- Inbuilt guidance in the case of a high service learning curve for users
- Multiple or interchangeable user capability
- Guarantee of privacy
- Reputable security protection

These emergent cues for trust in the integration of online and offline elements of business across new media are less well known to marketers but are evolving around three nodes – mobility, flexibility and interactivity. As we argued in the Critical Focus section of this book, today's consumer is, above all, agile, versatile and willing to define and search for their own multimedia mix of service and product requirements. This means that more services may become search-based in nature, if customers avail themselves of the online capability.

At another level, we need to identify better the sources of trust. Consumer theorists (Evans, Jamal, Foxall, 2006; Solomon, 2007), suggest the importance of word of mouth, opinion leaders and reference groups as key influencers of our choices. This remains valid, but perhaps the question of where reference groups are located and how they influence us has evolved with new media technology. Word of mouth may be personal recommendation, but might also be viral or random chatter; opinion leaders may equally be an influential friend of long standing or a planted blogger on our favourite social network site; our reference group may be our work colleagues or a virtual chat community with similar shopping addictions as ourselves.

With the online environment evolving from being functionally sophisticated to becoming socially important to us, many consumers are now placing more trust in sources located through this medium. Customers rely on interlinked circles of trust and the sources may not be easy to uncoil for marketers. For younger consumers, these may mix strong personal sources such as college friends with widely available impersonal sources such as search-engine listings (see Figure 7.2).

For the new service consumer their first source of trust is themselves as savvy and confident consumers; the second might be their mobile sms messaging network (which might include family) or blog responses with selected friends on Bebo or Youtube; and their third source might be search listings on Google or Yahoo. Depending on the stage of decision-making, alternative sources at this level might be feedback and comment on e-Bay or Expedia or a similar kind of site; bite-sized data on Wikipedia; online product/service reviews; tips from celebrity-watching

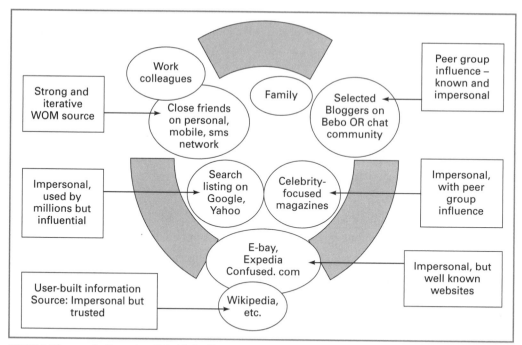

FIGURE 7.2 Sources for Trust – Interlinked Coil of Personal/Impersona Sources, developed by Broderick, author

media; best-buy indicators or guidance on sites such as confused.com; or search-result landing pages of recognized brand names. We need, as marketers to consider the blurring of personal and impersonal sources of influence and the multiple cues that exist in simultaneous online-offline modes for trust-building.

Task 7.3

Look at Figure 7.2 above.

1 Draw a diagram for yourself that identifies key sources you trust when making purchase decisions.

2 Look at the diagram you have drawn. Whose opinion do you value most when selecting the following services?

- A restaurant in which to take your partner or a friend
- Music concert to attend in summer
- Insurance for your car
- A retail store to visit when buying something to wear to an interview
- Planning a month long holiday in Canada

You may identify more than one source for each.

Cues that customers might use for increased trust in the online perception of products and brands are also critical in another key technological development in new media: the growth of Search Engine Marketing (SEM).

Search Engine Marketing and Relationship Development

One of the most critical technology-driven challenges to some of our implementation of relationship-development strategies is the growth in importance of search engines as the customer's first access point for gathering information and purchasing many products and services.

The emergence of search engines

We know that information-retrieval search engines existed long before the Internet. Electronic Card Catalogs, travel reservation systems and private search databases have existed a long time. Lee (2005) identifies that there were search engines running a variety of programmes and protocols before the Internet evolved to include Web browsers. After the browser was invented as a graphical way to displaying information, it became an interface for search. More recently professional search-engine development has created a powerful option for customers to use when gaining information, evaluating alternatives and actually purchasing products and services. Search engines are consulted and results used at each stage of the consumer buying process.

The power of these engines is in the search-engine traffic that it generates and this has led a number of forward-thinking practitioners and academics to look at SEM. Lee (2005) argues that search engine results generate some of the best sources of targeted customer traffic, whether that traffic originates from "organic" unpaid search listings or paid advertising listings. On the one hand, unpaid (otherwise known as organic) search-engine traffic has evolved significantly over the past ten years and on the other, paid listing is now a lucrative business.

Lee (2005) attributes this growth in paid search results advertising to

- search engines' need for alternative revenue sources;
- marketers' increasing requests for search results traffic;
- the high value of the traffic generated through search results.

INSIGHT: "With the hidden value in search listings, it is wise to extend your branding efforts through SEM campaigns" (Bruemmer, 2005).

Text link search results can now be purchased on all of the top 15 search sites as ranked by Media Metrix and NetRatings. Sectors where customer search activity is most prominent are IT, cars, shopping, travel services, pharmaceuticals and movies. Internet-linked communication sites are also searched extensively: Internet-facilitator sites such as Paypal; sites on which to advertise; broadcast media sites and personal blogs and websites. Most frequent search terms are shown in Table 7.2 below.

TABLE 7.2 Top 10 Search Terms by Category, Four Weeks Ending 26 August (%)

IT and Internet		Automotive Manufacturers	
Search Term	**Search Volume**	**Search Term**	**Search Volume**
Paypal	4.56	toyota	2.83
paypal.com	1.16	honda	2.47
people search	0.80	nissan	1.85
white pages	0.73	ford	1.70
Mapquest	0.70	dodge	1.15
www.paypal.com	0.56	suzuki	0.97
Ups	0.50	mazda	0.94
Experian	0.49	hyundai	0.93
pay pal	0.44	jeep	0.92
people finder	0.27	chevrolet	0.89
Movies		**Internet Advertising**	
Search Term	**Search Volume**	**Search Term**	**Search Volume**
imdb	1.09	free samples	0.56
netflix	1.00	free stuff	0.36
movies	0.73	work from home	0.34
blockbuster	0.57	work at home	0.25
fandango	0.37	free	0.24
snakes on a plane	0.29	unclaimed money	0.21
channing tatum	0.27	napster	0.20
harry potter	0.25	download music	0.19
movie times	0.24	adwords	0.16
netflix.com	0.23	www.smcorp.com	0.16
Food and Beverage Brands and Manufacturers		**Pharmaceutical and Medical Products**	
Search Term	**Search Volume**	**Search Term**	**Search Volume**
pizza hut	1.86	lexapro	0.89
starbucks	1.26	cymbalta	0.51
mcdonalds	1.13	viagra	0.49
candystand	0.91	depression	0.47
subway	0.69	herpes	0.41
drpepper.com	0.61	zoloft	0.39

dominos pizza	0.55	pfizer	0.39
candystand.com	0.52	cialis	0.34
burger king	0.50	merck	0.32
dominos	0.49	phentermine	0.32

Blogs and Personal Websites		**Broadcast Media**	
Search Term	**Search Volume**	**Search Term**	**Search Volume**
xanga	3.00	cnn	2.63
xanga.com	0.93	msnbc	1.25
myspace	0.84	cnn.com	1.10
www.xanga.com	0.60	fox news	0.87
yahoo 360	0.45	news	0.77
livejournal	0.39	bbc	0.67
myspace.com	0.37	bbc news	0.45
perez hilton	0.28	aljazeera	0.42
360	0.24	good morning america	0.33
yahoo360	0.24	al jazeera	0.31

Shopping Rewards and Directories		**Travel Destinations and Accommodations**	
Search Term	**Search Volume**	**Search Term**	**Search Volume**
consumer reports	0.26	hotels.com	0.68
mycokerewards.com	0.18	hotels	0.50
coupons	0.16	holiday inn	0.39
froogle	0.09	six flags	0.22
free stuff	0.09	motel 6	0.21
free samples	0.09	best western	0.21
pch.com	0.08	disneyland	0.21
webkinz	0.08	las vegas	0.20
mycokerewards	0.07	days inn	0.19
consumer report	0.06	cedar point	0.18

The top 10 search terms in IT and Internet: automotive; movies; Internet advertising; food and beverage; pharmaceuticals and medical; blogs and personal websites; broadcast media; shopping; and travel. Clickstream data are collected by Hitwise, ranked by volume of searches that successfully drove traffic to listed websites.

Characteristics of Search Engine Marketing

Search Engine Marketing is described as the act of marketing a website via search engines, whether this be improving the rank in the organic listings or purchasing paid listings or a combination of these and other search engine-related activities (Webmaster World Forums, September, 2006).

Lee's (2005) key argument is that marketers need to leverage power contained within this targeted traffic source, and learn to use both paid and organic SEM effectively. He sees its uniqueness as twofold – its non-intrusive nature and its ability to tap the searcher at the exact moment they are seeking knowledge or a solution.

INSIGHT: Lee (2005) identifies three key characteristics of SEM:
෯

- Search engine traffic is a non-intrusive method of Internet marketing.
- Search engine traffic originates from a voluntary, audience-driven search.
- Search engine traffic results from a fixed inventory of searches. To qualify as search engine traffic (or pure search traffic), the search must be one that the searcher initiated as a search, either by clicking a search link in a directory style portal or by filling out a search query box.

Lees' (2005) ideas are parallelled by Stephen Turcotte, president of Backbone Media. He argues (2004) that the increase in typical downloading speed has not only given designers the freedom to create more complex and imaginative sites, but also encouraged corporations to develop resource materials that may be helpful to prospects and customers. In this way, the initial stages in relationship building with customers can be enhanced by giving attention to the search listings and ensuring the result of the search (the landing page) is attractive.

Turcotte (2004) of Backbone Media sees search-engine optimization as one cost-effective way to boost ROI. He argues that marketing departments are realizing that that their first Web contact with a new prospect may be via Google or Yahoo; therefore, search engine optimization can offer a strong ROI, especially when it enables B2B companies with expensive products to reach key audiences.

MINI-CASE: ZOOM AND GO

Toronto-based *Zoom and Go* is a website that gets content from consumers, including hotel and resort reviews, images, and video clips that can be viewed online or downloaded to an iPod. Consumers are compensated for submissions in points that can be redeemed for cash, or a video, for example. They're encouraged to submit as often as they'd like. The idea is to provide a more authentic analysis of travel destinations around the world.

Customers seem to like the experience – since fully launching last year, the site has received over 10 000 videos and over 50 000 pictures. In 2006 it was getting about a million unique visitors per month, split fairly evenly between Canadians and Americans. According to the site's founder, Jonathan Haldane, it's one of the largest on the Internet.

Zoom and Go is also appealing to advertisers. Display advertising is available and access to such an active and engaged audience of travellers is of value. Another feature of the site is the space to set up a webpage. If you don't have a website of your own or are looking for a new distribution channel, for example, the company will build and host a site for you within its network for an annual fee.

Hotels and resorts can use this feature as a staging area for email campaigns by uploading their guest lists and deploying HTML messages that encourage past and recent guests to fill out an online review.

The microsites can generate additional email communication and CRM initiatives. Results can be comparable to a standard online or email media buy. Marketers are still communicating with their target audience; the difference is the conversation takes place after the initial transaction. With this approach marketers have the opportunity to retain customers.

Questions

1 What makes this site popular?

2 Why might users trust this site more than other sources?

By sending in their own ideas and clips and sharing others by downloading, customers are, to some extent, extending their holiday experience.

3 Is there another service where a customer content site would be popular with customers?

4 These sites are attractive to advertisers. Will such sites build loyalty?

Search Engine Marketing and relationship development

The relevance of search engine marketing for RM theory is that search engine traffic is a strong mediator of the opportunities customers have to be exposed to particular services, products, brands and to experience any relationship development. The website design (the site the customer lands on) can be seen, within the IMP model (Ford, 1990) discussed in Chapter 2 above, as an important mediator in any provider–client relationship, as it controls the environment in which the relationship might start. It is the meeting point.

The search engine is a gateway to *who* is being brought together as provider and client. If customers are at the information search stage of their decision-making, they may be gathering relevant data to give them potential alternatives from which to choose. However, clients are exposed to a limited number of potential suppliers of what they want by virtue of the search listings. The search engine also controls *how* provider and client are brought together – they meet in an intangible environment, where the selected webpage is the "surrogate" space – it shelters and holds the important elements that represent the company, its offer, its personnel and its customer profile to the client. On the listed and accessed webpage different parts of the site are respectively setting a good initial impression though the servicescape for consumption; encouraging interest, reciprocating customer advances, offering a comfortable space in which to deepen interest and ties, act finally as the point of consummation of the exchange. It needs to be welcoming, attractive, to demonstrate sought-after qualities, be able to communicate enough to secure further interaction and offer a measure of security for payment offered.

The challenge in search engine marketing is that, if our initial knowledge and exposure to a company is via the listing of their website, the biggest challenge may be to create effective technical and functional cues that encourage customers to go further. This places the emphasis on search engines as means of brand building.

Task 7.4

Undertake a search on Google, Overture or Yahoo. Decide on one search term. Use Google for one keyword search. Then use Yahoo or Overture for the same keyword search.

- Look carefully at the first two pages of listings you get on each search engine. Note the differences in ranking.

- Now, look at the sponsored links at the side of the page. Note the names of the these websites. Check to see how many appear for both search engines (on the first two pages).

  The differences that you have found depend on whether the algorithms used by each search engine are different.

- Read the following statement and circle what best describes your own approach to search engine listings.

When I get a listing:

	Always	Sometimes	Occasionally	Rarely	Never
I click on sponsored links at the side	5	4	3	2	1
I just click on the first 4 or 5 entries on the list	5	4	3	2	1
I click on most listings on the first page	5	4	3	2	1
I click on a few listings on the first three pages	5	4	3	2	1

- Now, ask nine of your classmates to read the statements and to circle what best describes their own approach. Note the patterns of responses.

If some classmates tick 5 for statement 4, what might this indicate about their approach to search engine information? If, on the other hand, some classmates tick 1 for statements 3 and 4, what might this indicate about their approach to using search engines?

For the above task, you can see that search engine perceptions and patterns of use may vary across different users. If so, in what way do customers view search engines? Are the search engines themselves a source of trust? If I search for information using Google and see a listing, do I experience more trust in those listed sites because they have been listed so strongly on Google?

In addition, are those businesses that are not apparent on the listing missing out on an implied sense of trust – if some advertisers on Google are regarded with a certain level of trust, due to their presence on the search engine?

Search engines – online brand building at early stages of relationship

In 2004 Interactive Advertising Bureau (IAB) and Nielsen/NetRatings conducted a study on "Internet Search Brand Effectiveness". The study looked at various branding attributes of search engine listings: unaided brand awareness, aided ad awareness, familiarity and brand image associations. Results indicated that search engine results listings were stronger than placed or tiled ads and were particularly effective when the brand holds a top position in the listings. Some

SEM is not just targeted traffic to your site for lead generation and online or offline conversions: it is equally a strong vehicle for brand awareness building, according to Bruemmer (2005).

> INSIGHT: "Better branding can be achieved when all ad elements encourage maximum awareness *GeV* upon click-through to the landing page" (Bruemmer, 2005).

A key conclusion is that companies might need to spend more time on the early stage of relationship building online – building the actual exposure and awareness of the company, services, products or brands. If the search engine listing is the introductory point in a company's relationship with customers, it places a lot of importance on search engine optimization as being essential in a firm's attempts to initiate relationships with customers.

Challenge in shorter client evaluation periods

The "getting to know" phase that emerged from search engine listings – history of company, range of products, evidence of past value, evidence of customer satisfaction and worth is condensed into a short evaluation period, a few clicks after which the customer may exit *or*, a preliminary level of interest may be encouraged and the customer visits later, *or* a swift purchase decision may be made. This relatively swift move from preliminary interest to conviction and potential purchase is critical to e-commerce sites. The visitors from a search results link have selected one listing from among many others. It is where this takes them in terms of further interaction that is quite uncertain. This is where the argument for optimization of search engines takes root.

E-commerce and customer retention – search engine optimization

The technology behind search engines mediates our experience of potential relationships with brands and companies. Consumers use search engines to research and buy products online. They read reviews and descriptions, analyse ratings, and research pricing as they compare products and vendors. A successful e-commerce site must offer a positive customer experience and build trust. To do this, search engine optimization (SEO) is important.

High rankings in the search engines are essential to the success of an e-commerce site, because high rankings make the products more visible and accessible to online shoppers. Downhill and Peggie (2006) of Elixir Systems see two primary methods for achieving high rankings in search engines. One is to optimize your website naturally, i.e. organically, so that search

Task 7.5

It is worth examining Table 7.1 above and looking at the search terms used by customers.

■ Consider what level of brand awareness it shows.

(Most sites are well-known facilitator sites – Napster, Paypal or very well-known brands (McDonalds, Pizza Hut, Honda, Toyota).

■ What does this indicate for marketers seeking to establish and deepen the brand relationships they have with customers?

engines rank it highly for your important terms on their search results pages. The second way to achieve high rankings is to buy Pay-Per-Click (PPC) ads that appear on search results pages.

The case of Silkflowers also examines this pattern (see Chapter Case below). This first highlights that natural optimization for an e-commerce site can have a profound impact on the performance of the website and profitability of the business.

In searching to optimize search engines the importance of expert advice is apparent – to successfully optimize an e-commerce site for search engines requires specialized techniques and processes. Online retailers and e-commerce site owners need to consider what success they are getting with PPC campaigns, and evaluate (or re-evaluate) possible gains from integrating organic search optimization. For e-commerce sites, as opposed to content-only sites, repeat custom and retention can only be evaluated by powerful tracking programmes that can then permit adjustments.

Search listings are a gateway to customer connection – in its many-to-many mode the listing permits serial introductions to customers that are frequent and random; and it creates challenges in terms of where, within this brief encounter with the provider the customer is prepared to place trust. Building on this virtual introduction requires new ways of utilizing virtual, mobile media. It demands closer cooperation and engagement with online customer groups, understanding the online cues that site visitors respond to and being well informed about the determinants of satisfaction with websites and other related media (as noted by Feinberg and Kadam, 2002). Only through more integration of RM activities with new media capabilities can long term customer retention and loyalty evolve.

Chapter Summary

In this chapter, we explored how new media developments are influencing relationship development significantly; particularly in the online environment. It highlighted the need to adapt to information-based competition and incorporate intelligent processes when seeking to develop online relationships. The importance of recognizing the expansion of and the emergence of the customer as co-designer and initiator of relationships was explored. Taking some of the specific developments in the virtual environment, it explored how more dynamic websites are emerging which can show greater commitment to varying customer needs. Finally, it examined in detail the implications of search-engine technology: how it is currently influencing the early stages of relationship development and the future challenge for customer retention. Where the impact of new media has evolved even further is in the growth of customer-generated media (CGM): blogs, wikis, forums, chat communities – and the emergence of social networks. Both of these will be considered in the next chapter.

Review Questions

1 What challenges does information-based competition generate for online publishers?

2 In what ways are the levels of customer participation and customer control growing in online products and services? What is the potential impact of this on relationship building with customers online?

3 In what ways can SEM improve brand awareness and brand reputation for small hotels? How would effective SEM support relationship development?

Further Reading

Surjadjaja, H., S. Ghosh and J. Antony (2003) "Determining and Assessing the Determinants of E-service Operations", *Managing Service Quality*, vol. 13, no. 1, pp. 39–53.

Tapscott D. and A. Williams (2006) *Wikinomics: How Mass Collaboration Changes Everything*, London: Portfolio. (Buzzword bingo comes to mind . . . 'peer pioneers', 'ideagoras', 'the prosumers'!)

For some further explanation of Search Engine Marketing:
http://www.webmasterworld.com/glossary

For commentary, see online sources such as ClickZ, SitePoint and ISEDB.

END OF CHAPTER CASE AND KEY QUESTIONS

Silkflowers.com

When Silkflowers went live with a new search engine listing, it was listed in one of the top ten search listing positions within weeks, after keying in a chosen keyword. After just three months the company had recorded more than 175 top 10 positions for their keywords. That number grew to 220 by the first quarter of 2006. "This campaign was a great success since we were a new site and started with no positioning on these search engine results pages," says Chris Corelli.

After six months the growth in positions had reached a plateau – a point where many website owners and designers scratch their heads and begin a potentially dangerous process of tinkering with a successful site and strategy. "What many online marketers fail to recognize is the dynamic nature of search engines and their indexing protocols," notes Oneupweb CEO Lisa Wehr. "And with the addition of thousands of new sites daily, the Internet is itself in a state of constant change. It takes an experienced eye to see the trends and know what adjustments need to be made to stay ahead of the curve."

Working with Silkflowers.com's creative team, Oneupweb has helped them implement some minimal design and copy changes that have shown some big results, leading to continuing growth of the company's search engine positions. "We look at this as 'a natural progression," notes Wehr. "Grow, learn and grow some more. It's working for Silkflowers.com and many of our natural search clients."

Integrating paid advertising pays off

Early in the planning process Oneupweb and Silkflowers.com developed an online marketing strategy integrating organic search and PPC advertising to build traffic and create conversions leading to steadily increasing sales. Silkflowers.com has seen steady month-after-month growth in conversion rates leading to greater net revenues. Each new ad is tested, measured for performance and, where necessary, revised for maximum impact. During the first quarter of 2006 the number of clicks on the Silkflowers.com ads increased 18 per cent over the previous quarter, raising the overall click-through rate (CTR) from 4.9 to 6.86 per cent. The result: a growth in revenues of 13.6 per cent over the preceding three months.

Tracking success

Key to the ongoing performance of Silkflowers.com is their ability to measure and adjust performance. Silkflowers.com was able to track, by the hour if necessary, the way each PPC ad was performing in every medium in which it appeared.

Chris Corelli: "We use a marketing analytics tool; this allows us to clearly identify what is working and what is not in the online marketplace. It provides us with statistics, reports and graphics on our pay-per-click ads by keyword and competitive comparison."

By any measure, the programme has been a success, according to Chris, "The time to market was a big benefit, since we had no previous online presence. And thanks to the tracking of ROI, we can base our planning and adjustments on good information."

Questions

1 What planning has led, in this case, to the successful expansion of the customer base?

2 Why is a good positioning important on these search listings? How has good positioning been achieved by Silkflowers on the search engines?

3 Are there any likely future challenges for Silkflowers in terms of developing relationships with customers further?

4 Does SEM pose any challenges for relationship development with customer groups over time?

References

Aldrich, D. (1999) *Mastering the Digital Marketplace*, Chichester, England: John Wiley and Sons.

Broderick, A. (2003) "The New Marketspace: Key Implications for Classifying Service Encounter Online", *Conference of American Marketing Association SERVSIG* (Services Marketing Speed Interest Group), Reims Management School, Reims, 12–14 June, 2003.

Broderick, A. and S. Vachirapornpuk (2002) "Service Quality in Internet Banking: The Importance of Customer Role", Market Intelligence and Planning, vol. 20, no. 6, pp. 327–335.

Bruemmer, P. (2005) "Branding with Search Marketing", SEMPO website.

Chaffey, D., R. Mayer, K. Johnston and F. Ellis-Chadwick (2003) *Internet Marketing: Strategy, Implementation and Practice*, 2nd edn, Harlow: Financial Times Prentice Hall.

Chandler, K. and M. Hyatt (2003) *Customer-centered Design: A New Approach to Web Usability*, Harlow: Prentice Hall.

Daniel, E. (1999) "Provision of Electronic Banking in the UK and Ireland", International Journal of Bank Marketing, vol. 17, no. 5, pp. 211–232.

Derringer, P. (2004) "Under The Hood: More Web Sites Valuing Good Content", *American Executive Magazine*, October.

Devlin, J. and S. Azhar (2004) "Life Would be a Lot Easier if We Were a Kit-Kat, Practitioner Views on the Challenges of Branding Financial Service Brands Effectively", *Brand Management*, vol. 12, no. 1, pp. 12–31.

Downhill, F. and J. Peggie (2006) "Online Reputation Management", SEMPO site, April.

Dutta, S. and A. Segev (1999) "Business Transformation on the Internet", *European Journal*, vol. 17, no. 5, pp. 466–476

Evans, M., A. Jamal and G. Foxall (2006) *Consumer Behaviour*, Chichester: Wiley.

Feinberg, R. and R. Kadam (2002) "E-CRM Web Service Attributes and Determinants of Customer Satisfaction with Retail Web Sites", *International Journal of Service Industry Management*, vol. 13, no. 5, pp. 432–51.

Ford, D. (1990) "Introduction: IMP and the Interaction Approach", in D. Ford (ed.), *Understanding Business Markets: Interaction, Relationships and Networks*, London: Academic Press.

Gamet, V. (1996) "Twisting Servicescape: Diversion of the Physical Environment in a Re-Appropriation Process", *International Journal of Service Industry Management*, vol. 8, no. 1, pp. 26–41.

Jayawardhena, C. and P. Foley (2000) "Changes in Banking Sector – The Case of Internet Banking in the UK", *Internet Research: Electronic Networking Applications and Policy*, vol. 10, no. 1, pp. 19–30.

Jiang, P. (2000) "Segment-based Mass Customizations: An Exploration of a New Conceptual Marketing Framework", *Internet Research: Electronic Networking Applications and Policy*, vol. 10, no. 3, pp. 215–226.

Kellog, D., W. Youngdahl and D. Bowen (1997) "On the Relationship Between Customers Participation and Satisfaction: Two Frameworks", *International Journal of Service Industry Management*, vol. 8, pp. 206–219.

Lee, K. (2005) "Introduction to Search Engine Marketing", through SEMPO website, September.

Leverick, F. *et al.* (1997) "The role of IT in shaping of marketing", *Journal of Marketing Practice*, vol. 3, no. 2, pp. 87–106.

Peattie, K. and L. Peters (1997) "The Marketing Mix in the Third Age of Computing", *Marketing Intelligence and Planning*, vol. 15, no. 3, pp. 142–150.

Rayport, J.F. and J.J. Sviokla (1994) "Managing in the Marketspace", *Harvard Business Review*, vol. 37, no. 3, pp. 60–77.

Shih, C. (1998) "Conceptualizing Consumer Experiences in Cyberspace", *European Journal of Marketing*, vol. 32, no. 7/8, pp. 655–663.

Solomon, M. (2007) *Consumer Behaviour, Buying, Having and Being*, 7th edn, New Jersey: Pearson Prentice-Hall.

Sterne, J. (1999) *World Wide Web Marketing*, New York: John Wiley and Sons Inc.

Turcotte, S. (2004) cited in P. Derringer "Under the Hood: More Web Sites Valuing Good Content", *American Executive Magazine*, April.

Vandermerwe, S. (1997) "Increasing Returns: Competing for Customers in the Global Market", *Journal of World Business*, Winter, pp. 333–350.

Wang, F., M. Head and N. Archer (2000) "A Relationship-building Model for Web Retail Marketplace", *Internet Research: Electronic Networking Applications and Policy*, vol. 10, no. 5, pp. 374–384.

Weiber, R. and T. Kollmann (1998) "Competitive Advantages in Virtual Markets Perspectives of 'Information Based Marketing' in Cyberspace", *European Journal of Marketing*, vol. 32, nos 7/8, pp. 603–615.

Customer-generated Media, Social Networks and Relationship Development

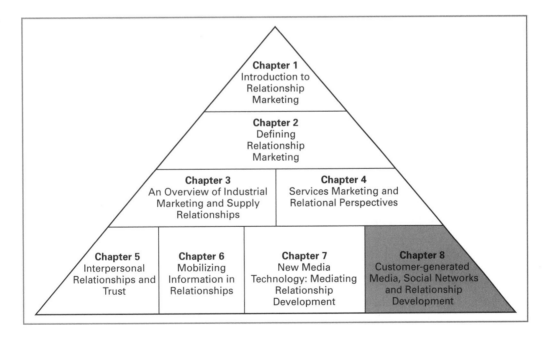

❖ LEARNING OBJECTIVES

At the end of this chapter, you should be able to:

1 **understand** the emergence of increased customer control in current online marketplace

2 **explore** self-customization and how it might influence online relationships

3 **appreciate** the growth of customer-generated media and how marketers view it

4 **identify** the value of online brand communities as a means to develop brand loyalty

Chapter Contents

Introduction

The last chapter has examined selective elements of new media technology and identified the way that they are affecting customer relationships:

- Increased opportunities for intelligent customer interactivity

- An expanded customer role in consumption that affects their evaluation

- An adaptation in the sources of trust for customers prior to, during and after purchase

- An increased importance of initial cues evident in search engine listings

When examining RM in new media environments, it is also important to consider two underlying developments. First, customer participation and control of their consumption patterns is increasing. To understand the real impact of these changes it is necessary to understand the level of customization and interactivity that impact on relationship development. As a result of consumers' ability to research and design product and service combinations, many consumers no longer see themselves wholly as customers, but as "co-producers" of the service.

At the same time, there is a need to embrace some of the social developments that virtual and mobile technologies are bringing. The growth of customer-generated media and how this is encapsulated in the current burgeoning of social networks at global level (blogs, chat rooms) is now a major preoccupation for marketers seeking to develop loyalty with key customer groups. Results are, as yet, inconclusive.

Particular focus in this chapter is on how customers are engaging with other customers and contributing to development through the virtual medium. Brand web communities are examined as examples of how new forms of social organization are emerging in the virtual marketspace and how social interaction within communities may pose a serious threat if negatively oriented or alternatively may foster increased customer loyalty.

> INSIGHT: Blogs – "For individual brands, this is an online phenomenon that still plays by offline rules. People will only gather round and get engaged with a brand if they have good reason to love it and appreciate it. You have to earn the right to have people want to treat you as a badge brand and flag their affiliation with you publicly ..." Cindy Gallop (2006 former chairman of Bartle Bogle Hegarty.

New Communication Possibilities Online

One of the most important dimensions of the digital marketspace is the conception of the customer as becoming the central source of communication. Hoffman and Novak (1996) proposed a new model for hypermedia, computer-mediated environments, based on a many-to-many communication model as operative in virtual environments, where the possibilities of communicating to multiple audiences with one keystroke creates powerful communication nodes. Kiani (1998) sees mutual communication as the key, identifying four kinds of mutual interaction that take place in online marketing.

- Company to consumer
- Consumer to company
- Consumer to consumer
- Company to company

Of the four modes of communication above, the real growth in communication in terms of new media is in customer to company and in customer to customer communications.

Customer to customer

Marketing academics and practitioners are actively seeking to be involved in and to influence customer-generated media (CGM). The implications for product and service relationships arise in the emergence of social networks online. This is covered in a later section (see p. 185).

Task 8.1

Note ten sites of customer to customer communications that you are familiar with online.

- Draw a map of the four kinds of mutual communication that exist online for Cisco, their suppliers and customers. Identify some likely content of the communication. You may wish to visit the website <Cisco.com>.

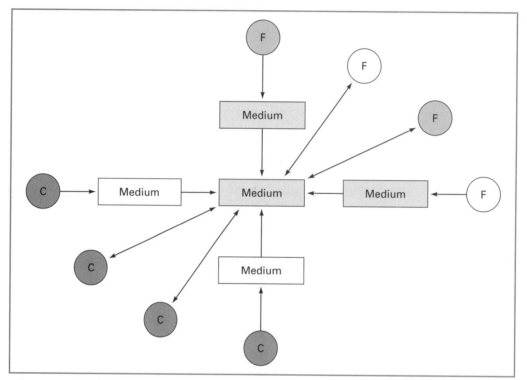

FIGURE 8.1 Hypermedia Computer-mediated Environment Communication Model
Source: Hoffman and Novak (1996).

Customer to company

First, looking at the customer–company interactions, we noted in Chapter 7 that this linked to the level of customer participation in the online processes made available to them. In new media, the relationship to the medium is also a critical one. The customer interaction with the medium itself is multidimensional. Browsing the Net was seen to create a level of concentration or "flow" – a state that engaged the customer fully. Hoffman and Novak, (1996), drawing on Csikszentlmihalyi (1990), suggest that flow occurs when a motivated consumer perceives a balance between their skills and the challenges of their interaction with the computer-mediated environment. Flow, they argue, is crucial to online consumer relationship with firms and products.

Earlier studies of banking services (Jayawardhena and Foley, 2000), identified the importance of the website menu options, the navigation, the icons, all the tangible elements of the site as mediators of further customer engagement with the firm. The same strategic impetus is put forward by Chaston (2001). More recent thinking, however, has identified that customer interaction within the virtual environment is complex – and is increasingly motivated towards social rather than merely economic or functional goals.

Customer-centric Services

There is now a recognition that customers have more opportunities to self-select and self-determine aspects of their consumption online. This links to ideas on customer participation covered in Chapter 7 and the services-dominant paradigm thinking, recently proposed by Vargo and Lusch (2004). Customer-centric services have emerged and this is changing the way in which customer relationships with firms are maintained, as originally argued by Mols (2000). This greater customer management of communication affects not just the initiation of contact with firms and the scope, depth or duration of the relationship that develops, it also changes the nature of relationship development. As can be seen in Figure 8.2, the customer has control over their level of engagement and can effectively determine the level of interaction they seek.

From Transactional Offerings to Co-development in Services

We saw in Chapter 7 that technological developments have encouraged greater strategic awareness of information-driven structure(s). Nonetheless, online products and services vary in the degree to which the scope of service delivery, as experienced by the customer, moves from being transactional, to being integrated and transformational, i.e. that there is co-development of products with clients. This is already occurring in business-to-business buyer exchanges and reverse marketing linkages. However, not all products and services require transformative levels of interactivity:

- Some customer groups may never require more than a transactional interaction mode with automatic execution of service processes.
- In other service environments, greater levels of self-customization are encouraged through the online possibilities.
- In products/services where strong brand relationships emerge, the virtual space actively fosters customers as co-creators of the brand (product and service).

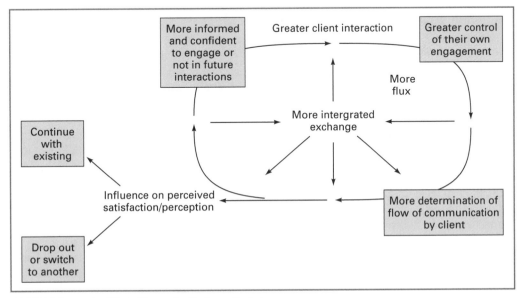

FIGURE 8.2 Cumulative Effect of Increasing Customer Control
Source: developed by A. Broderick.

MINI-CASE: REAL.COM (1)

A very good example of this is the entertainment site, Real.Com. On that site, the critical factors are the user interface, the availability of demos and the online community. Factors such as easy downloading, clear navigation, error-free access, and availability of different languages are important to encourage initial use, but regular, pop-up advertisements can detract from the experience for some users. Demos promote products, but also smooth the way for customers evaluating the products. With regard to entertainment product demos, most of them only provide limited available time. However, in order to evaluate demos carefully and make a right decision in the decision-making process, customers expect longer demo time than the limited time allocated. Some users will try to get to the developer's site to try it. For a customer using the site regularly, the pop-up ads and the limited demo time may lead to switching to another site. On the other hand, if the customer enjoys the online community, their level of engagement with that community may be the motivation for feeling loyal to the site. It is the customer's own participation which determines their feelings of loyalty or commitment.

Questions

Visit Real.com and browse the website.

1 **Looking at three kinds of communication noted above: (customer to customer; customer to company; and company to customer), which kind of communication has most influence on a new user? Which is most important for a regular user?**

2 **What other factors might encourage a user to switch to another site?**

3 **Can you identify a similar online product/service, where it is your choice to become more involved or not?**

Sequence dependency and the Sand Cone Model

A useful framework to illustrate the areas where the customer may experience varying levels of participation or different input possibilities emerges from the Sand Cone model, first proposed by Ferdows and De Mayer (1990). They suggested that there was a sequence dependency in the developments of manufacturing. They proposed that without setting the foundations of service quality, i.e. reliability, no other aspects of service quality can be successful. More recently, Voss (2003) adapted this idea and suggested a sequence dependency in e-services.

As Figure 8.3 illustrates, there are three levels in the service – foundation, customer centred and value added. Unless the lower level qualifiers meet customer needs, other capabilities or features will not be effective. The foundation level mainly depends on three factors: website responsiveness and ease of navigation, website effectiveness and the fulfilment of basic expectations. The first level determines "what is expected" at the minimum level; if it is inadequate, the customer tends to leave and go for other alternatives. At the second level are the differentiating elements of trust, information and status, configuration and customization that determine the customer-centred level of e-service. The final stage is adding value through the e-service design, the service experience. To excite customers and encourage commitment, websites need to surprise the customer with elements of the experience. In online dating, recent studies have identified the virtual dating space as offering a fantasy world, an arena for developing other selves (Hardey, 2002). On the other hand, online dating has been interpreted as commodifying the mating process and reducing the choice of partner to a marketplace exchange (Bauman, 2003).

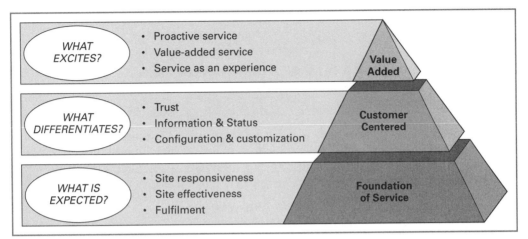

FIGURE 8.3 Sand Cone Model and Sequence Dependency in E-Service
Source: Voss (2003).

Transactional Interaction mode – limited relationship

As discussed in Chapter 7, many online booksellers, music sellers and aggregator reservation sites such as Opodo.com offer a comparatively process-limited online service. It is relatively simple in transaction possibilities and in outcomes. Satisfaction and added value emerge in small changes in micro-processes. Amazon.com has built a reputation for remembering your reading interests and informing you about books you may have expressed interest in before. It offers online customer evaluations of books. Each of these elements create added value but do not require significant creative input from you, as customer. The processes can generate trust and loyalty, if not a strong emotional bond.

Self-customization and Relationship Development

Pine and Gilmore (1999) identified that different levels of customization can be achieved on a relatively large scale through mass customization (see Figure 8.4). Some online products and services will have a standard product/set of products (as in IKEA) where there is no change to the product range, but there is self-selection. Such a product lends itself to adaptive customization. Other products can offer more potential for change and for collaborative customization, such as corporate-event planning online.

An increased capacity for self-customization by customers clearly fulfils level two of the Voss (2003) framework – that service is customer centred and, in some services, it also matches level three, the area of service as a proactive experience.

A useful example of this adaptive customization, which allows consumers to customize their own product through standard format, is illustrated through Expedia's range of flights, accommodation and car hire, which the consumer can select as appropriate. This self-service approach to customization is delivered by customer experimentation with numerous possibilities. Travel services are experience-based services and were traditionally dependent on strong face-to-face interaction and personalized attention in a travel agent office as a means to generate loyalty with clients. How can an experience-based service generate the same level of satisfaction and loyalty online? What is the customer response to this particular form of customization and how does it

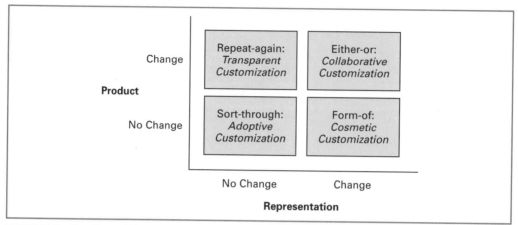

FIGURE 8.4 The Four Faces of Mass Customization
Source: Pine and Gilmore (1999).

affect relationships with service providers? In a recent study of UK customers (Barritt and Broderick, 2006) some interesting attitudes emerged. Individuals are now seeking a travel experience which is individual – preferred destinations for respondents in this study tend to be more exotic than in previous years with many enjoying holidays to Borneo, South Africa and the Philippines as opposed to the more accessible European countries. Additionally, individuals are choosing not to remain in one location for the duration of their vacation, but are instead visiting several different areas of a country, or even extending their holiday to another country. It is no longer simply the destination that creates a holiday, it is the entire atmosphere that surrounds the individual which forms the experience. Clients now seek more individuality and choice with their holidays. Early stages of participation involved in the preparation and creation of a holiday are key factors for customers. Illustrated in Figure 8.5 below is a diagram displaying the range of information that consumers now seek prior to booking their holiday (based on research, Baritt and Broderick, 2006) .

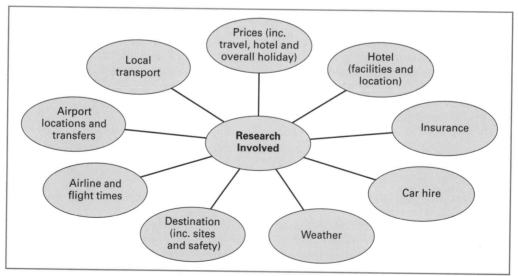

FIGURE 8.5 Customized Travel Information Search Online

The level of customer participation involved in the creation of a customized holiday online is high and includes customer research and design. Through availability of self-service options through Expedia.com the customer research phase is an important and lengthy part of the service consumption. The Chapter case (see pp. 194–5) highlights the experiences of some customers when researching their holiday. Results show an interesting set of interpretations by customers of their own contribution to their holiday.

Social Process of Content Sharing and Relationship Elements

Within digital marketing possibilities, sociologists (Slevin, 2000) and other commentators predicted change in the way in which individuals within new media are interpreting and responding to the social world. Sites such as MySpace, Facebook, YouTube and Bebo in the UK and Hyves in the Netherlands are now well-known social network sites and seem to validate Slevin's view. Thanks to the accessibility of the Internet, many of these social network sites are attracting significant international audiences.

Online social networks are similar to offline member groups. The purpose of a social network is to bring together a group of individuals with something in common. They perhaps went to the same university, have the same hobby, are obsessed about Harley-Davidson, work in the same industry, or simply want to make some friends. Whatever this common thread is, members can create a collective sense of identity within the community. Collective memories centre on shared experiences network members have with one another. This is achieved through collaborative discussions and exchanges of information online, through sms, in blogs, etc.

For marketers, social networks offer a ready-made segmentation for targeting, since they are based on shared interests and thus offer already segmented groups with identifiable interests and behaviours. These represent significant opportunities for behavioural targeting and they are viewed as good advertising opportunities, given potential access to blogs and *message boards*. For many brands the potential link to social networks can be important to future brand strength; but there is still a wariness towards it.

> INSIGHT: eMarketer Senior Analyst Debra Aho Williamson: "The challenge for marketers developing their own networks will be to entice consumers to participate. Some brands may have more success than others." (2006)

From a relationship perspective, the challenge is to become knowledgeable about these new modes of social interaction and to explore how the content generated by users may be enabling or hindering the development of strong brand relationships (as originally noted by Wang *et al.*, 2000).

Customer-generated Media (Blogs, Podcasts, Forums, Chat Rooms)

One of the most significant areas of current and future challenge for RM is the emergence of CGM. There has been a CGM explosion that includes social media, user-generated content at many levels, citizen journalism, regular writing to blogs, forums and chat communities.

At present, blogs are the most obvious development in CGM. Based on data from Technorati, (2004), almost half a million blogs were identified in June 2003. By the end of 2004, this had risen to 10 million (McGann, 2004). Today, some estimates are suggesting that 50 million blogs exist, although many are not live. Calcanis (2005) found only 200 blogs with monthly traffic of 1 million pageviews per month. In terms of viewership, Pew Internet & American Life Project have estimated that about 11 per cent (approximately 50 million) of Internet users are regular blog readers. The demographic profile of bloggers is not clear, but one estimate suggests that most bloggers are under 30 (see Figure 8.6 below).

> INSIGHT: There are millions of blogs, but I would say that less than 1 million are updated regularly (Calcanis, 2005).

While advertisers are keen to get involved with social networks through being involved in blogging, not all blogs are positive for relationship development . Companies can sometimes find that a negative campaign has been waged against their reputation online by a disgruntled employee or customer. If a negative blog establishes itself high in a search list it can be detrimental to a company's reputation and cause aggravation. Due to the high rate of click, the information or message spreads quickly and the damage gathers pace. Customers do not really distinguish good PR from malicious PR and a hostile message in a search engine can damage a reputation very quickly, sometimes before companies are aware of it.

Downhill and Peggie (2006) advise that companies get to know what is being said about them. They suggest the need to check information actively in the public domain, to monitor blogs and manage the search engine listing carefully. A three-step strategy of Analyse, Monitor and Influence is suggested by Downhill and Peggie (2006) to keep the company's reputation clear. In addition to being hard to measure and control, blog traffic is also asymmetrical – it spikes sharply when certain popular stories are circulated.

A related development to blogs are podcasts. Citing a study by Nielsen/NetRatings, Newcomb (2006) noted that more people in the US had downloaded a podcast than have published a blog or engaged in online dating. The study of 30 000 Internet users in the US found that 6.6 per cent of the US adult online population, or 9.2 million Web users, had downloaded an audio podcast in the previous 30 days (July 2006). In contrast, a Forrester Research report

Blog Demographics		
Age range	**Blogs Created by Age**	**Percentage**
10–12	55,500	1.3%
13–19	2,120,000	51.5%
20–29	1,630,000	39.6%
30–39	241,000	5.8%
40–49	41,700	1.0%
50–59	18,500	0.4%
60–69	13,900	0.3%
Total	4,120,000	100%

FIGURE 8.6 Demographic Profile of Bloggers
Source: Perseus Development Corporation (2005)

MINI-CASE: SMALL WORLD LABS

Not all blogs are large scale. One firm enabling a niche approach to blog development is Small World Labs (SWL). The company has created entire social networking interfaces for professional and interest-based communities like ClassicalLounge.com, a community for classical musicians, and Sacramento-based PBS affiliate KVIE – not only to help them connect with their community, but also use the space to push their own brand. SWL has picked up 15 clients in just under two years since its official launch.

"We tailor the content, look, and feel [of] each customer's site, giving them a fully branded offering", explained SWL CEO and Founder Michael Wilson. "This is the main difference between using SWL and MySpace, LinkedIn, or Yahoo Groups to connect together your constituents. With SWL you control the social or professional network, you control the look and feel, you control the structure of interactions, and most importantly, you get the credit for offering this important service to your constituents."

The Austin, Texas-based company offers a range of features commonly associated with social networking, including a rich text editor to add text or html to blogs, photo albums, RSS news feeds, and Evite-like functionality. For community owners the platform can monitor ad placements and analytics, while enabling interactions with site members.

"Branded social networks offer marketers an excellent opportunity to test social networking without worrying about whether their ad will appear next to unsavory content – which has happened on larger networks such as MySpace."

Once a critical mass of site visitors has been reached, advertising can be highly targeted. As Wilson put it, "Having rich user profiles gives [KVIE] much more detailed demographic, behavioral, and interest information about their users which is valuable to their advertisers, driving more advertising revenue."

Marketers are trying to keep a closer watch on the content associated with their campaigns. One way to do that is by targeting smaller, home-grown communities.

Questions

1 Find out the difference between a branded social network and a natural social network.

2 What are the potential difficulties in managing a branded blog over time (with ongoing customer input)?

(April 2006), based on a survey of 5051 online users in North America, found that only 3 per cent of users had ever downloaded a podcast, and only 1 per cent did so regularly.

By comparison, Nielsen/NetRatings' data shows that 4.8 per cent of the US adult online population publish blogs. These activities are low compared with the main Internet activities – online job hunting, at 24.6 per cent, and paying bills online, at 51.6 per cent and 3.9 per cent engage in online dating.

Podcast listeners tend to be younger, with Web users between the ages of 18 and 24 nearly twice as likely as the average Web user to download audio podcasts. This makes podcasts, in some practitioners' eyes, a real future opportunity for targeted messages to specific customer groups that can build interest and loyalty.

INSIGHT: "The portability of podcasts makes them especially appealing to young, on-the-go audiences", Michael Lanz, an analyst with Nielsen/NetRatings, said in a statement: "We can expect to see podcasting become increasingly popular as portable content media players proliferate" (Lanz, 2006).

The value of customer chat to marketers

Customer chatting, whether embraced through text or video, is growing. In association with this, there has been a growth in advertising which links to customer chatter in chat rooms and bulletin boards. Basically advertisers are piggybacking on consumer talk. For marketers, advertising on CGM sites builds on consumer conversation and creates a positive link to target groups.

According to Blackshaw (2006), customer to customer conversation is more trusted, and more engaging than other content against which advertising might be placed or integrated. It can include brands creating blogs or sponsoring communities, and some companies are seeking to integrate advertising with CGM. This kind of advertising is evident in buttons, banners, and sponsorships in social media sites and ads on Technorati in blog search results. The potential for advertising on social network sites is a driver behind the $900 million deal between Google and MySpace. Google sees a huge potential for placed ads on the MySpace network.

As ads seek to penetrate social networks, questions are raised by customers about marketer-sponsored content and this raises some ethical issues. It is quite a cheap method of securing a presence with a target audience and is not always transparent. A question arises as to the openness of customers to advertising within their social network and whether it is always appropriate to openly seek to influence consumption decisions of members in a social, relaxed environment.

The issue of original content of the network is also central – content providers want to ensure that their own CGM or user-generated content areas are not viewed as less real or authentic. An interesting example of CGM being adopted by marketers is the CGM-linked promotions by Hewlett Packard, discussed below in the mini-case.

CGM and non-profit environments

CGM is sometimes a very valuable tool in non-profit environments as a means to develop interest and commitment towards an event or cause and as a means to promote events and to secure support for key events. A very good example of this is the Race for Life campaign in the UK which runs each Summer and is supported by hundreds of thousands of women nationally. Some very encouraging, supportive material is posted each year and this serves to create ongoing loyalty from year to year. A sense of community emerges from postings, as does a sense of solidarity and conviction about the cause (see Case 7 – Race for Life in Contexts). It is a very good forum for relationship development and commitment to the Race for Life brand across organizers and participants. To a lesser extent, the CGM offers some valuable exposure for the sponsor.

Social network communications and brand relationship development

How effective is communication in social networks in terms of relationship development? The future of many products and services is linked to customer engagement with the brand or the

MINI-CASE: HEWLETT PACKARD – DEVELOPMENT OF CGM

Hewlett Packard (HP) has added new rich media and CGM elements to its "The Computer is Personal Again" campaign. HP began its global campaign in May 2006 with TV, print and Web, with new components set to roll out later. HP's agency Goodby, Silverstein & Partners, handled most of the work.

Web ads display visuals of laptop computers and silhouette cut-outs of hands with messages on them. The mostly rich media executions will appear on Real Guide, Rhapsody, UGO, MySpace, RollingStone.com, Facebook, YouTube, MTV.com, E Online and sites in Blue Lithium's network. ZenithOptimedia handled media for all channels in the campaign.

"We are adding a series of unique and interesting ad units that are more integrated than what we've done before", said HP Worldwide Director of Consumer Advertising, Tracey Trachta.

The buy also includes homepage takeovers, including one on Yahoo scheduled for August 7 and 8. That particular creative will appear to suck all the content off the page, similar to a placement that ran last summer. "It shows you just how much entertainment you can get with the notebook, and connects back to the HP site for information and [the ability to] purchase", said Trachta.

A viral component dubbed "Lights. Camera. You." was recently added to the online campaign. Users can go to the microsite, upload a personal photo and create a commercial starring themselves. Personiva provides the facial animation technology. People then specify their interests from a list that includes sharing photos, listening to music, traveling, IM and gaming. The end product is a personalized spot featuring the visitor's visage. Once a video is created, users can post it to their blogs or email it to a friend.

Once word got out, a significant number of people were using it. "We are seeing phenomenal activity on the Web site", said Yogesh Sharma, co-founder and CEO of Personiva. "The kind of sharing we're seeing is above industry standard, and people are having fun with it."

The CGM spots echo HP's broadcast commercials featuring celebrities like Jay-Z, Olympic snowboarder Shaun White, Mark Burnett and Mark Cuban.

Some assets also appear in the open and close segments on MTV's Web-based show "Meet or Delete," a reality show where people choose dates, band mates and roommates based only on the content of a person's hard drive.

Source

E. Burns (2006) "HP adds CGM to 'Personal' Campaign", www.clickz.com, 14 July 2006.

Questions

1 For HP, what is the value of advertising on CGM media site?

2 In what way do companies hope to influence users of CGM sites?

3 Why was the viral component with potential personalized video added?

4 The CGM spots in this case are echoes of broadcast commercials – why would the company use consistent spots?

Follow-up task

Visit hp.com/personal and see some of the approaches being taken.

firm's reputation. What has been most influential on brand relationship development to date has been the emergence of brand-centred online chat communities. The importance of online brand communities in brand development was noted by Muniz and O'Guinn (2001) and McAlexander *et al.* (2002). With its ability to provide a global meeting place through bulletin boards, discussion lists and chatrooms, the Internet has facilitated the growth of many online communities that are now devoted to particular product classes or brands. These are groups of consumers who share a common understanding and experience of a particular brand and use these meanings as a way to communicate with each other. Many of the strongest brand communities centre on iconic brands. Different to blogs, they centre on loyalty and interest in a specified interest (a car, campaign, a location), and are not just chatting. In many cases, they emerged from offline communities of interest or clubs and they predate blogs, wikis and podcasts. Some have been in operation for over fifteen years. As a live and ongoing network of communication and feedback: if marketers can collaborate with it, it offers an opportunity to extend traditional relationships online. It may also pose a threat if the brand is losing reputation.

INSIGHT: In this fertile arena of social networks, blogs, bulletin and chat forums, traditional marketer-dominated flows of information are now mediated by customers, who:

- collectively gather brand/organization messages online through comparison of website offerings and reflect these to other customers;
- share, interpret and sometimes re-interpret their service experience(s) to other customers in chat communities;
- seek to engage with, modify, re-create service episode(s) through active engagement with service personnel and other customers in real-time mode. (Broderick, author)

Characteristics of brand communities

Schouten and McAlexander (1995: 43) defined distinctive subgroups of consumers that self-select "on the basis of a shared commitment to a particular product class, brand or consumption activity" as "subcultures of consumption". In an ethnographic study of Harley-Davidson owners they showed that a major characteristic of such subcultures is a unique set of shared beliefs and values about brands. Members create a collective sense of identity within the community. Acknowledging the importance of inter-customer relationships in building customer loyalty, McAlexander *et al.* (2002) suggested that the community should have a wider web of relationships with marketing agents, the company. Each online community will have its own specific cultural composition and structure (Kozinets, 2002), that will be brought about by the unique collective identity that its members share. It is that collective interest and identity which is a great source of loyalty towards the brand. Brand communities are social groups and Muniz and O'Guinn (2001) highlighted how certain brand community members may hold more influence over meaning creation of brands through their perceived status over other members of the community. This role interaction was also seen in the Real.Com case.

Level of marketer engagement

Unlike blogs, where monitoring and some placed advertising is the key mode of engagement, the objective for marketers in their links with brand communities is to actively discuss and consult with their brand communities, seeking to establish and strengthen deeper ties with their core followers. The loyalty comes through the shared interest; therefore relationship development is to some extent an implicit process. Company contributions are not necessarily welcomed; therefore some linked advertising or PR are used to keep a presence on community sites. Nonetheless, brand communities will express important sentiments about the company and brand – so it is a live source of feedback on firm decisions and a dynamic source of customer data.

Online communities now exist as an integral part of the online product or service environment, where users exchange experiences of the product or service and develop ties of friendship that may not mean they are a brand advocate, but are nonetheless loyal and open to customer offers and membership status that cements their interest in the site. A good example of integrated online communities as facilitating elements of brand commitment is an online entertainment site – Real.Com.

MINI-CASE: REAL.COM (2)

By definition, there is a high level of customer to customer interaction possible on entertainment sites. Each player can interact with other players when they are playing the game by using mobiles, web links, email, or SMS messages. It might involve simple card games or board games to complicated role-playing games. Exchanging own entertainment collections, MP3 music might be offered by service providers generally or between individual customers in the online community. In some research undertaken in 2005, this was noted as very important by community members:

> Because in that website ... when you are online and I am also online, you have some music I can download from you. For example, if I want to find a specific song, Robin William's songs, if I find you have this song, I can download from you. It's very interesting. (Interviewee 006F)

Activity in the online community led to interaction using many different Internet resources, such as Yahoo's briefcase, online photo album or FTP (stands for "File Transfer Protocol"). For example, in terms of exchanging music collection, one music fan interviewee describes the process and experience clearly as follows:

> I have thirty megabytes [of space] in Yahoo briefcase. I can share every thing with my friends or other people ... When I visit message boards, people may ask for some songs they like of, when I found I've got, I just put in my briefcase and they can feel free to download it from my briefcase. Also, I have this problem because I have some kinds of collections, I like collect music, different kinds of music, pop music or classic music, but some old, out-of-date music I cannot find in the market or websites, so I often ask people they have got or

not. Fortunately, many people respond to me and tell me I can download from their web-sites ... I found it's very interesting, you just exchange music with other people and also fulfil your needs ... (Interviewee 003F)

The offering of online community is very important for many customers, with a place for interacting with each other and making friends with others who have the same interests and hobbies. For those people who participate frequently, the advantages and enjoyment of online communities are clear.

However, members of chat communities are self-selecting. One respondent who never par-ticipated in the online community, did not see it as helpful and noted:

in my place when ... they have chatting rooms, a so-called small, small community. From the marketing point of view, it doesn't help much, I feel. Because, the people just talk, just for fun they come and go out, so I don't think it helps a lot. (Interviewee 008M)

Online community as micro-society

Online communities can be regarded as micro-societies. In the online community different interaction behaviours exist, such as enquiries, suggestions, appreciations, discussions and arguments. An analysis of the chat community of Real.Com showed that a positive customer to customer interaction in the online community was able to increase customers' satisfaction towards the service offering.

Customer to customer interaction took the form of knowledge sharing or gaining, problem-solving and engaging in activities. Knowledge sharing or gaining was common and took place not only in the real-time chat rooms and on message boards, but also in product reviews.

... I just want to see what is feeling from other people ... I never see them before we just talk on the Internet, so it's quite a good experience I can see other people their thoughts and what they think the comic should be. (Interviewee 004M)

From this interaction, customers receive suggestions, recommendations and other related entertainment product information, such as game cheats, tips, song lyrics, etc. Moreover, during the interaction, customers can make friends, as noted from one respondent :

Apart from the game secrets, sometimes I can make friends and I can get other knowledge, maybe about travelling, different culture of nationalities. Last time, I chatted with a Japanese guy, he talk to me about Japan, he said if next time I go to Japan he will wait for me in the airport and then play video game together. I think I might go in October or November later on, he will be my tour guide. I think it's quite good in the online community. (Interviewee 002M)

Different customer roles in online communities

Customer roles in online communities can be classified into three categories: help seeker, proactive helper and reactive helper. In the study, most people participating in the Real.Com community were help seekers, who actively seek solutions or advice from other customers who have the experiences. A few people play the role of proactive helper. For instance, in the online community of Real.com games homepage a participant, who calls himself a member of X-man

'Wolverine', not only proactively provides solutions to most queries but also shares some information with others. On Real.com's message board, as KNIGHTofPAIN had a problem that others were discussing, he unwittingly plays the role of reactive helper in terms of providing solutions. :

> I am now on the sniper level that you spoke of. I don't see any fog on mine, perfectly clear. Did you look under video options and disable FOG? (Message Boards, Police Tactical Training, HEY SILKY, KNIGHTofPAIN).

In the above cases, Wolverine and KNIGHTofPAIN become important advocates of some of the games because they offer help, just like a staff member. Their help is valued as they are trusted members of the community.

Questions

1 In what way is the online community contributing to the success of Real.Com?
2 Why are online community interactions an important element of the service experience in this case?
3 What gaps would exist in the service experience without the online community?

Task 8.2

L ocate a chat community for one of the following:

Harley-Davidson

Volkswagen Golf

Apple iPod

- Observe some of the discussion points on their forums or bulletin boards.
  Identify the themes and nature of interactions between members.
- See if you can locate members who are adopting different roles with members of the site or with newcomers to the site.

The Real.Com case demonstrates the importance for online entertainment service providers to not only promote their products and services, but also encourage customers to participate, interact and communicate in the online community. Good interaction in the online community clearly seems to increase customers' engagement and commitment to the service.

An online brand community provides an ideal site to monitor the dynamics of ongoing interrelationships between marketers, their customers and the brand. As brands come under greater competitive pressure, it will become increasingly important for marketers to understand the power of the brand community, its influence on brand-meaning formation and its capacity to generate greater loyalty among members. Marketers will need to think strategically about how to ensure they are developing effective relationships with their key brand communities.

Chapter Summary

In this chapter, some recent critical changes in customer approaches in online markets have been reviewed. The chapter examined in detail the emergence of customer-generated media and social networks and highlighted their increasing influence on customer relationships with brands and organizations. In particular, the chapter highlighted the emergence of increased customer control in the current online marketplace and how this is creating more difficult relationship development processes for companies. Second, the possibilities of customer self-customization and how that may change customer outlook on traditional relationships with service providers has been examined. The growth of customer-generated media and how marketers are viewing it in terms of potential targeting opportunities were then discussed, with the focus on blogs and podcasts. Finally, the importance of online brand communities was identified, with an illustration of the way brand relationships with customers and loyalty to brands is emerging though the social interactions within such communities.

Review Questions

1 What do we mean by customer-generated media (CGM)? What kinds of CGM are most influential when choosing a holiday?

2 Identify the differences between blogs, social network sites and online brand communities. Why do some marketing practitioners suggest that companies must not ignore the growth in social chat networks?

3 Blogging is a powerful tool for customer advocacy. How can a company monitor and engage with blogs to enable closer customer interaction? What are the difficulties when a company experiences negative blogging about its brands or services?

Further Reading

Maclaran, P. and M. Catterall (2002) "Researching the Social Web: Marketing Information from Virtual Communities", *Marketing Intelligence & Planning*, vol. 20, no. 6, pp. 319–326.

Muniz, A. (1997) "Brand Community and the Negotiation of Brand Meaning", *Advances in Consumer Research*, vol. 24, pp. 308–309.

Wright-Isak, C. (1996) "Communities of Consumption: A Central Metaphor for Diverse Research", *Advances in Consumer Research*, vol. 23, pp. 265–266.

END OF CHAPTER CASE AND KEY QUESTIONS

Online travel services – customer self-customization

In a recent study of UK online travel customers (Baritt and Broderick, 2006), research and design of the holiday by consumers proved to be far more significant than standard information search by consumers during the typical consumer decision-making process. Findings showed that extensive research was not a problem for most consumers. In fact, customers often enjoy the aspect of participation involved and are motivated by the sense of control it provides them with.

The control enjoyed by consumers provided respondents with their expectations of the holiday. The research possibilities online for a holiday that a customer is planning to take abroad are non-restrictive. The abundance of choice gives customers power to select a holiday that meets their exact requirements without the need to sacrifice any of their chosen features. The study (Baritt and Broderick, 2006), shows that customers enjoy the *opportunity* to create a holiday that meets their requirements; they are focused on the freedom and independence that customization offers as opposed to experiencing a holiday that is organized by others to perfection.

Interpretation of customized experience

When customers in the study interpreted their experience of the researching of holidays online, some common aspects that were noted in the respondent comments were self-reliance, sense of responsibility, sense of personal achievement and enjoyment of self-discovery. For some consumers, this meant the opportunity for more control over their own decisions : "... it's quite nice to travel half way across the world and control everything, you know, knowing that you've done it all yourself. You don't have to rely on other people to get you to the destination" [R3]. A consequence of self-reliance was responsibility to others. Consumers appear to feel more responsible when booking a self-customized holiday – feeling that their fellow holidaymakers are more dependent on them: "you do take the responsibility for it. I mean ... you're the one who's got to do something about it." [R5]. Although the responsibility placed upon an individual may be more stressful if things become problematic, some respondents found it a very rewarding activity and felt a certain degree of self satisfaction when a customized holiday has reached or exceeded expectations. Consumers congratulated and praised themselves on what they believe to be an achievement: "... when you've booked it all and it all turns out to be right, I suppose you do feel kind of proud because you think 'I did this!'" [R5]. Additionally, while reminiscing upon a particularly satisfactory moment of the holiday, consumers were seen to remind themselves that they had produced that experience themselves. This appears to make the experience even more unique to that individual: "It was really nice when we went to the Grand Canyon because we got there after all the tour buses had been ... we got there about five thirty in the evening ... and, because we'd got there at that time, *I think it was really special, it felt more ... we'd done that ourselves*" [R2].

Self-customization was freedom – offering an opportunity to satisfy their own needs on a more individual basis and was a source of pleasure : "... *because it was our own holiday we could do what we wanted.* We had a sort of itinerary that we drew together that we followed. It was mainly walking about and seeing the sights like going up the Empire State Building and Wall Street" [R1]. And "... it's the feeling that you have arranged it all yourself and *you know you've just booked exactly what you want and no more, no less*" [R5]. Consumers viewed this self-discovery as part of the excitement of an independent holiday.

In particular, consumers enjoyed the wide range of choices offered online and felt more uninhibited, thereby adding to the independence and control sought after. Much of the success of the holiday was attributed to their own efforts and the freedom in this form of customization allows customers to create the individual service they want.

Participation is key: in online travel services it is the customer conduit to customization. Some consumers see themselves as co-designers of the service and interpret the customization possibilities in travel services as opportunities for self-reliance, for self-discovery and obtaining a sense of personal achievement.

Questions

1 Looking at some of the respondent comments in this case, what particular elements appear to have excited some customers or reached level three in the Sand Cone Model (Voss, 2003)?

2 How can a firm who has created and delivered some parts of this holiday build a further relationship with these customers?

This case demonstrates that online relationship building differs from offline relationship development.

3 Is it easy for travel firms to encourage increased loyalty online for those customer groups who are very keen on self-customization? Consider attitudinal loyalty and suggest actions that might encourage this.

4 If clients attribute the success of the holiday to their own efforts, what implications does this create for building customer commitment?

Follow-up

Consider you own holiday travel patterns. Do you research and plan holidays online? If yes, what sites do you use to get initial information? Do you feel any loyalty to these sites?

References

Baker, A. (1998) "Cyberspace Couples Finding Romance Online Then Meeting For the First Time in Real Life", *Journal of Computer-Mediated Communication*, pp. 1–4.

Baritt E. and A. Broderick (2006) "Customer as Service Co-Designer: Mass Customization in the travel sector", Competitive Paper in Proceedings from Academy of Marketing Conference, July, Middlesex University, UK.

Bauman, Z. (2003) *Liquid Love: On the Frailty of Human Bonds*, Oxford: Blackwell Publishing.

Blackshaw, P. (2006) "The Pocket Guide to Chatterbacking, Internet Inferno", *Marketing Management*, February.

Calcanis (2005) Silicon Alley Reporter, Blogosphere, accessed through SEMPO site.

Chaston, I. (2001) *E-Marketing Strategies*, New York, NY: McGraw-Hill.

Csikszentlmihalyi, M. (1990) *Flow: The Psychology of Optimal Experience*, New York: Harper and Row.

Downhill, F. and J. Peggie (2006) Online Reputation Management, SEMPO site, April.

Ferdows, K. and A. De Mayer (1990) "Lasting Improvements in Manufacturing Performance: In Search of a New Theory", *Journal of Operations Management*, vol. 9, no. 2, pp. 168–84.

Hardey, M. (2002) "Life Beyond the Screen: Embodiment and Identity Through the Internet", *The Sociological Review*, vol. 50, no. 4, pp. 570–585.

Hoffman D. and T. Novak (1996) "Marketing in a Hypermedia Computer-mediated Environments: Conceptual Foundations", *Journal of Marketing*, vol. 60, no. 3, pp. 50–68.

Jayawardhena, C. and P. Foley (2000) "Changes in Banking Sector – The Case of Internet Banking in the UK", *Internet Research: Electronic Networking: Application and Policy*, vol. 10, no. 1, pp. 19–30.

Kiani, G. (1998), "New Game, New Rules: Will Traditional Mentality Work in the Marketspace"? *Management Research News*, vol. 21, no. 6, pp. 1–13.

Kozinets, R.V. (2002) "The Field Behind the Screen: Using Netnography for Marketing Research in Online Communities", *Journal of Marketing Research*, vol. 39, February, pp. 61–72.

Lanz (2006) *American Executive Magazine*, June.

McAlexander, J.H., J.W. Schouten and H.F. Koenig (2002) "Building Brand Community", *Journal of Marketing*, vol. 66, pp. 38–54.

McGann, R., (2004) "The Blogosphere by the Numbers, Traffic Patterns", commentary based on Clickz data, posted 22 November through Search Engine Watch online magazine.

Mols, N.P. (2000) 'The Internet and Bank's Strategic Distribution Channel Decisions', *International Journal of Bank Marketing*, vol. 17, no. 6, pp. 295–300.

Muniz, A.M. and T.C. O'Guinn (2001) "Brand Community", *Journal of Consumer Research*, vol. 27, no. 4, pp. 412–432.

Newcomb, K. (2006) "Downloading Podcasts More Popular than Blogging", *Marketing Management*, July.

Pew Internet and American Life Project (2004), cited in R. McGann, "The Blogosphere, traffic patterns".

Pine II, B.J. and J.H. Gilmore (1999) *The Experience Economy: Work is Theatre and Every Business a Stage*, Boston: Harvard Business School.

Schouten, J.W. and J.H. McAlexander (1995) "Subcultures of Consumption: An Ethnography of the New Bikers", *Journal of Consumer Research*, vol. 22, June, pp. 43–61.

Slevin, J. (2000) *The Internet and Society*, Massachusetts: Polity Press.

Vargo, S. and R. Lusch (2004) "Evolving to a new dominant logic for marketing", *Journal of Marketing*, vol. 68, no. 1, pp. 1–17.

Voss, C.A. (2003) "Rethinking Paradigms of Service-service in a Virtual Environment", *International Journal of Operations and Productions Management*, vol. 23, no. 1, pp. 88–104.

PART II
Contexts for Relationship Development

Introduction to Contexts

This section of the book presents a series of case contexts that highlight marketing relationships between customers and organizations in some detail. The cases encourage application of ideas to reflect how relationship theories vary across relationship contexts, notably professional services, consumer products, b2b partnerships, loyalty-based sports services, and the non-profit virtual environment. In addition, not all sectors absorb RM theory effectively and some reflect the contextual pressures placed upon relationships

The case contexts have been chosen to reflect three things – first, a range of marketing environments that draw on b2b, b2c and c2c and professional, consumer and virtual contexts. For instance, two Context (6 and 7) look specifically at the virtual marketspace and how c2c communications are influencing client relationships with brands and firms. Second, the contexts deal with areas of particular challenge in current marketing decision-making (Contexts 1 to 4). As an illustration, Context 1 examines how some of the dimensions of RM may be selectively applied in markets where complex processes are involved. Similarly, in highly competitive markets, the challenges in building relationships through strong client-focused processes and interactions is covered in Context 2, where the focus is on where value can be generated to encourage customer retention. Third, Contexts 5 to 7 try to reflect newly emerging trends that impact on the degree of relationship that can be developed with firms – issues such as technology-enabled communications and customer to customer communication (see Contexts 6 and 7). This is also evident in how firms need to deal with emerging consumer power in Context 5.

How Can the Reader Use the Case Contexts?

Some of these contexts may form the focus of class activities set by tutors. The questions set at the end of each chapter may help to orient the reader in sifting through the key issues. In some cases we encourage the reader to apply a bounded set of classical RM theories established in the first five chapters of this text.

The case contexts are also suitable for independent study. The intention is that the reader should reflect upon the material covered in the chapter where the theories are explained in order to answer the questions at the end of each context. Some suggested theoretical starting points for each context are illustrated in Table 9.1 below and some specific frameworks suggested for analysis are included in some context questions.

TABLE 9.1 Summary of In-depth Case contexts

Specific case context, chapter it links to	Area of relationship theory focused on	Key frameworks that might be used	Some relevant learning points
Whitesides LLP and the Corporate Legal Services Market Chapters 2, 5	Dimensions of relationship – marketing exchange and management and process elements Trust building	Typology of relationship, Brodie, Coviello and Brooks (1997) Morgan and Hunt (1994)	Complexity of relationship development in credence-based b2b environments
Travel Services Travelsphere Chapter 4	Building good client relationships in competitive markets. Interaction through the client experience Critical points for relationship development in service process analysis	Service quality dimensions – Grönroos (1990) Parasuraman et al. (1995); Pre-, during and post model – Fisk et al. (1981); Service blueprint – Shostack (1977); Hoffman and Bateson (1998)	Importance of ongoing service managing to optimize client interactions in experience-based b2c environments Specific uses of a blueprint or process focus to highlight client relationship fail points
Sports Management Leicester Tigers Rugby Club Chapters 1, 4, 5	Characteristics of relationship approach Generating loyalty and increasing customer retention	Characteristics of RM and ladder of loyalty Christopher, Payne and Ballantyne (1991) Trust building in relationships (Morgan and Hunt, 1994)	Challenges of creating a relationship around a non-traditional product and building a loyal customer database
Supply Relationship Between an Organization (Co-Med) and its Advertising Agencies Chapters 2, 3	Dynamics of relationships within supply chain Stakeholder management and risk	Supply risks Kraljic (1982) Relationship development cycles (Wilson, 1996; Evans et al., 2004) Suppy relational model, (Morgan and Hunt, 1994)	The variation in industrial marketing relationships Challenges in managing relationships with stakeholders
Utility services – British Gas Residential and the Impact of Consumer Power Chapters 2, 5	Type of relationship and marketing implications Customer power Influence of this on switching and on loyalty to firms	Donaldson and O'Toole (2002) Relationship dissolution (Tynan et al., 1997; Evans et al., 2004)	The way power in b2c is now shifting towards consumers and challenges to improving trust and retaining a relationship focus in this environment
Car branding Consumer roles and brand relationships in Mini online brand community Chapters 7, 8	Relationship development through brand communities. Hierarchy of influence, WOM and how it affects attachment to brands	Brand communities McAlexander, Schouten and Koenig (2002); Maclaran and Catterall (2002); Muniz, A. (1997)	Understanding the role that brand communities play in brand and firm relationship development based on c2c
Social Network in non-profit context: Race for Life campaign Chapters 7, 8	Examining elements of social networking Specific focus on blogging as part of WOM and means of customer engagement	Experience-based services (Zeithaml and Bitner, 1981) Building advocacy (Kozinets, 2002; Barritt and Broderick, 2006; Hardey, 2002)	Function of blogging and social networks in influencing customer perceptions of a non-profit cause Level of relationship development

Note: Potential areas of analysis noted in the columns in Table 9.1 correspond with author references in the relevant chapters.

Context 1
Professional Services (b2b)

Whitesides LLP and the Corporate Legal Services Market

Introduction

Corporate and commercial law is an area of law that encompasses law firms providing legal advice to business organizations on issues ranging from flotations, mergers and acquisitions to ownership issues such as selling, investing or buying in or out of commercial organizations. Similar to other professional services, corporate legal services have a number of distinctive characteristics: there is a defined field of knowledge. (i.e. the law) which is usually acquired by a qualified provider (e.g. lawyer) through a number of years' training and experience. Clients use lawyers in an ongoing advisory capacity to help them solve their business problems and, to practise their profession, lawyers are required to be members of a professional body known as the Law Society. The Law Society sets out levels of competence, controls its members' practices and enforces codes of ethics where appropriate.

Because of these features, corporate legal services embody many of the characteristics that engender a favourable environment for the development of relationships between firms and clients. More specifically: corporate legal services are required on a periodic, ongoing basis over an extended period of time; they tend to be intangible, complex, require a relatively high degree of technical expertise and adaptability and are difficult to evaluate even after purchase.

The legal services market has traditionally had a reputation for being a product-focused market. However, the legal services market has changed dramatically in recent years with a range of complex and interrelated factors driving these changes.

The Law Market

The legal services market in general within the UK is estimated to be valued at £15,987 million (The Law Society *Key Facts on the Solicitors' Profession*, 2005 annually). A number of factors affect the demand for lawyers and legal advice. These include:

- globalization;
- the increasing frequency and complexities of business transactions (e.g. flotations, mergers, etc.);
- increases in wealth levels leading to, for example, greater home ownership which in turn increases demand for legal services (e.g. conveyancing);

- emerging technologies requiring new legislation (e.g. the Internet);
- greater population diversity (e.g. anti-discrimination legislation);
- European Union legislation;
- social changes in terms of increased crime rates, divorce rates, etc.

This has resulted in a marked increase in the demand for legal services. As a result, the number of practising solicitors has increased from 23 565 to 126 142 in 2005 and continue to increase.

These lawyers can work for one of three generic types of law firms that have emerged in recent years. The "elite firms" consist of the largest law firms in England and Wales. Their primary location is within the financial centre of London ("the City") and their location reflects the services they provide. These may include legal advice on such matters as finance, corporate affairs, property, tax, company, commercial, banking and capital insurance, intellectual property, etc. Their clients are often large, publicly quoted firms or state organizations.

The second type of firm are medium-sized, regional firms and these focus on local business-to-business market needs within distinct geographic regions. However, there is an increasing tendency for these firms to compete nationally as a result of advances in information technology making accessibility more important than physical distance. This, coupled with the increase in fees charged by "City"-based firms (£500–1000 per hour for a partner) has made them more attractive from a commercial-client perspective. Many regional firms have also established national reputations in niche markets such as shipping law, immigration, insurance law, commercial fraud, etc.

Small firms and sole practitioners (less than five partners) are primarily "general practice" solicitors who focus on the provision of legal advice on such matters as family, criminal, personal injury ("trippers and slippers") and conveyancing to private individuals. As a result, a large proportion of their income may be dependent on Legal Aid. They are often referred to as "High Street lawyers" because of their location and accessibility.

The Corporate Legal Services Market

The market for business-to-business legal services has expanded rapidly. This, in turn, has led to the expansion and consolidation of many law firms specializing in this area. A key driver behind this has been the transformation of the nature of the relationship between law firms and clients. Historically, the relationship between clients and lawyers, whether in terms of a commercial or private professional capacity, was essentially between individuals. This was because, historically, most business organizations were effectively operated as private companies with the owners and a small number of managers running it.

However, increases in the number of flotations, mergers, acquisitions and takeovers taking place since the 1960s has meant larger companies are more likely to be publicly quoted enterprises than privately owned ones. The organizational structure of such companies has moved away from that of an owner-manager structure to that of a large, multidivisional management structure increasingly dominated by professional, non-owning personnel.

Many of these organizations have in-house legal departments to manage the outsourcing of legal services. They therefore possess a high degree of legal knowledge and may be in a position to make increasing demands in terms of the commercial and legal criteria that law firms are required to fulfil in order to supply them with such services. The result of this is that the purchase of legal services is increasingly being treated in a way similar to other commodities, with price, reliability and speed of delivery being viewed as increasingly important. Such organizations are using a number of law firms simultaneously to ensure they maintain checks and balances on their legal suppliers. Until recently, these types of companies used the large City-based law firms. However, as has already been indicated, there is an increasing tendency for smaller regional law firms to compete nationally against these firms for larger clients.

Whitesides Solicitors

Adrian Smith is an equity partner in the corporate commercial department of Whitesides, a medium-sized law firm based in the East Midlands. The firm has seen phenomenal double-digit growth in recent years and has trebled its turnover since 1996. Much of this growth has come from the acquisition of large, blue-chip companies as clients.

However, attempting to attract these larger clients has not been without its challenges. Historically, Whitesides' client base consisted of managing directors and owner managers of SMEs within the Midlands area. With a number of blue-chip companies on its books, the client base may no longer be viewed as being heterogeneous in terms of the client service requirements. This has fundamental implications for the way service expectations are set, evaluations of service delivery are made and the relationship is managed. At one extreme, smaller owner-managed organizations that are largely unfamiliar with the law may require a different type of interaction and relationship with Adrian's department than larger, more sophisticated clients with in-house legal expertise. To quote Adrian:

Quite a lot of larger clients will use more than one firm of solicitors. They consider it commercially advantageous and they will usually have sophisticated ways to know exactly what is involved in terms of the service they require. They will have a pretty good idea as to what the cost of that service is in the market place. They will also have a pretty good idea of what the expertise is of the firms that they might want to use. That is a very different situation if, for example, you have a chap who's built up a business which is his sole asset and he's thinking of retiring and he wants to sell it. In terms of the corporate Plc client, the relationship element of the transaction between them and the professional advisor is less important by quite a long way than it would be with the man who's selling his life's work. He needs to have confidence in the relationship.

A survey (Garry, 2007) conducted into the switching behaviour of clients between law firms in the corporate legal services market in general provided Adrian with some interesting reading. The majority of clients (around 75 per cent) had been with the same law firm for five years or more.

Poor quality or poor value was the reason most cited for changing law firms. What was unclear from the survey, however, is how an owner manager of an SME would gauge the quality of the legal advice they receive when they do not possess any legal qualifications. A change in the client's contact solicitor was cited as another main reason for changing firms. What was not clear from the survey is whether the switching behaviour of the respondents is related to pull or push factors. It is frequently implicit practice within the corporate legal services market that when a solicitor is "headhunted" from one law firm to another, they will attempt to take key client accounts with them to their new firm. This may have culminated in their clients "following" their solicitor to another firm. Many public sector organizations, particularly at a local government level, are compelled to undergo a re-tendering process for legal services every three to five years as part of the Government's initiative on "best value". From Adrian's experience, it is therefore quite possible to lose a client in this manner even if they are completely satisfied.

Another reason cited for changing law firms was takeovers and mergers. This may occur because the dominant partner in the takeover or merger uses different law firms and a rationalization process occurs where law firms are "dropped" from the panel (a panel is a short list of law firms that are given most preferred supplier status). This in turn may have implications for the law firms still used. To quote Adrian:

> Buying power with sophisticated clients is a concern. They are reducing the number of law firms on their panels. The law firms that are left are in a much weaker position than they were because they're reliant upon an awful lot of work from a major buyer which is in turn encouraging solicitors who provide their service to be more "flexible" and once the clients encourage that debate we're almost into competitive tendering.

Far from being a co-operative, "win win" situation, some of the relationships with larger clients were increasingly lose-win as far as Adrian was concerned. This was evident in a recent decision by the partners within the department to terminate a high-profile client account. As Adrian states:

> With the bigger client organizations, they know very well that we like to be seen doing work for them and they end up getting work done extremely cheaply. As a matter of fact, we have decided recently, in the past week, to terminate the relationship with a large client on the basis that the client had gone too far in dictating not only the fees but also the extra services which must be provided for nothing. There comes a point when you do a cost–benefit analysis and you cannot do the work to the required quality for the price they are demanding. I am also acutely aware of how my departments resources are being used in this way, possibly to the detriment of smaller but more loyal clients.

Sources

Garry, T. (2007) Affect and the role of client sophistication on satisfaction judgements with business-to-business professional service, unpubished PhD, University of Nottingham.

Questions

1 How would you classify the relationship between client and law firm in the
   corporate legal services market using Brodie *et al.* (1997) classification system?
   Justify your answer by applying the dimensions identified in Brodie *et al.* (1997) to
   corporate legal services (by completing the template below):

Marketing Exchange Dimensions	Application to Corporate Legal Services
1. Focus	
2. Parties involved	
3. Communication patterns	
4. Type of contact	
5. Duration	
6. Formality	
7. Balance of power	

Management and Process Dimensions	Application to Corporate Legal Services
1. Managerial intent	
2. Decision focus	
3. Managerial investment	
4. Managerial level	
5. Time frame	

2 What is the role of trust and commitment within such relationships and how might
   it vary according to the sophistication of the client?

Context 2
Travel Services (b2c)

Travelsphere and Customer Retention in a
Competitive Market

Introduction

The travel trade was in a state of shock after the terrorist attack on the World Trade
Center on September 11th, the effects of war in Iraq, further terrorist atrocities and
the impact of SARS. It was not a good time for travel companies like Travelsphere of
Market Harborough. After years of double-digit growth, the guided tour specialist had to
move quickly to keep sales at the previous level of £92 million. Achieving stability was
a triumph. It then wanted to seize the opportunity for growth. It could grow by overseas
expansion or by acquiring companies that had been weakened by the industry-wide
problems. It would be risky though. Maybe the best route to growth would be to invest
the funds in building brand awareness. The directors were spoiled for choice – just like
the holidaymakers they served. But the stakes were higher.

"We thought we would have a meltdown year after September 11", admitted managing
director Mark Watts. Yet when the US was hit, Travelsphere's customers just delayed
travelling or turned to its brochures for alternative destinations. The company actually
saw sales climb as customers bought more expensive holidays elsewhere. "When there's a
problem somewhere in the world, people simply go somewhere else," said Watts.

Outbound Tour-Operator Market Size

Travelsphere operated in the UK outbound tourism market, competing with UK tour
operators and travel agents. Research shows the size of the total outbound tourism market
in 2002 was £27.1 billion (Keynote Report 2002: Ch. 1). According to the same research tour
operators/travel agents captured 59 per cent of this market (£16.0 billion). According to
ABTA, in 2002 there were 706 tour operators registered with ABTA, with a concentration
among the top four of 53 per cent. The top four companies in this market compared to
Travelsphere (Hg Annual Report, 2003) in terms of total turnover were as follows:

Company	Turnover £ billion	Profit Margin %
MyTravel	5.1	1.6
First Choice	2.4	2.3
Thomas Cook	1.6	9.2
TUI UK	1.5	(0.8)
(Travelsphere)	0.1	11.0

The above data show that Travelsphere was small relative to the main players in the market. However, the niche market model of Travelsphere was more profitable than its rivals. The total size of the UK outbound market 1988–2002 was as follows:

Year	1998	1999	2000	2001	2002
Market Valuation (£m)	19 489	22 020	24 251	25 332	27 073

The travel market was growing at a rate faster than growth in the UK economy: over the period from 1998 to 2002 the market grew a total of 38.9 per cent. The implications of this for Travelsphere were good, with an increasing number of customers across all market sectors, and an increasing level of profit. Travelsphere's commitment to pay for seats and hotel rooms was usually less than eight weeks prior to departure, a major advantage at a time when the Foreign Office was issuing travel warnings over increasingly large areas of the globe. "We're not like a typical large operator with heavy forward commitments, we don't have our own coach fleet or airlines. If we can see a product is not doing well we can shift our effort into other areas", said Watts. It was not all plain sailing, however. The SARS outbreak devastated Travelsphere's hugely popular China tours. A pioneer into the region in the 1980s, it expected to take 14 000 visitors into China, making it the largest European escorted operator in the country. Final numbers were well down on that figure. This is the main reason why Travelsphere expected flat sales in 2003, at around its 2002 level of £92 million. Yet profits before tax rose sharply in the same period, up by 12 per cent in 2002 to £10.7 million and up 50 per cent from 2001–2003.

Travelsphere was determined to stick to the market it knew: essentially holidays for older customers. It was a niche player, looking after 150 000 customers a year, with a brand that was far from being a household name; passenger numbers and brand awareness needed to grow if it were to hit its target of annual, double-digit growth in the years 2003–2006. Yet its strengths also derived from the market it served. Its customers were a resilient, silver-haired bunch. Seventy-five per cent were over 55, most were affluent and all had an insatiable and unshakeable enthusiasm for overseas travel. "Our clients view travelling not as a luxury but as a necessity", said Watts. "They want to go on holiday every year, they need their fix."

This is one reason the company always made money and enabled it to become one of *The Sunday Times* Top 100 most profitable companies in 2000. This contributed to attracting venture capitalist Hg, which bought a 40 per cent share from its two surviving founders Mike Edwards and Richard Mackay in 2000. Seeing a chance to sell its tours directly, and cut travel agents out of the loop, Edwards and Mackay had launched Travelsphere in 1977. Since then the company built its reputation for value-for-money holidays for adults only all over the world. Its products ranged from £99 breaks in Paris right up to £3000 round-the-world trips in 2003. The firm has been broadening its appeal with new products: accompanied tours for single people; attracting a slightly younger crowd (30s upwards), for more active cycling and walking tours.

Travelsphere was not prepared to venture far beyond the customers it knew so well. Deputy managing director David Clemson said the company would not create holidays for twenty-something customers, for example, nor would it seek to enter the mass market.

As the UK population aged, the number of potential clients in the company's target market grew. With 1.7 million households on its database, direct marketing was the most direct and cheapest way to win business. "The reason we are successful is that the vast majority of our bookings come from our database marketing", said Clemson. Selling a holiday to a database customer costs about 10–15 per cent of what it costs to attract a new customer through newspaper advertising, which means Travelsphere's marketing budget in 2003 accounted for just 5 per cent of turnover.

While the website www.travelsphere.co.uk was bringing in some new business, newspaper ads remained the most important way to grow the customer base. But financial director Sue Simmons hated the imprecision of mass media. "Chasing new customers is expensive," she said, "and simply increasing the advertising budget may not be a cost-effective way to bring in new business, particularly at a time when travellers are more cautious."

Challenges

The challenge facing Travelsphere was how to unlock the potential within its existing customer base. If the company were to stick to the "silver" customers, they would have a large slice of the lucrative 50-plus market.

Why jeopardize that and start targeting the highly competitive younger audience? The 20- and 30-year-olds are after a completely different holiday from the silver travellers. Would it be possible to carry this brand across the entire 20 to 70 age range? Would Watts be better off developing his existing market by increasing awareness of Travelsphere among the over-50s?

Options for Expansion

One solution was to raise Travelsphere's profile as a brand. Watts thought it could, and should, be much better known that it is: "We are not a household name and yet we are bigger than a lot of companies that are." Was there some way to overcome that and develop the brand so that it became more widely known? "If you asked people in our demographic group: 'Who are the leading escorted coach touring operators?' they would say Shearings or Wallace Arnold, purely because they've got hundreds of coaches flying round the country with their names on the side. Spending more on advertising is something we may have to consider to heighten awareness of the brand. It's difficult to know what else we can do." A longer-term, slow-burning campaign may be the solution, Simmons felt.

"Maybe we have to be a little bit bolder, create a sustained media campaign using other media as well as newspapers." Travelsphere tried advertising beyond the national press, such as in weekly magazines, but with limited success.

Another source of expansion may come from partnerships or acquisitions. Although the mass travel market has long since consolidated, there was scope for some consolidation in Travelsphere's niche, where a number of other specialists operated.

Travelsphere could acquire another UK travel specialist selling to the same kinds of customers but with a different product range or perhaps specializing in a specific geographical area, said Clemson. He argued that there were many struggling operators that would welcome the opportunity to sell out.

Overseas expansion was also a possibility. The company had already looked at the Irish market and would consider Continental tie-ups too. Efficiencies could be created by using Travelsphere's operations in the UK and taking advantage of greater buying power of older customers. As air travel continued to grow in popularity, there was also scope to expand this regionally, said Watts. "It would be beyond our means to take a weekly charter to South Africa for example, but if we could partner with one or two other operators, it could be a really interesting proposition." Many customers would jump at the chance to avoid the crowded south-eastern airports, said Watts. "People are tired of getting up at one in the morning to transfer on a coach down to Heathrow."

Sources

www.travelsphere.co.uk
The Sunday Times, 31/08/2003
Keynote Report, 2002
Hg Annual Report (2003)

Questions

1 Develop a diagram showing the key relationships that Travelsphere has with different stakeholders.

2 Identify ways in which the company can extend the relationship with existing customers (over-50s seeking organized travel packages). (You may wish to consider the nature of experience services, discussed in Chapter 4.)

3 In this market, a lot of companies are selling similar holidays, so it's the "holiday experience" that differentiates one from the other. Using Fisk's (1981) model of pre-consumption, during consumption and post-consumption, identify key points in the travel experience where customers might become dissatisfied and discontinue using the company.

4 Using the information in the case, draw a service blueprint that shows the frontstage, backstage activities for an individual customer as they select and experience one of Travelsphere's tours. What would you consider to be important visible elements of the service?

Follow-up Activity

This case looks at Travelsphere at a critical point in their development (end of 2003). Now, switch to the current year and gather information on Travelsphere. Start by visiting the website www.travelsphere.co.uk. Discuss their present approach to RM.

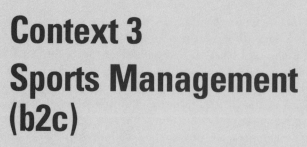

Context 3
Sports Management (b2c)

Leicester Tigers Rugby Club – Building Loyalty

Introduction

Historically, rugby union was a minority sport epitomized by "its amateur ethos, ramshackle facilities and administration, its condescending 'toffs' social profile, and its apparent determination to rule out any contact or compromise with the tainted professionals from the 'north'" (Gill and Welch, 2005). However, its transition from amateur to professional status in 1995 brought about huge changes both at a national and club level. One of the most successful clubs to emerge from this transition both from a business and sporting perspective has been Leicester Rugby Club or Leicester Tigers. Leicester Tigers is an English rugby union club that plays in the Guinness Premiership. The club has been the most successful club of the professional era, winning the Heineken cup twice and the league five times in the space of five years. As far as its Managing Director, David Clayton is concerned, a club is a "brand", a team a "product" and fans "customers". Based on this ethos, he attributes the club's success to developing a loyal 'customer' base and the resultant financial foundations which enables sound investment in its "product". Leicester Tigers has seen season ticket sales rise from around 10 000 in 2000/2001 to 13 000 in the 2006/2007 season, and every home game is sold out with attendances of 16 815 (up from 10 884 in 1999/2000).

Tigers Club History

Leicester Tigers was formed in 1880 as the result of the merger of three smaller teams: Leicester Societies AFC, Leicester Amateur FC and Leicester Alert. They moved to their present ground at Welford Road in 1892 when it accommodated just 1100 spectators in sharp contrast with today's capacity of nearly 17 000.

The origin of the Tigers' nickname is uncertain although a match report of 1885 shows that the name was already established. This is in contrast to its competitors in the premiership (such as the Newcastle Falcons, Leeds Tykes and Sale Sharks) who adopted their nicknames with the advent of the professional game in the mid-1990s. Some believe that it may have come from the Leicestershire regiment after they acquired the nickname on their return from service in India. Others believe that it emerged from the time the team wore a brown and yellow striped kit.

Leicester Tigers started to grow as a club towards the end of the 1970s. At the start of the decade the club had between 600 and 700 members and regular attendance for home games was around 1000. Between 1978 and 1983, the club reached five Cup finals.

Success continued in the 1990s, with Leicester Tigers winning a series of titles including cup final titles, consecutive premiership titles and the Heineken cup in 2001 and 2002 (see below). Between 30 December 1997 and 30 November 2002 they went 57 games unbeaten at home (losing only 14 games out of 92 played). In the 2003 Rugby World Cup the club had seven representatives in the winning England squad, including the captain.

Leicester Tigers Football Club Titles

Midland Counties Cup
Winners: 1897–1898; 1898–1899; 1899–1900; 1900–1901; 1901–1902; 1902–1903; 1903–1904; 1904–1905; 1908–1909; 1909–1910; 1911–1912; 1912–1913
Finalists: 1888–1889; 1890–1891; 1893–1894

English Cup Winners
Winners: 1978–1979; 1979–1980; 1980–1981; 1992–1993; 1996–1997
Finalist: 1977–1978; 1982–1983; 1988–1989; 1993–1994; 1995–1996

League Championships
1987–1988; 1994–1995; 1998–1999; 1999–2000; 2000–2001; 2001–2002

European Champions
2000–2001; 2001–2002

The Switch from Amateur to Professionalism

In 1995 the status of rugby union changed from amateur to professional and there followed a period of great turbulence. Many of the owners of clubs were "rich fans" and had a very product-focused approach to the game, believing that success on the pitch (and thus profitability) could be only be guaranteed by buying the best players. Many clubs did have good players but their stadiums were dilapidated and too small to hold the numbers required to balance the books. Some clubs made losses of millions of pounds. By the 2001–2002 season only two Premier clubs (Leicester and Northampton) had made a profit. The rest made combined losses of £11.5 million.

As a result, clubs started to appoint professional managers. These were chief executives able to ensure that a passion for sporting triumph was not indulged at the expense of basic business principles. This, coupled with England's success in the World Cup in 2003, has altered the fortunes of many clubs. As Mark McCafferty, chief executive of Premier Rugby, comments: "The collective turnover of the business is now approaching £100 million. Attendances have doubled in the last ten years and now average more than 10 000 a game and we have high-profile, end-of-season games that attract crowds of 50 000 plus."

Marketing at Leicester Tigers

David Clayton, the managing director of Leicester Tigers is typical of the new breed of managers brought into the game. Clayton was appointed MD in 2001. While he was not especially interested in rugby before his appointment, what he did bring to the club were proven marketing skills in a sporting context, as he had previously been commercial director of both Wolverhampton Wanderers and Nottingham Forest football clubs.

The marketing of sports teams brings its own unique challenges: the product itself is intangible and the outcome of the product is unpredictable (the team may lose!) A large proportion of the product is based on subjective emotions and experience.

Despite these marketing challenges, under Clayton's five-year stewardship Leicester's turnover has risen from £4.5 million to £12.6 million per annum while profits have soared from £56 000 to just over £1 million. Before 2000 the club was running at a loss – now it owns the freehold to its ground and has £4 million in the bank. Achievement of this financial stability has meant cultural change.

The Club's vision is for Leicester Tigers to be the most successful and best-supported rugby club in the world with an international global-brand recognition on a par with Manchester United Football Club. "We recognize that we operate in the leisure and entertainment industry, so we have to be focused on supporters – whether they are sponsors, businesses or individuals", says Clayton. Over 50 per cent of income is commercial, and corporate sponsors include Next, Alliance and Leicester, Hewlett Packard, Bradstone, FloGas and Aggregate with corporate box holders including Barclays Bank, HSBC, Orange, and Price Waterhouse Coopers. "One of our core values is that quality is the key to customer satisfaction and business success. Whether it's on or off the field, our focus is on delivering that."

Clayton sees his mission as making the club sufficiently profitable to invest in its own future without recourse to owners' funds. He is committed to the belief that the core business revolves around ticket sales and stadium occupancy and these depend upon success on the pitch.

As McCafferty, a former head of car rental giant Avis, puts it: "As with any consumer product, you try to create a higher level of appeal, attachment and loyalty to that product – clubs are brands in their local communities. If you try to increase the appeal and so sell more tickets, your rights are worth more money and you create a higher return." McCafferty wants the top clubs in Rugby Union to be rewarded by audience increases of "20 to 30 per cent" and by being able to renegotiate sponsorship and broadcast contracts.

As with every rugby club, Leicester has worked hard to build loyalty through a number of strategies. The club is keen to convert casual attenders into season ticket holders and keen to retain existing season ticket holders. Postcards are sent to existing season ticket holders reminding them to renew their tickets. A telesales team will contact individuals in cases of non-renewal. This is followed by a "we're missing you" postcard with an empty stadium seat with the 'lapsed customers' name on it. This is followed by an exit interview if the customer does not renew.

Critical to the success of this approach is a centralized, integrated, user-friendly MIS system with comprehensive and accurate data and employees with "the right skills and attitude".

Clayton is also keen to keep the Tigers at the customers "front of mind" throughout the week and an award winning website has been developed to help achieve this. The Tiger's website (*www.leicestertigers.com*) has over 4500 pages and delivers over 2 million page impressions to 60 000 visitors a month. An average of four news stories are published on the site everyday ensuring fans are kept up to date with the latest news and gossip about the team and club. Featuring live match statistics, regular news updates and a 300-item online shop, online ticket bookings and charity auctions of club memorabilia, it is the largest official club site in the premiership. Traffic on the site has doubled in twelve months. The club has also boosted its profits after introducing an e-commerce arm to sell merchandise. It now contributes 20 per cent of the club's turnover.

Customers can also receive an online magazine entitled *Tigerzine* direct to their inbox, download Tigers wallpaper, watch video highlights and have live match audio. Younger fans are encouraged to join the junior Tigers club and can receive a number of bonuses including having a birthday celebration at the club and becoming a mascot for a game.

Additionally, many premiership players have a clause in their contract requiring them to perform some "community service" each month. Some fulfil that obligation by taking coaching clinics, while others choose to spend time in local schools.

Sources

"Aspects of Marketing and income generation at Leicester Tigers", a presentation by David Clayton, De Montfort University, November 2003.
Gill, K. and M. Welch (2005) "The Organisation of Sport and Recreation in the UK, National Governing and Representative Bodies" available at http://www.yorkshiresport.org.uk/ccpr/c7.htm.
Leicester Tigers Football Club website at *www.leicestertigers.com*
Simpson, J. (2006) "Tackling Change", *Director Magazine*, April.

Questions

1 Explain the nature of the relationship between the club and its "customers".

2 Why is RM appropriate within this context?

3 Apply and evaluate the ladder of loyalty within this context.

4 How could Leicester Tigers improve its customer retention strategy?

Follow-up Activity

Examine the RM activities of a football or other sports club with which you are familiar. How does it appear to manage its relationship with its "customers"?

Context 4

Professional Supply Relationship (b2b)

A Supply Relationship Between an Organization and its Advertising Agencies

Introduction

This case context investigates the business-to-business marketing relationships between a medical company, referred to as CoMed, and its two creative advertising agencies, Ballad and Candy (all are fictional names, but based on real companies).

CoMed is part of a large public limited organization, registered as a FTSE 100 company. It produces market-leading medical solutions in two major areas: anaesthesia and safety devices, including medication delivery and patient monitoring. Its products range from single-use devices to capital equipment. It operates in a number of separate markets and sells to a variety of customers such as emergency services, hospitals and surgeries. The global and international marketing department of the organization are based in the Midlands in the UK.

Ballad is a relatively large agency, based in Birmingham, with a new office recently opened in the centre of London. The agency specializes in medical advertising with major accounts comprising both CoMed and a competitor, Dragoncare. They produce high quality illustrations, marketing support and can work internationally through their network of contacts, helping with exhibitions and conferences globally. CoMed originally appointed Ballad to produce material for all their medical devices.

Candy is a new agency, founded in 2001. It is small, based in Birmingham and owned by a manager who worked within CoMed as a senior employee before leaving to start the business. As such, the manager has a firm understanding of the products, the industry market segments, CoMed's customers, their routes to market and the company's budgeting, etc. After the formation of Candy, he began working with CoMed as their creative agent only on one product line. However, over the course of the last two years he has received a number of requests to become involved in other ranges produced by them.

CoMed's Relationship Preferences

In discussion with CoMed, they have identified a range of factors they determine as being particularly important to the ongoing success of the relationships they have with both Ballad and Candy:

- Two-way communication
- Openness and honesty, especially in problem-solving, such as perhaps arising from a misinterpretation of a creative brief

- Working together to achieve
- Understanding and empathy – the agencies know what CoMed require without them necessarily having to explain in great detail
- Verbal and non-verbal behaviour – behind-the-scenes communication that impacts on the day-to-day relationship between the account managers in the organizations
- Listening rather than making assumptions about their needs

As well as these interpersonal preferences, CoMed is of course looking for good creative delivery of its messages, which are of a high quality, genuinely innovative and represent value for money. Factors which sit alongside these include responsiveness, accuracy and a certain market knowledge that underpins the work the agencies produce.

Recent Events: Ballad

Although CoMed have a clear understanding that the working relationship with Ballad takes time to build into a good rapport with strong trust, they have recently felt 'let down'. When it was first appointed as creative agency, Ballad produced excellent creative work; the team were enthusiastic, excited and very fresh in the ideas they produced for CoMed's promotional literature. However even though the finished work produced by Ballad is of a very high quality, CoMed do feel that it's a long and often "arduous" process to get to where they want to be – they feel that they miss out on opportunities as a result of the rigour imposed by the agency, and some urgent briefs have apparently been completely ignored.

As a result, one manager of a core product line at CoMed has commented: "I've been completely frustrated in my job and, in the end, I've had to take my work to another agency." On top of this, some other key managers within the organization feel that their work is expensive, and ultimately does not represent good value for money: "you know, there are so many inconsistencies, you want things done in a certain time, and you don't get them done in a certain time … I feel let down and I can't understand why!"

Both the marketing manager for CoMed and the account manager for Ballad recognize there is a serious problem: "I think the differences are more about individual personalities – the biggest problem is personality clashes", says George Drury, account manager for Ballad. "I think he has a very low attention span – he couldn't focus and because of this he switches off half way through meetings when we are talking about strategy …", comments Claire Timmins, marketing manager for CoMed. Furthermore, Claire suggests that her relationship with the manager of Candy is much closer to what she expects: "culture and values will guide you. You need to know their boundaries, so you know what you can get away with, how creative you can be and also you need to understand the structural boundaries within the organization …", epitomizes her feelings about how well Stephan Babani, Candy's account manager, understands CoMed's business. Such issues are further compounded by the physical distance between the organizations – "everyone tends to be busy and having to take the time to travel is a pain; if the agency comes to you then it costs you their time so you already feel under pressure".

In summary, CoMed have identified a pattern to their relationship with the two agencies (see Figure 9.1).

Source

Shotton, A.M. (2006) "An investigation into the marketing relationship development process between an organisation and its advertising agency suppliers", BA dissertation, De Montfort University, Leicester.

Questions

1 Discuss the risk associated with the supply of services (Kraljic's model) by Ballad and Candy to CoMed.

2 Identify and discuss the factors that appear to be influencing the relationship between CoMed and its creative agencies.

3 With reference to the relationship development cycles presented in Chapter 3 of this text, discuss which stage of the classic relational development cycle best characterizes the relationships between:

■ CoMed and Ballad

■ CoMed and Candy

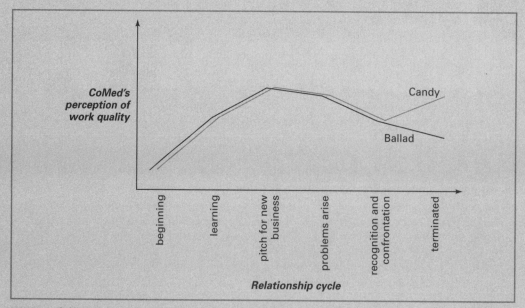

FIGURE 9.1 CoMed's Relationship Pattern with Ballad and Candy
Source: adapted from Shotton (2006).

Follow-up Activity

Have a look at the website of a major advertising agency (for example, McCann Erickson, Ogilvy and Mather). Identify its major clients and discuss the issues that may arise in the management of the agency's relationship with its customers. How might these issues be overcome?

Context 5
Utility Services (b2c)

British Gas Residential and the Impact of Consumer Power

Introduction

By 2007 British Gas (BG) was the market leader within the energy sector. Its strategic vision was to "build on this heritage but move the business forward" with its aim to be the "the people the nation turns to first for value and service" (wwwbritishgasnews.co.uk). However, having lost over 2.5 million customers between March 2004 and March 2007 and with BG's profits plummeting, its ability to achieve its aims was consistently being questioned.

British Gas Residential – Brand Heritage

The postwar gas supply structure comprised over a thousand private and municipally operated gas companies. However, with the 1948 Gas Act came a single nationalized industry consisting of twelve autonomously run boards with each one literally referred to by customers as "the gas board". During the 1950s and 1960s demand for gas continued to grow and in 1966 the decision was taken to tap into the reserves of natural gas under the North Sea. This required a national conversion programme which entailed visiting over 13 million household and factories to convert over 34 million individual appliance from town gas to natural gas.

The 1972 Gas Act paved the way for greater centralization with the creation of the British Gas Corporation presiding over twelve geographical-based sub-boards, the names of which reflected their geographical responsibility (e.g. EMGAS was responsible for the East Midlands and NEGAS was responsible for the North East).

The 1986 Gas Act returned the gas industry to the private sector and saw the emergence of British Gas Plc (BG) with £9 billion worth of shares being floated on the global stock markets. At the same time Ofgas was formed to protect the interest of customers

On 29 April 1996 the market was deregulated in the South West and 500 000 existing BG customers had the option to choose an alternative gas supplier. By the end of May 1998 the entire market had been deregulated and BG also started to supply its first electricity customers.

As part of Centrica Plc, BG expanded its portfolio of domestic services to include telecommunications and cover for over 4 million draining, heating and kitchen appliances. This enabled them to gather a wealth of data and information on its customers.

The Development of Customer Relationship Strategies

In September 2003, at a seminar on creating value, Centrica's Director of Marketing highlighted how the company was able to optimize the data it had on its customers. Perceived as a critical and appreciating asset, BG's database comprised over 30 million separate customer accounts which were used by the company to "drive value out of their relationships" (British Gas Transformation: transcript of seminar delivered by Nick Smith (Director of Marketing and Strategy, British Gas Data, available at www.centrica.co.uk/index.asp?pageid5484&sub5transcript-Nicksmith) by profiling 12 segments based on current and potential customer value. Examples provided to highlight this included some profiling.

One segment was described as "active BG customers", defined as holding two or more BG products. Another segment were viewed as medium current-value customers with the potential to become high current-value customers holding five product relationships with the organization. High-risk defectors could also be identified and appropriate retention strategies implemented. British Gas also recognized the importance of customer VALs (Value and Lifestyle) profiling. One example identified a young and wealthy segment that was cash rich but time poor and were innovative in their thinking. "Brand tarts" described a segment that were after a good deal; were confident purchasers, unimpressed by logos and brands; had a high house value and had acquired a broad portfolio of savings and investments. This segment were four times more likely to switch than the average BG customer!

From optimizing its data, BG claimed it was able to develop strategies based on an understanding of their current relationships and the potential future behaviour of its customers, and were thus in a position to build prosperity models that predict the likelihood of creating or destroying customer value. Indeed, it was anticipated that by 2006 there would be an overall reduction in customer churn of 30 per cent. However, as early as January 2004 BG was reported to be losing 3000 customers a day after steep rises in domestic gas prices that were caused by recent global increases in wholesale oil and gas prices and declining North Sea oil and gas reserves, making remaining reserves increasingly difficult to tap.

Prices Rise and Complaints Rise!

By the end of 2005 BG was not only the most expensive but was also the worst-regarded for customer service. While complaints about its main competitors were decreasing, BG complaints were increasing. Between April and September 2005 energywatch received 15 433 complaints about British Gas compared to 6222 for the same period in the previous year. Inaccurate billing, sometimes leading to a threat of debt collectors, together with a lack of response to enquiries were the main focus of the complaints. By September 2005 BG had been featured on BBC1's *Watchdog* programme a total of 29 times – more than any other company except British Telecom. While BG suggested it endeavoured to answer calls within 60 seconds, researchers for the programme found that it took an average of nine minutes, and on one occasion it took 47 minutes to have their calls answered.

In March 2006 BG raised its prices by another 22 per cent and in September 2006 prices were increased a third time by a further 14.2 per cent, thus increasing prices by 32.6 per cent in total since the beginning of 2004. Encouraged by the media, utility comparison websites were doing a roaring trade with over 4 million customer switching energy suppliers in 2006. BG alone lost 1 million residential customers, leaving it with 16 million. Despite losing customers, BG's residential arm made an operating profit of £95 million after turning around a loss for the first six months of the year. However, with 600 000 consumers already changing energy supplier in the first two months of 2007 alone, consumer power and switching behaviour was a feature of the market.

Price Reductions and the Rise of Consumer Power

In February 2007 BG became the first company to announce price cuts after substantial falls in wholesale energy prices. Phil Bentley, BG's Managing Direct said "We've taken the lead on lower prices and we are committed to restoring our customer service to an industry leading level" (Bland, 2007). However, by early 2007 Ofgem, the energy regulator, was highlighting the increasing power of consumers who were prepared to shop around to find the best deals: "Customers should continue to turn up the heat on energy suppliers by taking advantage of the savings available by switching suppliers", said Alistair Buchanan, Chief Executive of Ofgem. In April 2007 Ofgem "named and shamed" (Brodie, 2007) two leading power companies, the French group EDF and Spanish-run Scottish Power, for failing to pass on the benefits of cheaper gas prices to customers. While reluctant to intervene directly with regards to pricing issues, Ofgas instead focused its attention on an awareness campaign highlighting to consumers the potential premium they may be paying for remaining loyal. The intervention from the gas regulator followed complaints from customers and consumer groups about the delays by the energy companies in passing on to consumers the benefits of falling wholesale gas prices. With financial analysts estimating that companies are "sitting on" £4 billion due to customers, BG cut its prices for the second time in two months. In an attempt to cut costs further, BG announced the loss of 700 jobs from its back-office operations and a further 340 job losses from its service teams responsible for installing and repairing central heating systems.

However, while wholesale prices fell by 50 per cent, the price cuts announced by the energy suppliers cut the average household bill by only 16 per cent. Many consumers perceived that, while energy suppliers were quick to increase prices, they were slow to pass on any savings.

Rebuilding the Brand

In early 2007 Phil Bentley took over the helm of BG and immediately set the priority of "re-building the brand in the eyes of British consumers who have been deserting in droves" (Reece, 2007) by putting the company back at their heart.

Bentley's strategy for rebuilding the brand and turning BG' fortunes around revolved around three key factors. First, customer attraction and retention. "Every customer counts. We've got to hang on to all the customers we can and we have to win new customers" (Reece, 2007), stated Bentley. Indeed, as a result of the implementation of the Spring 2007 price cuts BG saw a record number of households returning to the company (an estimated average of 80 000 a week).

The second factor revolved around adding value. The focus was not on being the cheapest in the market but on offering improved levels of customer service that were better than the competition. As a result, BG invested in the largest billing system in the world. The average time taken to answer phones was reduced by half, and BG invested in over 800 better-trained employees "in the front line".

The third factor revolves around repositioning the organization so it is perceived as an energy expert rather than purely involved in gas. British Gas is now in a position to help consumers "green" their lives and reduce their carbon footprint not only at a macro energy generation level through, for example, its investment in on and offshore wind farms, but also at a micro-level through the greening of individual households through the supply of domestic wind turbines or supplying light bulbs that last 50 years. How successful BG is in its branding strategy remains to be seen.

Sources

"British Gas cuts prices again", B. Bland, the *Daily Telegraph*, 26 April 2007.

"British Gas Transformation", transcript of seminar delivered by Nick Smith (Director of Marketing and Strategy, British Gas Data. Available at www.centrica.co.uk/index.asp?pageid=484&sub=transcript-Nicksmith

"Devoting his energy to customers", D. Reece, the *Daily Telegraph*, 12 March 2007.

"Cut prices or be shamed", S. Brodie, the *Daily Telegraph*, 23 April 2007.

Questions

1 What are the unique customer challenges that face utility companies such as BG?

2 How relevant is Donaldson and O'Toole's relationship classification schema (see Figure 2.10) in evaluating the relationships that exist between BG and its domestic customers?

3 How would you classify "active BG customers" and "brand tarts" using Donaldson and O'Toole's classification schema? Justify your answer!

4 Do you think BG is adopting the correct strategies to rebuild its brand image?

Follow-up Activity

Have a look at some "independent" websites that claim to compare and contrast product and service prices. What do you think their motivation for providing such a service is and how might a utility company such as BG manage such activities?

Context 6
Virtual Services (c2c)

Customer Roles and Brand Relationships in Mini
Online Brand Community

Introduction

The Mini was first launched in 1959 in two different versions, the Morris Mini-Minor and the Austin Seven. Being "a noteworthy breakthrough in small car design" (Brooke, 1999), its advertising at that time emphasized its design/wheel revolution and its practical value. However, later advertisements developed the idea of the Mini being associated with happiness and fun, as illustrated by the memorable strapline from the 1960s: *"You don't need a big one to be happy. Happiness is Mini shaped"*. The core brand meaning, that of fun, has remained unchanged since the 1960s, when the then young baby-boom generation used the Mini to differentiate themselves from their elders (Filby, 1981). Throughout the 1960s the Mini became associated with contemporary pop stars such as The Beatles, actors such as Michael Caine, Peter Sellers and fashion designers such as Mary Quant (Filby, 1981; Steward, 1989). This encouraged young people to associate the mini with pop and style icons as we can see from the following advertising campaign that used the singer Lulu's love of the Mini to make these associations:

> Once upon a time, Lulu drove a Mini. And loved it so much she nearly cried when she sold it. Recently, we showed Lulu a new Mini Clubman. She said it was like falling in love all over again ... Some things Lulu found easy to recognize. Like the Mini's famous economy and the sheer fun of Mini Motoring.

In addition, a new version of the Mini, the Mini Cooper, was developed with some of the features of a sports car, a development that attracted rally drivers involved in international motor racing events (Clausager, 1999). This added excitement to the brand and helped to extend the British love affair with motor racing glory. Two groups of Mini enthusiasts emerged from these early brand developments: first, the general Mini community lover whose bonds to the brand and other members are based on emotions – those of happiness, fun, and a sense of style; and second, those who bond because of the shared excitement of the Mini in motor racing events (Rees, 1994).

How Mini Brand Communities were Formed

Original offline brand communities formed largely on a regional basis, as a collection of like-minded car enthusiasts, who met occasionally at car rallies and formed loose affiliations. Many communities were self-forming and were set up with the independent resources of the enthusiasts. These subsequently evolved into the web communities through the development of their own web pages (e.g. Bernese Mini Club, Switzerland). In turn, these enthusiasts acquired an almost legendary status on club webpages: "The Mini Car Club of NSW was started some 38 years ago when a bunch of motoring enthusiasts pooled their resources in celebration of the small car that would redefine motoring forever" (club webpage).

It is interesting that, from an early date, each group of enthusiasts centred around specific models, the Mini Clubman, and the Mini Cooper. The essence of the two groups was, nonetheless, similar in that both shared the fun and style aspects and both recognized the Mini as heralding something new in motoring and something that went beyond just technical details, specific features or driving performance – it was also about how they lived or aspired to live and, as such, a symbol of a particular lifestyle (Laban, 1999). As the Mini has aged, further brand values emerged to strengthen the brand heritage; notably, its uniqueness, its tradition and its classic qualities.

More recently, Mini owners, rather than joining a regional enthusiast's group as a first step, often access both national and international Mini webpages and become members of Mini web communities directly online, shortly after acquiring their Mini. A broad range of websites can now be accessed online, for instance, the MiniWWW Directory (*www.comp.glam.ac.uk/~Minis*) contains several volumes, categorized as Enthusiasts; Parts and Sales; Technical and DIY; History; Motorsport, Models and Collecting. Some Mini owners thus begin to discover and share the diversity of meanings associated with the Mini brand at an early stage of ownership.

Brand Values that are Communicated through Brand Community

In research undertaken on mini brand communities, some interesting patterns emerged that show how brand communities are important spaces where relationships are built between customers. As those relationships develop around the brand, the nature of the brand and how it is experienced are discussed.

Findings from analysis of the online communities showed that brand attributes that emerged in the early years are still largely intact for members. Fun was the core brand meaning for most members (this is in line with the marketing message of the original model, as noted by Harvey, 1990 and Laban, 1999). As members exchanged views, they made references to the fun of driving and owning the Mini, as indicated by the following examples: "you can't measure the price just by the engine and metal. You're buying fun" (online bulletin board).

In the recent market positioning by the BMW marketing team behind the revived Mini of 2000–2001, one of the key brand values retained from the original 1959 brand was the motorsport success of the Classic Mini (*PR Newswire*, 2002). In relation to speed and racing, there were many references to the excitement of driving the car and the ability to keep up with and surpass other models: "I love Minis because I can outrun BMWs with a 2.5 litre engine … that makes the Beamer guys real angry" (online bulletin board).

An example of these enduring associations with speed, competition and anti-authoritarian status came from one board member who, while abroad, had been involved in racing the Mini with work friends. He describes his excitement at a daring drive through Tokyo:

> I was in Japan working on an animation project when I had my first encounter with a Mini and a completely insane motor gang ... It was a bozozoku gang, near terrorist motor gangs that zip around Tokyo with battle flags, crazy outfits and a complete disregard for cops. "Cool", I thought to myself ... They want to race ... Sho, when is the next time I am ever going to have the opportunity to do this again?" ... and I popped her into first and felt the acceleration hit me in the chest ... I could barely hear Sho's screams turn from fear to sheer enjoyment ... Sho's trick Mini was more than victor, we had dusted the entire gang. When they caught up with us, they were cheering and shouting. Then they asked to treat us to a beer. (online bulletin board)

This was interesting as it was reflecting back an important element in the marketing of the Mini – its strong international brand heritage. In Australia special Mini Moke models were under licensed production (Davis, 1990; Clausager, 1999); in Japan it developed a cult status (Clausager, 1999) and also in Italy. For instance the link to film stars in the use of the Mini in the film *The Italian Job* was reinforced by the licensing of production and the marketing of the Italian version, Innocenti models, used in the film (Steward, 1989). In the online community and chat forums, members were reflecting these international qualities. Many references were made to *The Italian Job* and some members had seen it over 30 times and commented on the car models. What emerged in their expressions of the excitement of driving the Mini was the joy of being unorthodox and "letting loose" as much as enjoying the speed rush: "Personally, I love retro'ed out MK3s and MK4s and 5s and 6s and so on – slap that moustache grille and bumper over-riders on, supercharge/turbo or even VTEC that mini and give the bird to them geezers as you pass them like they're going in reverse" (online bulletin board).

An additional important element that emerged was the historical/classic attributes of the Mini brand. This involved references to the engineering tradition, classic design style as well as Britishness: ranging from the comment "it's older than me" to "it enables me to get all pious about being British".

Furthermore, reflection of brand meaning seemed to occur between the content of the marketing messages of websites and the content of some online discussions. For instance, on some national Mini Club websites are brand information pages with a strong focus on the iconic status of the Mini: "When the Mini first appeared in 1959, it became an instant classic. Over time, its British style and international savvy has made it one of the world's most loved cars" (club web page). A further elaboration of the history behind the brand is noted on a different website:

> One of the greatest achievements of the Mini is it anticipated the changing social values that would come to the fore in the 1960s, when the postwar baby boomers were looking to express their independence from previous generations through the fashions of Mary Quant and the music of the Beatles, the Stones and the Who. Along with the miniskirt, the Mini Cooper became an icon of British modernity. (club webpage)

Personal Experiences of Brand

Online community members made many references to significant events that happened to them as owners of Minis, as one member recounted:

> trailing edge of the front wheel wells were completely rusted out. To remedy this, I used a combination of newspaper, chicken wire and roofing tar. I was not very successful, due to the fact that during the rainy season in Northern California, whilst driving on rain slickened roads in the winter, the water would seep in and collect on the floor boards. Since the MK 1 Mini had an extremely efficient heating system it provided a nice spa for my feet – hence my continual operation of the car in my bare feet. (online bulletin board)

The Mini often enhanced its owner's sense of self through making them feel that they stood out from the crowd and could thus draw attention to themselves. We see this very clearly in the following account as one member recalls the attention she received when she took her Mini car to a school: "Right after I got my Mini, I took it down to San Juan Capistrano to pick up my goddaughter from school. When the class bell rang, all the kids came running out of class and stood by the Mini. Soon the Mini was surrounded by about 50 kids looking at it and asking me questions" (chatroom participant).

Reminiscences were shared in the community. Some members, who had been a long time without a Mini, realized when they bought one again what they had lost; not just the car but the past life experiences that came with it.

> You never forget your first Mini. Yeah, it is up there with the other important firsts that come along in a person's life. It is a moment that comes and goes with little fanfare, but isn't it funny how many details you recall when you think about it years later. I have just rejoined the ranks of Mini owners. (online interview)

There were also nostalgic references to family traditions associated with the Mini: "the Mini is in my genes! My Grandad owned one. My Dad owned one ... for my first car ... a beautiful Mini Mayfair named (all my Minis have names) Oscar ... I spent an intimate and deeply loving year with Oscar" (online bulletin board).

Social Interaction in Brand Community

A sense of shared independence of Mini enthusiasts is also evident in the online Mini communities, in particular a shared belief that the Mini has redefined motoring. In the following excerpt the unusual and unique qualities of the brand are also accepted and projected onto the owners.

> ... a motto Sir Alec Issoginis would have been proud of 'to dare to be different'. This motto is not only reflected in the variety of weird and wonderful Minis that the members own, but also creative ability of the members. (personal webpage)

Status of a member in the Mini brand community depends on their strength of the member's devotion to the Mini, the historical value of their Mini, how they maintain the condition of their Mini and their overall knowledge about the Mini. The use of certain technical terms is common to display a member's knowledge and establish their status within the community, illustrated in the following quote from a member giving advice:

> Probably the best car you could get would be a mid-sixties Cooper S. They also more expensive to buy, but are the true Mini "muscle cars" of the 60s. All Cooper S are highly sought after, but my own personal preference is the 970 Cooper S. These were a special that were built around 64, 65 time period. They have loads of power, but are smoother and more reliable than long stroke 1275 Cooper S. (online bulletin board)

The following extract identifies how an experienced member discusses the essential values of the brand with a new member and at the same time asserts status in the community by denigrating the new member's model:

> A: I'm very new to Minis
> B: Welcome to the gang. Basically what you've got sounds like a lovely, superb car. You'll be hooked form now on so hold tight and enjoy the ride.
> A: I found out what it is . . . It's a Clubman. The poor man's Mini, someone called it..
> B: No, don't say that. It's just a sorry attempt at a Mini, but good thing you don't notice it when you're in the driver's seat.
> A: What do you mean "a poor excuse for a Mini". What's so markedly different between a Clubman and Cooper?
> B: NEVER compare Clubman to a Cooper . . . and remember the world is round, not flat. (chatroom participants)

This shows the way that members learn the nuances of opinion in the member community and build some social hierarchy. Overall, the online Mini community are a group of very loyal brand enthusiasts and their interactions are a rich source of brand evolution.

Sources

Broderick, A., P. Maclaran and P. Ma (2004) "Brand Meaning Negotiation – Case of Mini Brand Community", *Journal of Customer Behaviour*.

Brooke, L. (1999) "Little Car, Big Package", *Automotive Industries*, April.

Clausager, A.D. (1999) *Essential Mini Cooper – The Cars and their Story 1961–71 and 1990 to date*, Devon, UK: Bay View Books.

Davis, P. (1990) *Spotlight on Mini Minor Downunder, including Mini-Cooper and Moke*, Blakehurst, NSW: Marque Publishing Co.

Filby, P. (1981) *Amazing Mini*, UK: Haynes Publishing.

Harvey, C. (1990) *Mighty Minis*, UK: Oxford Illustrated Press.

Laban, B. (1999) *The Mini: Forty Years of Fun*, New York: Harper Collins Illustrated.

Rees, C. (1994) *The Complete Mini: 35 Years of Production History, Model Changes, Performance Data and Specifications*, Croydon, UK: Motor Racing Publications.

Schrader, H. (1989) *Mini, Austin Morris, CooperS, Special, Clubman, 1275GT 1959–1983*, Munich, Germany: Schrader Automobile Bucher.

Steward, K. (1989) *Mini*, London: Osprey Publishing Limited.

Questions

1 In what ways do members of the Mini brand communities in this case show involvement and commitment to the Mini brand?

2 Can you list other brands that might have such a strong brand community presence?

3 In what ways are members of the Mini brand communities contributing to ongoing brand development? Be specific about different online roles undertaken, and nature of contributions in the excerpts shown.

4 If you were Marketing Manager for Mini, in what way would you

a) monitor brand communities?

b) communicate with brand communities?

c) build further relationships between the company website and these other forums?

Follow-up Activity

Log on to two of the Mini websites noted in this case and take a look at the discussion threads. Identify customer roles being adopted.

Context 7
Non-profit Context (c2c)

The Influence of Social Networking on Loyalty –
Race for Life Blog

The Race for Life is an annual event in the UK that is designed to raise money for breast cancer. It involves thousands of participant (women) who run a 5k course in the main cities throughout the UK each June and July. It has been sponsored by strong brands; in the past by Flora and in 2006–2007 by Tesco.

It has generated some very active social networking activity online. It is interesting in that it is not a friendship network, neither is it a firm-initiated or managed social network site. The Race for Life is a series of races across the country predominantly run by ladies, raising money and awareness for Cancer Research.

Many blog pages are created each summer in association with the Race for Life event. In looking at online blogs for this event over a two month period over the summer of 2006, a significant number of blogs were posted. These showed a considerable range in style and motivation including:

- individual, self-affirmative accounts of those who had done the race;
- advocacy and celebration of the cause;
- direct requests for sponsorship;
- information posting and requests for help from local organizers of the event (e.g. Swindon Harriers, a town in southern UK).

Some Examples: Race for Life Blogs

hey – good to see the blog back. In celebration I donated. My daughter is running too so may see you ....A, Thursday, 1 June.

Why should I pay for other people to enjoy themselves? .... N, Friday, 2 June.

You're not paying, you're donating to a good cause, and you're also encouraging people to get some exercise and maybe just think about their health. But you knew that already. :-) ....M, Saturday, 3 June.

Some excerpts are shown below.

Excerpt from ... Running Blog (S)

Hi, This blog is all about me and my running! I started running in January 2006, and felt I wanted a way to keep track, so that hopefully one day, when I can run that marathon (a dream of mine!) I can look back and see how I first began! You're welcome to share my journey with me!

Well that was BRILLIANT!! I love every minute of it! Got up there too early really (40 minutes before race started) and so had some hanging around to do. Visited the loos (as you do!) twice, just to be sure. Didn't bother with the warm up aerobics, well I remembered the rule this time not to change anything on race day, and I don't USUALLY prance around just before going for a run ;) Managed to get quite near to the start (I SO was not going to get stuck behind "runners" who ran for 30 seconds and then walked!) Eventually, later than 11am, we set off, after having to do stupid Mexican waves for a few minutes first (excuse me its HOT out here, can we PLEASE get started???!!!). Anyway, I set off, at my own steady pace, didn't get carried away with the start, and within a short time was passing those who had rushed past me as we started!!

The course was beautiful. It's in the university ground, and we went over fields, under just a few trees, and past a lovely river. I've never been round there before, and I enjoyed the route very much. Three young boys of around 7–9 years old cheered me on just when I was finding it hard work, shouting "345, 345, 345" as I ran past, they got thumbs up from me as I so appreciated the support at that point!

I managed to run the whole thing (my original aim) and finished in a time of 28 mins 43 seconds, which considering it was VERY hot and quite an undulating course really, I was pleased with). I wanted to crack that 30-minute barrier. Met someone I knew from running club after the race, which was nice, chatted to her for a few minutes, but she was obviously with family. I then went back to the finish line to watch others come in, to see someone I know from church coming in! She was alone too, so we sat and chatted for a while. We went back to the start just before the last few crossed the finishing line to cheer them on.

Last person was a lady in an electric chair, with a friend or maybe relative walking along side her. Somehow that just summed up the whole day for me.

All in all a GREAT morning :)

S, on Sunday, 16 July 2006

Excerpt from ... Running Blog (Y)

Well, I'd just like to announce that **I did it!!** Sunday morning at 11am over 10 000 women set off in 28oC heat to run the 5km race, and I managed to jog the whole course (no stopping!!) in 44 minutes. Not very fast, but not all that surprising considering how bloody hot it was!

Still, I'm very happy that I managed to keep my word and run the whole race, and I'd just like to say a huge thank you to all the people who <u>sponsored me</u> for it. Simon was lovely and drove me to and from the race, and made me drink my body weight in water and lucozade!

Roll on Race for Life 2007!!

Y, on Sunday, 16 July 2006

Excerpt from ... Race for Life follow-up (C)

Last Sunday I completed the Race for Life 2006. My reasons for deciding to do the 5 km run (that's around 3 miles, give or take), can be seen on *this post*. Suffice it to say, I've lost lots of people I care about to cancer, and I know there many more who are battling the disease at the moment.

The Race for Life is an annual women only event organised by Cancer Research UK. All the money raised through sponsorship goes directly to the charity – all admin costs for the run etc are covered by the entry fee paid by all the runners – so you can be assured that any money you donate will go straight into funding the fight against cancer.

This is a cause I care passionately about and, I promise you, this will be the only time I ask you for money (till next summer rolls around). Several of you have already sponsored me and you have my heartfelt gratitude and thanks. Several more of you have said things along the line of "damn it, I missed it. I'll sponsor you next year". Why wait till next year? The *online sponsorship page* is still open and will be till the 30th of July.

So how did the Race go? Well, I managed to beat last years time and got home in under 50 minutes. The actual time is somewhere between 45 minutes and 50 minutes because the girl with the watch (M) and I got separated at about the 2 km mark and I'd been finished a little while before I remembered to nab someone with a watch and do a time check. M managed it in 43 minutes! (Big woot to M!) I was no where near as fit as I was last year, or as fit as I wanted to be – I had grand plans to run the majority – but it was just too hot and I'm just not built to move at any great velocity I am afraid.

My thanks also to those who looked after house-keys etc, waited around for an hour on a blazing hot Sunday afternoon, and met us at the finish with large bottles of water. I didn't take any pictures this year but *the ones from last year* basically tell the same story. Lots of women, lots of sun!

It's a cliché, but every little really does help, and I would love to reach my target of £180. Whether you decide to give 50p or £50, I appreciate it. Sponsoring is really simple – go to the *online sponsorship page*, click on the pink "sponsor me now" button at the bottom of the page, and follow the instructions. If needs must I'm also still accepting sponsorship via paypal – if you want to use this option (though I do recommend and prefer the official sponsorship page) contact me and I will let you know the details.

Thank you again to everyone who's already sponsored me, and thank you in advance to anyone else who decides they are going to do their little bit for a very worthwhile charity. The closing date for sponsorships is the 30th of July – just over a week left, so you'd better get a wiggle on

C, on 20 July 2006

Sources

Sources are drawn from live blogs online for the summer 2006 event. All contributors have been anonymized and excerpts selected are random.

Questions

1 What motivates participants to develop blogs in relation to Race for Life?

   What role do blogs play in awareness building for this event?

2 In what way do the blogs shown here encourage a relationship to develop with the event? (You might wish to consider ideas on the functions of social networks in Chapter 8.)

3 Looking at the selection of blog excerpts, what kind of relationship is being furthered here

   ■ with the cause of Cancer Research UK and the event?

   ■ with the event sponsor (in this case, Tesco)?

   (You may want to consider some of the relationship types or dimensions that are discussed in Chapter 3.)

4 Some comments in these blogs are already anticipating next year. In what ways do blogs encourage customer retention?

Follow-up Activity

This is an annual event. Locate some blogs on a different charity event in your region or country. Can you find any variation in motivations for the blog, for instance:

■ individual, self-affirmative accounts;

■ advocacy and celebration of the cause;

■ direct requests for sponsorship;

■ information posting and requests for help from sponsor organization.

Index